The Economics of Public Issues

FOURTEENTH EDITION

Roger LeRoy Miller
Institute for University Studies
Arlington, Texas

Daniel K. Benjamin
Clemson University
and PERC, Bozeman, Montana

Douglass C. North
Washington University, St. Louis

PEARSON
Addison
Wesley

Boston   San Francisco   New York
London   Toronto   Sydney   Tokyo   Singapore   Madrid
Mexico City   Munich   Paris   Cape Town   Hong Kong   Montreal

Editor-in-Chief: Denise Clinton
Acquisitions Editor: Roxanne Hoch
Editorial Assistant: Julia Boyles
Managing Editor: Jim Rigney
Sr. Production Supervisor: Katherine Watson
Design Manager: Gina Kolenda
Sr. Manufacturing Buyer: Hugh Crawford
Production House: Orr Book Services
Composition: Nesbitt Graphics, Inc.
Cover Image: Federal Reserve Board and © PictureQuest

Library of Congress Cataloging-in Publication Data

Miller, Roger LeRoy.
    The economics of public issues/Roger LeRoy Miller, Daniel K.
Benjamin, Douglass C. North.—14th ed.
        p.cm.
    Includes bibliographical references and index.
    ISBN: 0-321-30349-0 (alk.paper)
        1. Economics. 2. Industrial policy. 3. Economic policy. I. Benjamin,
Daniel K. II. North, Douglas Cecil. III. Title

ISBN: 0-321-30349-0
HB171.M544 2005
330.973'0931—dc22   2004028935
1 2 3 4 5 6 7 8 9 10—DOC—09 08 07 06 05

To Steve Jackstadt,
Thanks for being there in the beginning.
Thanks for staying around no matter how far
apart we've been.
Thanks for your humor and your lasting friendship.

R.L.M.

To Elijah Kelly Benjamin,
Like many his age, master and commander
of all he surveys.

D.K.B.

Contents

Suggestions for Use

At the request of our readers, we include the following table to help you incorporate the chapters of this book into your syllabus. Depending on the breadth of your course, you may also want to consult the companion paperback, *The Economics of Macro Issues, 2nd Edition,* which features macroeconomic topics and a similar table in its preface.

Economic Topics	Recommended Chapters in *The Economics of Public Issues, 14th ed.*
Introduction to Economics	1, 3, 5, 8, 9, 22
Opportunity Costs and Scarcity	1, 2, 3, 9
Demand and Supply	4, 5, 8
Demand and Supply Applications	4, 5, 6, 7, 8, 9, 11, 13, 14, 27
The Public Sector and Public Choice	2, 9, 12, 24, 26, 27, 28
Taxes, Transfers, and Public Spending	10, 12, 17, 20, 23
Consumer Behavior	2, 5, 6, 7, 10
Elasticity of Demand and Supply	5, 6, 7, 10, 11, 12, 13, 14
Rents, Profits, and the Financial Environment of Business	11, 15, 27
Firm Production and Cost	1, 3, 11, 20, 22
Perfect Competition	15, 20
Monopoly	16, 18
Monopolistic Competition	15, 17, 19
Oligopoly	17
Regulation and Antitrust	1, 3, 5, 16, 18
Unions and the Labor Market	13, 16
Income, Poverty, and Health Care	4, 12
Environmental Economics	1, 2, 3, 7, 14, 21, 24, 25, 26, 27, 28
International Trade	29, 30, 31, 32
Comparative Advantage and Trade	4, 23, 29, 31, 32

Preface

This book is about some issues of our times. Several of these issues are usually thought of as being inherently noneconomic. Others provide classic illustrations of the core of economic science. Many are controversial and thus are likely to evoke noneconomic reactions to what we have to say. In our view, however, the one feature that ties all of the issues together is that they illustrate the power of economics in explaining the world around us. And, we might add, we hope all of them illustrate that economics can be entertaining as well as informative.

Over the years, we have sought to select issues for this book that, in addition to the attributes just noted, possess a sense of immediacy. The same criterion was used in adding the following new issues for this edition:

- The Mystery of Wealth (*why some nations are rich and others are poor*)
- Expanding Waistlines (*why Americans are getting heavier*)
- Give Me MP3 or Give Me Death (*the real costs of "free" music downloads*)
- Frankenfoods (*the perils and promises of genetically modified crops*)
- A Farewell to Jobs (*why efforts to "save jobs" make us all poorer*)
- The Rise of the Dragon (*does the rise of China spell the demise of America?*)

In addition, numerous readers have requested that we bring back two chapters from prior editions, and so we have complied. The returning chapters (updated, of course) are

- Heavenly Highway (*how a simple market mechanism can eliminate traffic jams*)
- Raising Less Corn and More Hell (*how your tax dollars end up in farmers' pockets*)

This edition is also marked by one entirely new feature: a list of "Selected Readings," conveniently collected at the end of the book and organized by chapter. Although these readings only scratch the surface of the rich literature we have drawn upon in preparing this book, the interested reader will be able to use them as a springboard for as much research as she or he wishes to undertake.

Long-time users will recognize that Part Seven has a new title—"International Trade and Economic Prosperity"—that reflects a refocusing of the material in this section. Two of us have a new book (Roger LeRoy Miller and Daniel K. Benjamin, *The Economics of Macro Issues*, Addison-Wesley) that examines monetary and fiscal policy, as well as other topics typically covered in a Principles of Macroeconomics course. Hence, the material in this section, including two entirely new chapters, once again emphasizes the microeconomic foundations of some key economy-wide public policy debates on trade and jobs.

All of the other chapters in this edition have been partially or completely rewritten, and every chapter is, of course, as up-to-date as we can make it. What you will consistently find is a straightforward application of economic principles as they are taught in virtually all courses in economics, public policy, and the social sciences. This book can be understood by those who have taken a course in economics, are taking a course in economics, or have never taken a course in economics. In other words, we have made it self-contained, as well as accessible to a wide range of students.

The chapters are organized into seven parts. Part One examines the foundations of all economic analysis, including the concepts of scarcity, trade-offs, opportunity cost, marginal analysis, and the like. In a sense, the four chapters in this introductory part set the stage for the remaining twenty-eight chapters. The second through sixth parts of the book cover the topics—such as demand and supply, market structures, environmental issues, and the impact of government policies—that are integral to virtually every course in which economics plays a role. At the end of the book, Part Seven examines global affairs, because these matters are an essential part of the public issues of today.

Every part has a several-page introduction that prepares the reader for the material in the following chapters. These part openers summarize and tie together the relevant issues, thus serving as launchpads for the analyses that follow. We hope you will have your students read these part openers before they embark on any of the chapters they precede.

Every instructor will want to review the *Instructor's Manual* online that accompanies *The Economics of Public Issues*. This is available on supplements central, a secure and password-protected instructor web site (www.awl.com/suppscentral). For each chapter, this manual provides the following:

- A synopsis that cuts to the core of the economic issues involved in the chapter.
- A concise exposition of the "behind the scenes" economic analysis upon which the discussion in the text is based. In almost all cases, this exposition is supplemented with one or more diagrams that we have found to be particularly useful as teaching tools.
- Answers to the "Discussion Questions" posed at the end of the chapter—answers that further develop the basic economic analysis of the chapter, and almost always suggest new avenues of discussion.

The world of public issues continues to evolve. By the time you read this preface, we will be working on the next edition. If you have any particular subjects you would like included in the future, let us know by writing us in care of Addison-Wesley.

Several chapters in this edition draw on the "Tangents" column that Benjamin writes for *PERC Reports*. We are grateful to the Property and Environment Research Center (PERC) for permission to use that material. In addition, dozens of kind users of the last edition of this book, as well as several extremely diligent and thoughtful reviewers, offered suggestions for the current edition. They include

Tim Fuerst, Bowling Green University
John Horowitz, Ball State University
R. Ashley Lyman, University of Idaho
Roger Meiners, University of Texas at Arlington
Cyril Morong, San Antonio College
Michael Nelson, Texas A&M University
Ray Pepin, Stonehill College

Although scarcity precluded the adoption of all of their recommendations, we believe they will be able to identify the impact they each had on this edition. To them and to our users who wrote to us we offer our sincere thanks, and we hope that they see the end result as being worthy of their time and concern. We also thank Adrienne D'Ambrosio and Kirsten Dickerson for shepherding the project, Sue Jasin for her expert manuscript preparation, and Robbie Benjamin, whose editorial skills once again have improved the final product. All errors remain, of course, solely our own.

R.L.M.
D.K.B.
D.C.N.

Part One

The Foundations of Economic Analysis

INTRODUCTION

Our world is one of **scarcity;** we want more than we have. The reason is simple. Although we live in a world of limited **resources,** we have unlimited wants. This does not mean we all live and breathe solely to drive the fastest cars or wear the latest clothes. It means that we all want the right to make decisions about how resources are used—even if what we want to do with those resources is to feed starving children in developing nations.

Given the existence of scarcity, we must make choices; we cannot have more of everything, so to get more of some things, we must give up other things. Economists express this simple idea by saying that we face **trade-offs.** For example, a student who wants higher grades generally must devote more time to studying and less time to, say, going to the movies; the trade-off in this instance is between grades and entertainment.

The concept of a trade-off is one of the (surprisingly few) basic principles you must grasp to understand the economics of public issues. We illustrate the simplicity of these principles with Chapter 1, "Killer Airbags." It is possible you thought that the government mandated the use of automobile airbags to save people's lives. Indeed, that may well have been the motivation. But it turns out that airbags also kill some automobile occupants and induce drivers of airbag-equipped cars to drive in ways that endanger themselves and other persons. So, like many of the issues explored in this book, there is more to automobile safety—and government policy making—than meets the eye, but with the use of some simple economic principles, you can greatly expand both your vision and your understanding of such issues.

Chapter 2, "Terrible Trade-off," examines a behind-the-scenes trade-off made every day on our behalf by the U.S. Food and Drug Administration (FDA). This federal government agency is charged with ensuring that the new prescription medicines that reach the market are both safe and effective. In carrying out its duties, the FDA requires pharmaceutical companies to subject proposed new drugs to extensive testing before the drugs may be introduced to the market. Additional, exhaustive testing improves the chances that a drug will be both safe and effective, but it also slows the approval of new drugs, thus depriving some individuals of the ability to use the drugs to treat their illnesses. The drug-approval process undoubtedly reduces pain and suffering for some people, and even saves the lives of others, because it reduces the chances that an unsafe or ineffective drug will reach the market. Yet because the process also reduces the rate at which drugs reach the market (and may even prevent some safe, effective drugs from ever being introduced), the pain and suffering of other individuals are increased. Indeed, some people die as a result. This, then, is the terrible trade-off we face in Chapter 2: Who shall live and who shall die?

If trade-offs, or choices, are present in all our activities, we must face the question of how to make the best choices. Economists argue that doing so requires the use of what we call **marginal analysis.** The term *marginal* in this context means incremental, or additional. All choices involve costs and benefits—we give up something for anything that we get. As we engage in more of any activity (eating, studying, or sleeping, for example) the **marginal benefits** of that activity eventually decline: The *additional* benefits associated with an *additional* unit of the activity get lower. In contrast, the **marginal costs** of an activity eventually rise as we engage in more and more of it. The best choices are made when we equate the marginal benefits and marginal costs of activity; that is, we try to determine whether engaging in any more of a given activity would produce additional costs in excess of the additional benefits.

In Chapter 3, "Flying the Friendly Skies?", we apply the principles of marginal analysis to the issue of airline safety. How safe is it to travel at 600 miles per hour 7 miles above the ground? How safe *should* it be? The answers to these and other questions can be explored using marginal analysis. One of the conclusions we reach is that *perfect* safety is simply not in the cards. Every time you step into an airplane (or even across the street) there is some risk that your journey will end unhappily. As disconcerting as this might sound at first, we think you will find after reading this chapter that once the costs and benefits are taken into account you would have it no other way.

Every choice we make entails a **cost:** in a world of scarcity something must be given up to obtain anything of value. Costs, combined with the benefits of our choices, comprise the **incentives** that ultimately inform and guide our decisions. That these decisions—and thus the incentives—have real and lasting consequences is nowhere more evident than in Chapter 4, "The Mystery of Wealth." Here we seek to answer a simple but profound question: Why are the citizens of some nations rich while the inhabitants of others are poor? Your initial answer might be, "Because of differences in the **natural-resource endowments** of the nations." It is surely true that ample endowments of energy, timber, and fertile land all help raise wealth. But it turns out that natural resources are only a very small part of the answer.

Far more important in determining the wealth of the citizenry are the fundamental political and legal **institutions** of a nation. Institutions such as political stability, secure private property rights, and legal systems based on the **rule of law** create the incentives that encourage people to make long-lived investments in improving land and in all forms of physical and human capital. These investments raise the **capital stock,** which in turn provides for more growth long into the future. And the cumulative effects of this growth over time eventually yield much higher standards of living: They make us rich. Thus, incentives, comprising both costs and benefits, turn out to be an integral component of the foundations of economic analysis, as well as the foundations of society.

1

Killer Airbags

Federal law requires that new cars be equipped with devices that kill drivers and passengers. If this sounds odd, the story gets stranger when you realize these devices are supposed to—and sometimes do—*save* lives. The devices in question are airbags, and their saga illustrates almost all of the important principles you should know to understand the economics of public issues.

The airbag story begins in 1969, when the Nixon administration first proposed requiring "passive" restraints that would protect motorists during collisions even if they took no actions to protect themselves. The ideal system was thought to be airbags that would automatically inflate in the event of a collision. But a special government study commission found the airbags then available were not only extremely costly and unreliable but were in fact dangerous to the occupants of cars, especially to young children. So, instead of airbags, the government tried requiring seat belts that prevented cars from being started unless the belts were fastened. Inconvenienced consumers who disliked seat belts quickly rejected these, and the idea of airbags was revived and eventually mandated by the federal government. In anticipation of the requirements that 1998 cars have them on both the driver and passenger sides, automakers began installing airbags on selected models in 1989. By 1997, more than 65 million cars had driver-side bags, and about 35 million had them on the passenger side, too.

At first it seemed as though the earlier problems with airbags had been solved. The installed cost of about $400 apiece was far less than it would have been when the bags were initially proposed, and their reliability was dramatically increased. News reports soon began appearing with stories of seemingly miraculous survival by occupants of airbag-equipped cars in collisions. By the end of 1995, it was estimated that airbags had saved more than 1500 lives since 1989.

As the population of cars with airbags grew, however, another set of stories began to appear: Airbags deploy at speeds up to 200 mph and are designed to be most effective when used in conjunction with seat belts. It soon became apparent that people who failed to use belts, people who sat closer than the normal distance from the steering wheel or dashboard, and—most ominously—children anywhere in the front seat were at increased risk of serious injury or death due to airbag deployment. By late 1997 it was estimated by the federal government that although a total (since 1989) of perhaps 2600 people owed their lives to airbags, there were more than 80 people, most of them children, who had been killed by the force of normally deploying airbags.

The outcry over the deaths of children killed in low-speed crashes by the very devices that were supposed to protect them generated action by both the private sector and the federal government. Auto manufacturers and their suppliers began developing "smart" airbags that sense the severity of a collision, the size of the person in the front seat, and whether the person is properly belted. Then, depending on the results of those measurements, the bag decides whether to deploy and at what speed it will do so. As an interim solution, in November 1997 (four and a half years after the first documented airbag fatality) the Department of Transportation announced that consumers would be allowed to apply for permission to have airbag cutoff switches installed in their vehicles. The estimated cost to consumers who have the switches installed is $150 to $200 per car. State governments also got in the act, with many of them mandating that children under a certain age or size be prohibited from occupying the front seat of an automobile.

Beginning with the 1998 model year, manufacturers also began installing less powerful airbags that inflate 22 percent less quickly on the driver side and 14 percent less quickly on the passenger side. The result has been a sharp reduction in (although not an elimination of) airbag-induced fatalities. By 2004, more than 130 million autos equipped with airbags were on the road. The federal government had credited the devices with saving 10,300 lives in serious, high-speed crashes since 1989, at a cost of about 230 people—two-thirds of them children—killed by airbag deployments in low-speed crashes.

What can we learn from the airbag episode that will guide us in thinking about other public issues of our times? There are several general principles:

1. *There is no free lunch.* Every choice, and thus every policy, entails a **cost**—something must be given up. In a world of scarcity, we cannot have more of everything, so to get more of some things, we must give up other things. Simply put, we face trade-offs. In this case, although airbags increase the safety of most adults, there is both a monetary cost of $800 per car and a reduced level of safety for children riding in the front seat.

2. *The cost of an action is the alternative that is sacrificed.* Economists often express costs (and benefits) in terms of dollars, because this is a simple means of accounting for and measuring them. But that doesn't mean costs have to be monetary, nor does it mean economics is incapable of analyzing costs and benefits that are very human. In the case of airbags, the cost that induced action by consumers, manufacturers, and government officials was the lost lives of scores of children.

3. *The relevant costs and benefits are the marginal (or incremental) ones.* The relevant question is not whether safety is good or bad; it is instead how much safety we want—which can only be answered by looking at the added (or marginal) benefits of more safety compared to the added (marginal) costs. One possible response to the child fatalities would have been to outlaw airbags on new cars and mandate that all installed airbags be deactivated. That would have guaranteed that no more children would have been killed by airbags. But for many people (such as those without young children), this solution to airbag fatalities would not be sensible, because the marginal cost would exceed the marginal benefit.

4. *People respond to incentives.* A rise in the apparent costs of using airbags (due to airbag fatalities among children) reduced consumers' desire to utilize airbags and induced them to put pressure on the federal government—pressure that convinced the Department of

Transportation to change the regulations. Moreover, the simultaneous rise in the rewards of developing alternatives to today's airbags sent suppliers scurrying to find those alternatives, including "smart" airbags.

5. *Things aren't always as they seem.* Many analyses of the effects of government policies take an approach that doesn't fully recognize the behavior people otherwise *would* have undertaken. Thus, official pronouncements about the consequences of policies routinely misrepresent their impact—not because there is necessarily any attempt to deceive, but because it is often so difficult to know what would have happened otherwise. For example, the claim that 10,300 lives have been "saved" by airbags is portrayed as the benefit of the government mandate that all new cars have airbags. In fact, absent the airbag regulations, it is highly likely that automobile manufacturers would have devised other systems—better seat belts, vehicles with additional "crush space" in the passenger compartment, or perhaps even some form of optional passive restraint system—that would have saved many of the lives supposedly saved by government-mandated airbags. Moreover, as we discuss more fully in Principle 6 (below), individuals themselves would have behaved much differently absent the airbag regulations. Given the speculative nature of such hypothetical behavior, the people reporting the numbers are (justifiably) reluctant to estimate the effects; we are thus served up the far safer statistic of "10,300 lives saved."

6. *Policies always have unintended consequences, and as a result, their net benefits are almost always less than anticipated.* Information, like all goods, is costly to obtain, and sometimes the cheapest way to learn more about something is simply to try it. When it is tried, new things will be learned, not all of them pleasant. More importantly, in the case of government regulations, Principle 3 (above) fails to make good headlines. Instead, what gets politicians reelected and regulators promoted are fundamental, *absolute* notions, such as "safety" (and motherhood and apple pie). Thus, if a little safety is good, more must be better, so why not simply mandate that all front-seat passengers in all cars be protected by airbags that are all the same? Eventually, the reality of Principle 3 sinks in, but in this case not before scores of children had lost their lives.

Although these basic principles of public issues are readily apparent when looking at the children who have been killed by airbags, they are just as present in two other features of airbags that have received far less attention. First, most airbag deployments occur in relatively low-speed accidents (under 30 miles per hour), when the added safety benefits to properly belted occupants is low. But once the bags are deployed, they must be replaced, and often so must the windshield (blown out by the passenger-side bag) and sometimes even the dashboard (damaged as the airbag deploys). The added repair cost per car is currently estimated to be between $2000 and $2500. Thus, not only have automobile repair costs soared due to airbags, many cars that routinely would have been repaired are now written off completely because it is too costly to fix them.

Second, and more significantly, cars that are airbag-equipped tend to be driven more aggressively, apparently because their occupants feel more secure. The result is more accidents by such cars, more serious accidents (such as rollovers) that kill occupants despite the airbags, and a higher risk of pedestrian fatalities—none of which are accounted for in the lives-saved figures that we quoted earlier. In addition, when seat belts are worn, they are almost as good as airbags in preventing fatalities among automobile occupants. Belts reduce the fatality rate by 45 percent; adding an airbag increases this only to 50 percent. The net effect is that even though airbags are both better and less costly than they were when first proposed, it is still not clear that they yield benefits exceeding their costs.

Despite this uncertainty about the net benefits of front-impact airbags, manufacturers are now installing side-impact airbags on some new automobiles. (By the time you read this, the federal government may have issued regulations mandating these devices on all new cars.) These new bags deploy in the event a vehicle is hit from the side in a crash and are designed chiefly to protect the head. The privately operated Insurance Institute for Highway Safety estimates that these airbags can cut fatalities in side-impact crashes to about 1.5 per 1000 accidents from the current rate of roughly 3 per 1000 accidents. Whether these estimates will be borne out in the real-world experience with side-impact airbags remains to be seen. Nevertheless, one thing seems highly likely: the new airbags are almost certain to have unintended consequences for automobile occupants. One can only hope that not many of them are fatal.

DISCUSSION QUESTIONS

1. Under what circumstances is it appropriate to trade off human lives against dollars when making decisions about safety?

2. Do you think government action allowing airbag deactivation and depowered airbags would have been as swift or as likely if all the fatalities had been among adults rather than chiefly among small children?

3. Do you think government regulators do (or should) distinguish between the *voluntary* choices adults make for themselves (such as not wearing motorcycle helmets or seat belts), versus the decisions to which young children are *involuntarily* exposed by adults (such as being placed unbelted in an automobile or subjected to second-hand cigarette smoke)?

4. Most people, without any government regulation requiring it, have locks on their doors to protect them from intruders. If airbags are so good at protecting people from injuries and death, why were government regulations required to get them installed on automobiles?

2

Terrible Trade-off

How would you rather die? From a lethal reaction to a drug prescribed by your doctor? Or because your doctor failed to prescribe a drug that would have saved your life? If this choice is one you would rather not make, consider this: Employees of the Food and Drug Administration (FDA) make that decision on behalf of millions of Americans many times each year. More precisely, the FDA decides whether new medicines (prescription drugs) should be allowed to go on sale in the United States. If the FDA decides to allow a drug to be sold, doctors can prescribe it, in the expectation that the beneficial effects of the drug will outweigh any adverse side effects it may have. But if the FDA prohibits the drug from being sold in the United States, doctors here cannot legally prescribe it, even if thousands of lives are saved by the drug each year in other countries.

The FDA's authority to make such decisions dates back to the passage of the Food and Drugs Act of 1906. That law required, among other things, that medicines be correctly labeled as to their contents and that they not contain any substances harmful to the health of consumers. Because of this legislation, Dr. Hostetter's celebrated Stomach Bitters and Kickapoo Indian Sagwa, along with numerous rum-laden concoctions, cocaine-based potions, and supposed anticancer remedies, disappeared from druggists' shelves. The law was expanded in 1938 with the passage of the federal Food, Drug, and Cosmetic Act, which forced manufacturers to demonstrate the safety of new drugs before being allowed to offer them for sale. (This legislation was driven by the deaths of 107 individuals who had taken an elixir of sulfanilamide, which happened to contain diethylene glycol, a poisonous substance usually contained in antifreeze.)

The next step in U.S. drug regulation came after the birth of 12,000 deformed infants whose mothers during pregnancy had taken a sleeping pill called thalidomide. When these deformities first became apparent, the drug already was widely used in Europe, and the FDA was moving toward approving it in the United States. In fact, about 2.5 million thalidomide tablets were in the hands of U.S. physicians as samples. The FDA ordered all the samples removed and prohibited the sale of thalidomide in the United States. Using this incident as ammunition, Senator Estes Kefauver secured passage of a bill known as the 1962 Kefauver–Harris Amendments to the 1938 Food, Drug, and Cosmetic Act. This legislation radically altered the drug-approval process in the United States.

Prior to the 1962 amendments, the FDA usually approved a new drug application within a 180-day time limit, unless the application failed to demonstrate that the drug was safe for use in the proposed manner. The 1962 amendments added a "proof of efficacy" requirement and also removed the time constraint on the FDA. Thus, since 1962, manufacturers wishing to introduce a new drug must demonstrate to the FDA's satisfaction that the drug is safe to use in the proposed manner, and also that it will accomplish the intended therapeutic outcome. Moreover, the FDA is free to determine how much and what evidence it will demand before approving a drug for sale, and it may take as long as it wants before either giving or refusing approval.

The most noticeable impact of the 1962 amendments was a reduction in the number of new drugs coming onto the market. Researchers have estimated that the 1962 amendments cut new drug introductions by as much as two-thirds. This reduction occurred because the amendments sharply increased the costs of introducing a new drug and markedly slowed the approval process. Prior to the 1962 amendments, for example, the average time between filing and approval of a new drug application was seven months; by 1967, it was 30 months; and by the late 1970s, it had risen to eight to ten *years*. Although the average approval time has since dropped, it still takes ten times as long for a new drug to be approved as it did before the 1962 amendments. The protracted approval process involves costly testing by the drug companies and delays the receipt of any potential revenue from new drugs. Moreover, once all of the test data are in, the FDA may decide against the company's application. Overall, the expected profitability of new drugs has been sharply reduced by the 1962 amendments, so fewer of them have been brought onto the market.

The rationale behind the FDA regulations is presumably protection of consumers, because generally consumers do not have the ability to obtain or analyze the information necessary to make accurate choices about the safety or efficacy of particular drugs. Consumers are at the mercy of the physicians who prescribe the drugs. But the physicians are also, in a sense, at the mercy of the drug companies, for it is almost impossible for each individual doctor to keep up with all of the technical literature about drugs and be aware of the advantages and disadvantages of each of them. Doctors must rely on the so-called detail people sent out by the drug companies to inform physicians about new drugs and give them samples to dispense to their patients, so that doctors can see for themselves how effective the new drugs really are. Without FDA regulations, it is argued, the drug companies might introduce drugs that are not completely safe or simply do not work as well as they might.

Countering this argument is that doctors, hospitals, and drug companies have strong incentives to prescribe, market, and produce drugs that are both safe and effective. After all, if it can be proven that side effects from a drug cause harm to an individual, or that an individual was harmed because a drug did not perform as promised, the ensuing lawsuit can cost the doctor, hospital, or manufacturer millions of dollars. Moreover, doctors, hospitals, and drug companies rely heavily on their reputations, and serious errors in prescribing, marketing, or producing drugs can damage those reputations beyond repair.

Although debate remains over exactly how much regulation is appropriate to ensure that drugs are both safe and efficacious, there is little doubt that the 1962 amendments have resulted in a U.S. "drug lag." The number of drugs marketed in the United Kingdom that are not available in the United States, for example, is very much larger than the number marketed in the United States that are not available in the United Kingdom. Although the FDA and its supporters note that it takes time to ensure that patients benefit from rather than are harmed by new drugs, regulation-induced drug lag can *itself* be life-threatening. Dr. George Hitchings, a winner of the Nobel Prize in Medicine, estimated that the five-year lag in introducing Septra (an antibacterial agent) to the United States "killed 100,000, maybe a million people" in this country. Similarly, the introduction of a class of drugs called beta blockers (used to treat heart attack victims and people with high blood pressure) was delayed nearly a decade in this country relative to its introduction in Europe. According to several researchers, the lag in the FDA approval of these drugs cost the lives of at least 250,000 Americans.

Now we can see the terrible trade-off in the market for prescription drugs: Although lives are saved because unsafe or ineffective drugs are kept off the market, the FDA regulatory process delays (or even prevents) the introduction of some safe and efficacious drugs, thereby costing lives. If the only cost of FDA-mandated testing were the millions of dollars that drug companies must spend on those procedures, there probably would not be many critics of the FDA. But the fact is that many persons could have benefited greatly—perhaps to the extent of being alive today—had the 1962 Kefauver–Harris Amendments not delayed the introduction of so many drugs.

With this thought in mind, let us take a more systematic look at the trade-off we face. Every time a new drug is introduced, there is a chance that it should not have been—either because it has adverse side effects that outweigh the therapeutic benefits (it is not safe), or because it really does nothing significant to help the individuals who take it (it is not effective). When such a drug is introduced, we say that a **Type I error** has been committed. Since 1962, incidence of Type I error—the thalidomide possibility—has been reduced by increasing the amount of prior testing for new drugs. People have surely benefited from this reduction in Type I error by incurring fewer adverse side effects and by being spared the costs of taking ineffective drugs. But other people have been the victims of what is called **Type II error.** Their cost is the pain, suffering, and death that occur because the 1962 amendments have prevented or delayed the introduction of safe, efficacious drugs. Type II error occurs when a drug *should* be introduced but is not, because of FDA regulation.

Does the apparently high incidence of Type II errors by the FDA over the past 40 years imply that the regulatory process should be overhauled radically? Possibly, but even doing so would not eliminate the fundamental trade-off. The FDA's long, intensive review of new drug applications does produce benefits: The drugs that eventually reach the market are safer and more effective. As we have seen, the costs are that some safe, effective drugs never make it to the market, and many others are substantially delayed. Expediting the review process would enable more drugs to reach the market sooner, but it would also increase the chances that a harmful or ineffective drug might slip through the screening process.

It seems that for every benefit there is a cost. Indeed, this simple fact is so pervasive in our lives that economists have even coined a phrase summarizing it—*there is no such thing as a free lunch*—which simply means that in a world of scarcity, every choice we make entails a cost. By choosing to *reduce* the risk of introducing another thalidomide, we also choose to *increase* the risk of delaying another Septra or beta blocker. Trade-offs such as this are an inescapable fact.

The principles involved in making the best choices among trade-offs are discussed in Chapter 3. On the drug front, outcries over the high incidence of Type II errors by the FDA have in some cases induced the agency to shorten the testing period for drugs when the costs of Type I error are insignificant compared to the possible damage due to Type II error—as is the case with terminally ill patients. Thus, since the 1980s, the FDA has accelerated the approval process for several drugs used in treating patients with terminal diseases. One of the most famous of these drugs is azidothymidine (AZT), which emerged in 1986 as a possible treatment for AIDS. AZT received FDA approval after a testing period of only 18 months when it was found that the drug increased the life expectancy of AIDS patients. In effect, the FDA decided that the costs associated with Type I error—such as headaches and nausea—were outweighed by the many deaths that would result if the drug were not approved quickly.

In light of the expedited review that some drugs receive, it is worth asking two questions. First, how is it possible that the costs of delays for other drugs might greatly outweigh the benefits? The answer appears to be a principle called *rational ignorance*. The fact is that for most people most of the time, it doesn't pay to learn all there is to know even about important issues such as medical care. Thus, voters simply don't know enough to enable them to put sufficient pressure on their elected representatives or the FDA to improve the approval process: It is rational for most voters to remain ignorant and ineffective, because the costs of learning and doing more outweigh the likely benefits. But what, then, explains the outbreak of consumer interest and pressure leading to relatively quick approval on drugs such as AZT for AIDS and Taxol, used to treat breast cancer? The answer seems to reside in the existence of narrow, clearly identifiable groups of individuals who have enormous personal costs or benefits at stake. In the case of AZT, gay men took the lead in putting pressure on the FDA, while in the case of Taxol, women did, particularly those coming from families with a history of breast cancer. In each case, the potential benefits of learning about the advantages of the drug and acting on that knowledge were large relative to the costs. It was rational for consumers to be knowledgeable rather than ignorant in these cases. The result was pressure on the FDA, and expedited approval.

Ultimately, despite the expedited review of AZT and a number of other drugs used to treat AIDS or cancer, most of the agency's critics remain convinced that the FDA has too often weighed the terrible trade-off of drug regulation in a way that has produced tragedy for patients. As the battle against AIDS continues, there is little doubt that pressure on the FDA to expedite the drug-review process will increase. Only time and careful scrutiny will enable us to determine whether future choices by the FDA help us or harm us.

DISCUSSION QUESTIONS

1. Does the structure of the drug industry have any bearing on the types of errors that drug firms are likely to make? That is, would a drug industry comprised of numerous highly competitive firms be more or less likely to introduce unsafe drugs than an industry composed of a few large firms?

2. How could the incentives facing officials at the FDA be changed to reduce the incidence of Type II errors?

3. What would be the advantages and disadvantages of a system in which the FDA, instead of permitting or prohibiting new drugs, merely published its opinions about the safety and efficacy of drugs, and then allowed physicians to make their own decisions about whether to prescribe them for their patients?

4. Suppose, for simplicity, that Type I and Type II errors resulted in deaths only. Keeping in mind that too little caution produces Type I errors and too much caution produces Type II errors, what would be the best mix of Type I and Type II errors?

3

Flying the Friendly Skies?

Most of us hop into our car with little thought for our personal safety, beyond perhaps the act of putting on seat belts. Yet even though travel on scheduled, commercial airlines is safer than driving to work or to the grocery store, many people approach air travel with a sense of foreboding, if not downright fear.

If we were to think carefully about the wisdom of traveling 600 miles per hour in an aluminum tube seven miles above the earth, several questions might come to mind: How safe is this? How safe should it be? Because the people who operate airlines are not in it for fun, does their interest in making a buck ignore our interest in making it home in one piece? Is some form of government regulation the only way to ensure safety in the skies?

The science of economics begins with one simple principle: We live in a world of **scarcity,** which implies that to get more of any good, we must sacrifice some of other goods. This is just as true of safety as it is of pizzas or haircuts or works of art. Safety confers benefits (we live longer and more enjoyably), but achieving it also entails costs (we must give up something to obtain that safety).

As the degree of safety rises, the total benefits of safety rise, but the marginal (or incremental) benefits of additional safety decline. Consider a simple example: Adding exit doors to an airplane increases the number of people who can escape in the event of an emergency evacuation. Nevertheless, each *additional* door adds less in safety benefits than does the previous one; if the fourth door enables, say, an extra ten people to escape, the fifth may enable only an extra six to escape. (If this sounds implausible, imagine having a door for each person; the last door added will enable at most one

17

more person to escape.) So we say that the marginal (or incremental) benefit of safety declines as the amount of safety increases.

Let's look now at the other side of the equation: As the amount of safety increases, both the total and the marginal (incremental) costs of providing safety rise. Having a fuel gauge on the plane's instrument panel clearly enhances safety, because it reduces the chance that the plane will run out of fuel while in flight.[1] It is always possible that a fuel gauge will malfunction, so having a backup fuel gauge also adds to safety. Because having two gauges is more costly than having just one, the total costs of safety rise as safety increases. It is also clear, however, that while the cost of the second gauge is (at least) as great as the cost of the first, the second gauge has a smaller positive impact on safety. Thus, the cost per unit of additional (incremental) safety is higher for the second fuel gauge than for the first.

How much safety should we have? For an economist, the answer to such a question is generally expressed in terms of marginal benefits and marginal costs. The economically *efficient* level of safety occurs when the marginal cost of increasing safety just equals the marginal benefit of that increased safety. Put somewhat differently, if the marginal benefits of adding (or keeping) a safety feature exceed the marginal costs of doing so, then the feature is worth it. But if the added benefits of a safety device do *not* exceed the added costs, we should refrain from installing the device. Note there are two related issues here: How safe should we *be*, and how should we *achieve* that level of safety?

Both of these issues took on added urgency on the morning of September 11, 2001, when terrorists hijacked four U.S. commercial jetliners. The hijackers deliberately crashed two of the planes into New York's World Trade Center and flew another into the side of the Pentagon. The fourth plane crashed in a Pennsylvania field, probably in the midst of a struggle for control between the passengers and hijackers. Most people were stunned with the ease with which the hijackers were able to carry out their mission, for it suggested that air travel, particularly in the United States, was far less

---

[1] Notice that we say "reduces" rather than "eliminates." In 1978 a United Airlines pilot preoccupied with a malfunctioning landing gear evidently failed to pay sufficient attention to his cockpit gauges. Eight people were killed when the plane was forced to crash land after running out of fuel.

safe than previously believed. Immediately, it was clear that we should devote additional resources to airline safety; what was not clear was how *much* additional resources should be thus devoted, nor precisely *what* changes should be made. For example, some airline pilots wanted the right to carry firearms on flights, to help them prevent future hijackings. Other people objected, noting the high potential costs of such an action: an errant shot from a pistol could puncture a plane's skin, resulting in catastrophic cabin depressurization. Similarly, almost everyone agreed that more careful screening of passengers (and baggage) at airports would produce important safety benefits. But again, the question arose: how should we achieve this? Should carry-on bags be prohibited, or just examined more carefully? How thoroughly should checked luggage be screened for bombs? Our answers to these questions are evolving as we learn more about the extent of the threat and the costs of alternative responses to it. Nevertheless, throughout the process, economic principles can help us make the most sensible decisions.

In general, the efficient level of safety will not be perfect safety, because perfection is simply too costly to achieve. For example, to be absolutely *certain* that no one is ever killed or injured in an airplane crash, we would have to prevent all travel in airplanes. This does not mean it is efficient to have air disasters become a daily feature on the evening news. It does mean that it is efficient for there to be *some* risk associated with air travel. The unavoidable conclusion is that if we wish to enjoy the advantages of flying, we must be willing to accept some risk—a conclusion that each of us implicitly accepts every time we step aboard an airplane.

Changes in circumstances can alter the efficient level of safety. For example, if a technological change reduces the costs of bomb-scanning equipment, the marginal costs of preventing terrorist bomb attacks will be lower. It will be efficient to have more airports install the machines, and to have extra machines at large airports to speed the screening process. Air travel will become safer because of the technological change. Similarly, if the marginal benefits of safety rise for some reason—perhaps because the president of the United States is on board—it could be efficient to take more precautions, resulting in safer air travel. Given the factors that determine the benefits and costs of safety, the result of a change in circumstances will be some determinate level of safety that generally will be associated with some risk of death or injury.

Airplanes are complex systems, and an amazing number of things can go wrong with them. Over the century that humans have been flying, airplane manufacturers and airlines have studied every one of the things that has gone wrong thus far and have put into place design changes and operating procedures aimed at preventing recurring error. Of course, consumers have the greatest incentive to ensure that air travel is safe, and if information were free, we could assert with some confidence that the actual level of safety supplied by firms was the efficient level of safety. Consumers would simply observe the safety offered by different airlines, the prices they charge, and select the degrees of safety that best suited their preferences and budgets—just as with other goods. But, of course, information is not free; it is a **scarce good,** costly to obtain. As a result, it is possible that passengers are unaware of the safety records of various airlines, or the competency of the pilots and the maintenance procedures of an airline's mechanics. Indeed, it is possible that even the airlines themselves are uncertain about the efficient level of safety, perhaps because they have no way of correctly estimating the true threat of terrorist attacks, for example. Both of these possibilities have been used to argue that it is appropriate for the federal government to mandate certain minimum levels of safety, as it does today through the operation of the Federal Aviation Administration (FAA). Let's look at this issue in some detail.

One argument in favor of government safety standards rests on the presumption that, left to their own devices, airlines would provide less safety than passengers actually want to have. This might happen, for example, if customers could not tell (at a reasonable cost) whether or not the equipment, training, procedures, and so on employed by an airline are safe. If passengers cannot cheaply gauge the level of safety, they will not be willing to reward airlines for being safe or punish them for being unsafe. If safety is costly to provide and consumers are unwilling to pay for it because they cannot accurately measure it, airlines will provide too little of it. The conclusion, at least as reached by some, is that government experts—such as the FAA—should set safety standards for the industry.

This conclusion seems plausible, but it ignores two simple points. First, how is the government to know what the efficient level of safety is? Even if the FAA is fully knowledgeable regarding the efficacy and costs of all possible safety measures, it still does not have enough information to set efficient safety standards, because it does not know the value that people place on safety. Without such information, the FAA has no way of assessing the benefits of additional safety, and thus no means of knowing whether those benefits are greater or less than the added costs.

The second point is that it is likely that what people are really interested in is reaching their destinations safely, not whether they got there because of a good plane, a good pilot, or a good mechanic. Even if they cannot observe whether an airline hires good pilots or bad pilots, they can observe whether that airline's planes land safely or crash. If it is *safety* that is important to consumers— and not the obscure, costly-to-measure set of reasons for that safety—the fact that consumers cannot easily measure metal fatigue in jet engines may be totally irrelevant to the process of achieving the efficient level of safety.

Interestingly, evidence shows that consumers are indeed cognizant of the safety performance of airlines, and that they "punish" airlines that perform in an unsafe manner. Researchers Mark Mitchell and Michael Maloney have found that when an airline is "at fault" in a fatal plane crash, consumers appear to downgrade their safety rating of the airline (i.e., revise upward their estimates of the likelihood of future fatal crashes). As a result, the offending airline suffers substantial adverse financial consequences over and above the costs of losing the plane and being sued on behalf of the victims. These research findings suggest a striking degree of safety awareness on the part of supposedly ignorant consumers.

Of course, this discussion leaves open the issue of how to handle safety threats posed by terrorists and the like. For example, much of the information that goes into assessing terrorist threats is classified as secret, and its revelation to airlines or consumers might well compromise key sources of the data. Hence there could be an advantage to having the government try to approximate the efficient safety outcome by mandating certain screening provisions without revealing exactly why they are being chosen. Similarly, because airlines are connected in networks (so that people and baggage move from one airline to another in the course of a trip) one might argue that achieving the efficient level of safety necessitates a common set of screening rules for all airlines.

Even so, this does not inform us as to whether the government should impose those rules, or the airlines should come to a voluntary joint agreement on them.

We began this chapter with the commonplace observation that airlines are safer than cars. Yet many people still worry for their safety every time they get on an airplane. Are they being irrational? Well, the answer, it seems, is in the eye of the beholder. Measured in terms of fatalities per mile traveled, airplanes are some 15 times safer than cars (and 176 times safer than walking, we might add). But this number masks the fact that 68 percent of aircraft accidents happen on takeoff and landing, and these operations occupy only 6 percent of flight time. It is presumably this fact that quite sensibly makes people nervous whenever they find themselves approaching an airport.

DISCUSSION QUESTIONS

1. Is it possible to be too safe? Explain what you mean by "too safe."

2. Many automobile manufacturers routinely advertise the safety of their cars, yet airlines generally do not even mention safety in their advertising. Can you suggest an explanation for this difference?

3. Many economists would argue that private companies are likely to be more efficient than the government in operating airlines. Yet many economists would also argue that there is a valid reason for government to regulate the safety of those same airlines. Can you explain why (or why not) the government might be good at ensuring safety, even though it might not be good at operating the airlines?

4. Professional football teams sometimes charter airplanes to take them to their "away" games. Would you feel safer riding on a United Airlines plane that had been chartered by the Washington Redskins than on a regularly scheduled United Airlines flight?

4

The Mystery of Wealth

Why are the citizens of some nations rich while the inhabitants of others are poor? Your initial answer might be, "Because of differences in the **natural-resource endowments** of the nations." It is surely true that ample endowments of energy, timber, and fertile land all help raise wealth. But natural resources can be only a very small part of the answer, as witnessed by many counterexamples. Switzerland and Luxembourg, for example, are nearly devoid of key natural resources, yet the real incomes of citizens of those lands are among the world's highest. Similarly, Hong Kong, which consists of but a few square miles of rock and hillside, is one of the economic miracles of the last century, while in Russia, a land amply endowed with vast quantities of virtually every important resource, most people remain mired in economic misery.

A number of studies have begun to unravel the mystery of **economic growth.** Repeatedly, they have found that it is the fundamental political and legal **institutions** of society that are conducive to growth. Of these, political stability, secure private property rights, and legal systems based on the **rule of law** are among the most important. Such institutions encourage people to make long-lived investments in improving land and in all forms of physical and human capital. These investments raise the **capital stock,** which in turn provides for more growth long into the future. And the cumulative effects of this growth over time eventually yield much higher standards of living.

Professor Paul Mahoney of the University of Virginia has studied the contrasting effects of different legal systems on economic growth. Many legal systems around the world today are based on one of two basic models: the English **common law system**

TABLE 4–1   Differing Legal Systems

Common Law Nations	Civil Law Nations
Australia	Brazil
Canada	Egypt
India	France
Israel	Greece
New Zealand	Italy
United Kingdom	Mexico
United States	Sweden

and the French **civil law system.** Common law systems reflect a conscious decision in favor of a limited role for government and emphasize the importance of the judiciary in constraining the power of the executive and legislative branches of government. In contrast, civil law systems favor the creation of a strong centralized government in which the legislature and the executive branches have the power to grant preferential treatment to special interests. Table 4–1 shows a sample of common law and civil law countries

Mahoney found that the security of property rights is much stronger in common law systems, such as observed in England and her former colonies, including the United States. In nations such as France and its former colonies, the civil law systems are much more likely to yield unpredictable changes in the rules of the game—the structure of **property and contract rights.** This unpredictability makes people reluctant to make long-term fixed investments, a fact that ultimately slows the economic growth of these nations and lowers the standard of living for their citizens.

The reasoning here is simple. If you know that the police will not help you protect your rights to a home or car, you are less likely to acquire those assets. Similarly, if you cannot easily enforce business or employment contracts that you make, you are less likely to make those contracts—and thus less likely to produce as many goods or services. And if you cannot plan for the future because you don't know what the rules of the game will be in ten years, or perhaps even one year from now, you are less likely to make the productive long-term investments that require years to pay off. Common law systems seem to do a better job at enforcing contracts and securing property rights, and thus would be expected to promote economic activity now and economic growth over time.

When Mahoney examined the economic performance of nations around the world from 1960 until the 1990s, he found that economic growth was one-third higher in the common law nations, with their strong property rights, than in civil law nations. Over the 30-plus years covered by his study, the result was that the standard of living—measured by real per capita income—jumped more than 20 percent in common law nations compared to civil law nations. If such a pattern persisted over the span of a century, it would produce a staggering 80 percent real per capita income differential in favor of nations with secure property rights.

William Easterly and Ross Levine recently have taken a much broader view, both across time and across institutions, in assessing the economic growth of a variety of nations since their days as colonies. These economists examined how institutions such as political stability, protection against violence or theft, security of contracts, and freedom from regulatory burdens all contribute to sustained economic growth. They found that it is key institutions such as these, rather than natural-resource endowments, that explain long-term differences in economic growth, and thus present-day differences in levels of real income. To illustrate the powerful effect of institutions, consider the contrast between Mexico, with per capita real income of about $9400 today, and the United States, with a per capita real income of about $38,200. Easterly and Levine concluded that if Mexico had developed with the same political and legal institutions that the United States has enjoyed, per capita income in Mexico would today be *equal* to that in the United States!

Given the great importance of such institutions in determining long-term growth, Easterly and Levine went on to ask another important question: How have countries gotten the political and legal institutions they have today? The answer has to do with disease, of all things. The 72 countries studied by Easterly and Levine are all former European colonies, where a variety of colonial strategies were pursued. In Australia, New Zealand, and North America, the colonists found geography and climate that were conducive to good health. Permanent settlement was attractive, so colonists created institutions to protect private property and curb the power of the state. But when Europeans arrived in Africa and South America, they encountered tropical diseases, such as malaria and yellow fever, that produced high mortality rates. This discouraged permanent settlement and encouraged a mentality focused on extracting metals, cash crops, and other resources. As a result, there was little incentive to promote democratic institutions or stable long-term property rights systems. The differing initial institutions helped shape economic growth over the years and, because of the broad persistence of those institutions, continue to shape the political and legal character and the standard of living in these nations today.

Recent events illustrate also that the effects of political and legal institutions can be drastically accelerated—in either direction. Consider China, which in 1979 began to change its institutions in two key ways. First, as we discuss more fully in Chapter 32, on a very limited basis China began to experiment with private property rights for a few of its citizens, and under narrow circumstances. (This experiment even included amending its constitution to strengthen private property protections.) Second, the Chinese government began to clear away obstacles to foreign investment, making China a more secure place for Western companies to do business in. Although the institutional changes have been modest, their combined effects have been substantial. Over the past 25 years, economic growth in China has accelerated, averaging better than 6 percent per year. And if that doesn't sound like much, keep in mind that it has been enough over that period to raise real per capita income in China by a factor of nearly *five*.

For an example of the potential *destructive* impact of institutional change, we need look no further than Zimbabwe. When that country won its independence from Britain in 1980, it was one of the most prosperous nations in Africa. Soon after taking power as Zimbabwe's first (and thus far only) president, Robert Mugabe began disassembling that nation's rule of law, tearing apart the institutions that had helped it grow rich. He reduced the security of property rights in land, and eventually confiscated those rights altogether. Mugabe also has gradually taken control of the prices of most goods and services in his nation, and he even controls the price of its national currency, at least the price at which Zimbabweans are allowed to trade it. Moreover, the Mugabe government has confiscated large stocks of food and much of the value of anything that might be exported out of or imported into Zimbabwe. In short, anything that is produced or saved has become subject to confiscation, so the incentives to do either are—to put it mildly—reduced.

As a result, between 1980 and 1996, real per capita income in Zimbabwe fell by one-third, and since 1996 it has fallen by an additional one-third. Unemployment is rampant, investment nonexistent, and the inflation rate in Zimbabwe has exceeded 400 percent in recent years. In only 25 years, the fruit of many decades of labor and capital investment has been destroyed, because the very institutions that made that fruit possible have been eliminated. It is a lesson we ignore at our peril.

DISCUSSION QUESTIONS

1. Consider two countries, A and B, and suppose that both have identical *physical* endowments of, say, iron ore. But suppose that in country A, any profits that are made from mining the ore are subject to confiscation by the government of A, while in country B, there is no such risk. How does the risk of expropriation affect the *economic* endowment of the two nations? In which nation are people richer?

2. In light of your answer to the previous question, how do you explain the fact that in some countries there is widespread political support for government policies that expropriate resources from some groups for the purpose of handing them out to other groups?

3. If the crucial factor determining a country's low standard of living is the adverse set of legal and cultural institutions it possesses, can you offer suggestions for how the other nations of the world might be helpful in permanently raising that country's standard of living?

Part Two

Supply and Demand

INTRODUCTION

The tools of demand and supply are the most basic and useful elements of the economist's kit. Indeed, many economists would argue that the **law of demand**—the lower the price of a good, the greater the quantity of that good demanded by purchasers—is the single most powerful proposition in all of economics. Simply stated, the law of demand has the capacity, unmatched by any other proposition in economics, to explain an incredibly diverse range of human behaviors. For example, the law of demand explains why buildings are taller in downtown areas than in outlying suburbs, and also why people are willing to sit in the upper deck of football stadiums even though lower deck seats are clearly superior. The great explanatory power of the law of demand is almost matched by that of the **law of supply,** which states that the higher the price of a good, the greater will be the quantity of that good supplied by producers. The law of supply helps us understand why people receive a premium wage when they work overtime, as well as why parking places at the beach are so much more expensive during the summer months than they are during the winter.

When the laws of demand and supply are combined, they illuminate the enormous **gains from trade** that arise from voluntary exchange. In Chapter 5, "Sex, Booze, and Drugs," we examine what happens when the government attempts to prohibit the exchanges that give rise to these gains. The consequences are often surprising, always costly, and—sadly—sometimes tragic. We find, for example, that when the federal government made alcoholic beverages illegal during the era known as Prohibition, Americans responded by switching from beer to hard liquor and by getting drunk a larger proportion of the times when they drank. We also show that the government's ongoing efforts to prevent individuals from using drugs such as marijuana and cocaine cause the drive-by shootings that occur in many major cities, and also encourage drug overdoses among users. Finally, we explain why laws against prostitution help to foster the spread of acquired immune deficiency syndrome (AIDS).

Sometimes, as illustrated in Chapter 6, "Expanding Waistlines," we have to examine both demand and supply to understand a public issue. Obesity is rising in the United States, chiefly as a result of three separate economic forces at work. First, wages paid in sedentary occupations have risen relative to those in physically demanding jobs, inducing people to spend more of their time exercising their brains at work, rather than their muscles. An even more important factor, however, is that the entry of women into the workforce has increased the demand for prepackaged prepared foods—which have been gladly supplied by producers. This has sharply reduced the **full cost** of eating (especially the full cost of snacks), and so increased the amount of food consumed. Finally, developments discussed in more detail in Chapter 10 have raised the full cost of consuming cigarettes over the last 20 years or so. This cost increase has induced people to substitute food for cigarettes. On balance, the health effects of this last development likely have been positive. Nevertheless, because expanding waistlines today will almost surely generate adverse health effects in the future, we can expect this issue to become a widely debated one in the years to come.

In Chapter 7, "Is Water Different?", we dispel the myth that the consumption of some goods does not conform to the law of demand. Here we examine the demand for water, that "most necessary of all necessities," and find that—lo and behold—when the price of water is raised, people consume less of it—exactly as predicted by the law of demand. One important conclusion of this chapter is that the water shortages and water crises that afflict various parts of the nation are not the result of droughts, but in fact are caused by government officials who are unwilling or unable to accept the reality of the law of demand.

It is surely distasteful to think in terms of the supply and demand for human beings; yet that is what developments half a world away compel us to do in Chapter 8, "Slave Redemption in Sudan." Nearly a century after human slavery was abolished there by British troops, the slave trade has reemerged in Sudan, the largest nation in Africa. Following in the tracks of the slave raiders are slave redemptionists, who seek to alleviate the human suffering in Sudan by purchasing freedom for thousands of enslaved individuals. Yet the efforts of these well-intentioned individuals are having consequences surely not intended by them. Indeed, attempts to reduce slavery in Sudan actually have encouraged the slave trade and even may have resulted in more—not fewer—people in bondage. And so we see that sometimes the consequences of well-intentioned actions are not merely unexpected but tragic.

Medical matters form the focus of our analysis in Chapter 9, "Choice and Life," where we look at an issue seemingly unrelated to economics—abortion. Although the debate between a woman's right to choose and a fetus's right to live is usually cast in highly charged, emotional terms, we demonstrate that the dispassionate reasoning of the economist can illuminate some of the issues at stake. Economics can never be the ultimate arbiter of whether abortion should be legal or illegal, but it can help us understand more about what our choices cost.

The cost of a pack of cigarettes in the United States has more than doubled over the last few years, importantly because the federal and state governments have sharply increased cigarette taxes. These tax increases have reduced the supply of cigarettes and so pushed up prices. As we see in Chapter 10, "Smoking and Smuggling," this has led to a host of other developments. The number of smokers and the amount of smoking are both down, as would readily be predicted by the law of demand. Nevertheless, for people who continue to smoke in the face of higher taxes, things are worse: not only is a larger share of their income going to the "evil weed", they are also smoking stronger, more carcinogenic cigarettes. At the market level, higher cigarette taxes have also led to much more widespread smuggling of cigarettes, as consumers seek to minimize the costs of the higher taxes. On a variety of fronts, then, we see that the basic tools of supply and demand enable us to understand the sometimes unintended and often surprising economics of public issues.

5

Sex, Booze, and Drugs

Prior to 1914, cocaine was legal in this country; today it is not. Alcohol (of the intoxicating variety) is legal in the United States today; from 1920 to 1933 it was not. Prostitution is legal in Nevada today; in the other 49 states it is not.[1] All these goods—sex, booze, and drugs—have at least one thing in common: The consumption of each brings together a willing seller with a willing buyer, creating an act of mutually beneficial exchange (at least in the opinion of the parties involved). Partly because of this property, attempts to proscribe the consumption of these goods have (1) met with less than spectacular success and (2) yielded some peculiar patterns of production, distribution, and usage. Let's see why.

When the government seeks to prevent voluntary exchange, it generally must decide whether to go after the seller or the buyer. In most cases—and certainly when sex, booze, or drugs have been involved—the government targets sellers, because this is where the authorities get the most benefit from their enforcement dollars. A cocaine dealer, even a small retail pusher, often supplies dozens or even hundreds of users each day, as did speakeasies (illegal saloons) during Prohibition; a hooker typically services anywhere from three to ten tricks per day. By incarcerating the supplier, the police can prevent several, or even several hundred, transactions from taking place, which is usually much more cost-effective than going after the buyers one by one. It is not that the police ignore the consumers of illegal goods; indeed, sting operations—in which the police pose as

---

[1] These statements are not quite correct. Even today, cocaine may be obtained legally by prescription from a physician. Prostitution in Nevada is legal only in those counties that have, by virtue of local option, chosen to proclaim it as such. Finally, some counties in the United States remain dry, prohibiting the sale of beer, wine, and distilled spirits.

illicit sellers—often make the headlines. Nevertheless, most enforcement efforts focus on the supply side, and so shall we.

Law enforcement activities directed against the suppliers of illegal goods increase the suppliers' operating costs. The risks of fines, jail sentences, and possibly even violence become part of the costs of doing business and must be taken into account by existing and potential suppliers. Some entrepreneurs will leave the business, turning their talents to other activities; others will resort to clandestine (and costly) means to hide their operations from the police; still others will restrict the circle of buyers with whom they are willing to deal to minimize the chances that a customer is a cop. Across the board, the costs of operation are higher, and at any given price, less of the product will be available. There is a reduction in supply, and the result is a higher price for the good.

This increase in price is, in a sense, exactly what the enforcement officials are after, for the consumers of sex, booze, and drugs behave according to the **law of demand:** The higher the price of a good, the lower the amount consumed. So the immediate impact of the enforcement efforts against sellers is to reduce the consumption of the illegal good by buyers. There are, however, some other effects.

First, because the good in question is illegal, people who have a **comparative advantage** in conducting illegal activities will be attracted to the business of supplying (and perhaps demanding) the good. Some may have an existing criminal record and are relatively unconcerned about adding to it. Others may have developed skills in evading detection and prosecution while engaged in other criminal activities. Some may simply look at the illegal activity as another means of thumbing their noses at society. The general point is that when an activity is made illegal, people who are good at being criminals are attracted to that activity.

Illegal contracts usually are not enforceable through legal channels (and even if they were, few suppliers of illegal goods would be stupid enough to complain to the police about not being paid for their products). Thus, buyers and sellers of illegal goods frequently must resort to private methods of contract enforcement—which often means violence.[2] Hence, people who are relatively good at

---

[2] Fundamentally, violence—such as involuntary incarceration—also plays a key role in the government's enforcement of legal contracts. We often do not think of it as violence, of course, because it is usually cushioned by constitutional safeguards, procedural rules, and so on.

violence are attracted to illegal activities and are given greater incentives to employ their talents. This is one reason why the murder rate in America rose to record levels during Prohibition (1920–1933) and then dropped sharply when liquor was again made legal. It also helps explain why the number of drug-related murders soared during the 1980s, and why drive-by shootings became commonplace in many drug-infested cities. The Thompson submachine gun of the 1930s and the MAC-10 machine gun of the 1980s were, importantly, just low-cost means of contract enforcement.

The attempts of law enforcement officials to drive sellers of illegal goods out of business have another effect. Based on recent wholesale prices, $50,000 worth of pure heroin weighs about two ounces; $50,000 worth of marijuana weighs about twenty pounds. As any drug smuggler can tell you, hiding two ounces of contraband is a lot easier than hiding twenty pounds. Thus, to avoid detection and prosecution, suppliers of the illegal good have an incentive to deal in the more valuable versions of their product, which for drugs and booze mean the more potent versions. Bootleggers during Prohibition concentrated on hard liquor rather than beer and wine; even today, moonshine typically has roughly twice the alcohol content of legal hard liquor such as bourbon, scotch, or vodka. After narcotics became illegal in this country in 1914, importers switched from the milder opium to its more valuable, more potent, and more addictive derivative, heroin.

The move to the more potent versions of illegal commodities is enhanced by enforcement activities directed against users. Not only do users, like suppliers, find it easier (cheaper) to hide the more potent versions, there is also a change in relative prices due to user penalties. Typically, the law has lower penalties for using an illegal substance than for distributing it. Within each category (use or sale), however, there is commonly the same penalty regardless of value per unit. For example, during Prohibition, a bottle of wine and a bottle of more expensive, more potent hard liquor were equally illegal. Today, the possession of one gram of 90 percent pure cocaine brings the same penalty as the possession of one gram of 10 percent pure cocaine. Given the physical quantities, there is a fixed cost (the legal penalty) associated with being caught, regardless of value per unit (and thus potency) of the substance.

Hence, the structure of legal penalties raises the relative price of less potent versions, encouraging users to substitute more potent versions—heroin instead of opium, hashish instead of marijuana, hard liquor instead of beer. Penalties against users also encourage a change in the nature of usage. Prior to 1914, cocaine was legal in this country and was used openly as a mild stimulant, much as people today use caffeine. (Cocaine was even included in the original formulation of Coca-Cola.) This type of usage—small, regular doses over long time intervals—becomes relatively more expensive when the substance is made illegal. Extensive usage (small doses spread over time) is more likely to be detected by the authorities than is intensive usage (a large dose consumed at once), simply because possession time is longer and the drug must be accessed more frequently. Thus, when a substance is made illegal, there is an incentive for consumers to switch toward usage that is more intensive. Rather than ingesting cocaine orally in the form of a highly diluted liquid solution, as was commonly done before 1914, people switched to snorting or even injecting it. During Prohibition, people dispensed with cocktails before dinner each night; instead, on the less frequent occasions when they drank, they more often drank to get drunk. The same phenomenon is observed today. People under the age of twenty-one consume alcoholic beverages less frequently than do people over the age of twenty-one. But when they do drink, they are more likely to drink to get drunk.

Not surprisingly, the suppliers of illegal commodities are reluctant to advertise their wares openly; the police are as capable of reading billboards and watching TV as are potential customers. Suppliers are also reluctant to establish easily recognized identities and regular places and hours of business, because to do so raises the chance of being caught by the police. Information about the price and quality of products being sold goes underground, often with unfortunate effects for consumers.

With legal goods, consumers have several means of obtaining information. They can learn from friends, advertisements, and personal experience. When goods are legal, they can be trademarked for identification. The trademark cannot legally be copied, and the courts protect it. Given such easily identified brands, consumers can be made aware of the quality and price of each. If their experience does not meet expectations, they can assure themselves of no further contact with the unsatisfactory product by never buying that brand again.

When a general class of products becomes illegal, there are fewer ways to obtain information. Brand names are no longer protected by law, so falsification of well-known brands ensues. When products do not meet expectations, it is more difficult (costly) for consumers to punish suppliers. Frequently, the result is degradation of and uncertainty about product quality. The consequences for consumers of the illegal goods are often unpleasant, sometimes fatal.

Consider prostitution. In those counties in Nevada where prostitution is legal, the prostitutes are required to register with the local authorities, and they generally conduct their business within the confines of well-established bordellos. These establishments advertise openly and rely heavily on repeat business. Health officials test the prostitutes weekly for venereal disease and every month for AIDS. Contrast this with other areas of the country, where prostitution is illegal. Suppliers generally are streetwalkers, because a fixed, physical location is too easy for the police to detect and raid. Suppliers change locations frequently, to reduce harassment by police. Repeat business is reported to be minimal; frequently, customers have never seen the prostitute before and never will again.

The difference in outcomes is striking. In Nevada, the spread of venereal disease by legal prostitutes is estimated to be almost nonexistent; to date, none of the 9000 registered prostitutes in Nevada has tested positive for AIDS. By contrast, in some major cities outside Nevada the incidence of venereal disease among prostitutes is estimated to be near 100 percent. In Miami, one study found that 19 percent of all incarcerated prostitutes tested positive for AIDS; in Newark, New Jersey, 52 percent of the prostitutes tested were infected with the AIDS virus, and about half of the prostitutes in Washington, D.C., and New York City are also believed to be carrying the AIDS virus. Because of the lack of reliable information in markets for illegal goods, customers frequently do not know exactly what they are getting; as a result, they sometimes get more than they bargained for.

Consider alcohol and drugs. Today, alcoholic beverages are heavily advertised to establish their brand names and are carried by reputable dealers. Customers can readily punish suppliers for any deviation from the expected potency or quality by withdrawing their business, telling their friends, or even bringing a lawsuit. Similar circumstances prevailed before 1914 in this country for the hundreds of products containing opium or cocaine.

During Prohibition, consumers of alcohol often did not know exactly what they were buying or where to find the supplier the next day if they were dissatisfied. Fly-by-night operators sometimes adulterated liquor with methyl alcohol. In extremely small concentrations, this made watered-down booze taste like it had more kick; in only slightly higher concentrations, the methyl alcohol blinded or even killed the unsuspecting consumer. Even in "reputable" speakeasies (those likely to be in business at the same location the next day), bottles bearing the labels of high-priced foreign whiskeys were refilled repeatedly with locally (and illegally) produced rotgut until their labels wore off.

In the 1970s, more than one purchaser of what was reputed to be high-potency Panama Red or Acapulco Gold marijuana ended up with low-potency pot heavily loaded with stems, seeds, and maybe even oregano. Buyers of cocaine must worry about not only how much the product has been cut along the distribution chain, but also what has been used to cut it. In recent years the purity of cocaine at the retail level has ranged between 10 percent and 95 percent; for heroin, the degree of purity has ranged from 5 percent to 50 percent. Cutting agents can turn out to be any of various sugars, local anesthetics, or amphetamines; on occasion, rat poison has been used.

We noted earlier that the legal penalties for the users of illegal goods encourage them to use more potent forms and to use them more intensively. These facts and the uncertain quality and potency of the illegal products yield a deadly combination. During Prohibition, the death rate from acute alcohol poisoning (i.e., due to an overdose) was more than 30 times higher than today. During 1927 alone, 12,000 people died from acute alcohol poisoning, and many thousands more were blinded or killed by contaminated booze. Today, about 3000 people per year die as a direct result of consuming either cocaine or heroin. Of that total, it is estimated, roughly 80 percent die from (1) an overdose caused by unexpectedly potent product or (2) an adverse reaction to the material used to cut the drug. Clearly, caveat emptor (let the buyer beware) is a warning to be taken seriously if one is consuming an illegal product.

We noted at the beginning of the chapter that one of the effects of making a good illegal is to raise its price. One might well ask, by how much? During the early 1990s, the federal government was spending about $2 billion a year in its efforts to stop the importation of cocaine from Colombia. One study concluded that these efforts had hiked the price of cocaine by 4 percent (yes, 4 percent) relative to what it would have been had the federal government done nothing to interdict cocaine imports. The study estimated that the cost of raising the price of cocaine an additional 2 percent would be $1 billion per year.[3]

The government's efforts to halt imports of marijuana have been more successful, presumably because that product is easier to detect than cocaine. Nevertheless, suppliers have responded by cultivating marijuana domestically instead of importing it and bringing it in across the relatively open U.S.–Canadian border rather than from elsewhere. The net effect has been an estimated tenfold increase in potency due to the superior farming techniques available in this country and Canada, as well as the use of genetic bioengineering to improve strains.

We might also consider the government's efforts to eliminate the consumption of alcohol during the 1920s and 1930s. They failed so badly that the Eighteenth Amendment, which put Prohibition in place, was the first (and thus far the only) constitutional amendment ever to be repealed. As for prostitution—it is reputed to be "the oldest profession" and by all accounts continues to flourish today, even in Newark and Miami.

The government's inability to halt the consumption of sex, booze, or drugs does not in and of itself mean that those efforts have failed. Indeed, the "successes" of these efforts are manifested in their consequences—ranging from tainted drugs and alcohol to disease-ridden prostitutes. The message instead is that when the government attempts to prevent mutually beneficial exchange, even its best efforts are unlikely to meet with spectacular success.

---

[3] Federal attempts to prevent cocaine from entering the country are, of course, supplemented by other federal, as well as state and local, efforts to eradicate the drug once it has crossed our borders. To date, there are no empirical estimates of the extent to which these other efforts have increased prices.

DISCUSSION QUESTIONS

1. The federal government currently taxes alcohol on the basis of the 100-proof gallon. (One-hundred-proof alcohol is exactly 50 percent pure ethyl alcohol; most hard liquor sold is 80-proof, or 40 percent ethyl alcohol, whereas wine is usually about 24-proof, and most beer is 6- to 10-proof.) How would alcohol consumption patterns be different if the government taxed alcohol strictly on the basis of volume rather than taking into account its potency as well?

2. During Prohibition some speakeasy operators paid bribes to ensure that the police did not raid them. Would you expect the quality of the liquor served in such speakeasies to be higher or lower than in those that did not pay such bribes? Would you expect to find any systematic differences (e.g., with regard to income levels) among the customers patronizing the two types of speakeasies?

3. The markets for prostitution in Nevada and New Jersey have two important differences: (1) Prostitutes in New Jersey face higher costs because of government efforts to prosecute them; and (2) customers in New Jersey face higher risks of contracting diseases from prostitutes, because the illegal nature of the business makes reliable information about product quality much more costly to obtain. Given these facts, would you expect the price of prostitution services to be higher or lower in New Jersey than in Nevada? Which state would have the higher amount of services consumed (adjusted for population differences)?

4. According to the surgeon general of the United States, nicotine is the most addictive drug known to humanity, and cigarette smoking kills perhaps 300,000 to 400,000 people per year in the United States. Why isn't tobacco illegal in the United States?

6

Expanding Waistlines

Americans are putting on the pounds. In the 1960s the average American male weighed 168 pounds; today he tips the scales at about 180. Over the same span, the average American woman put on ten pounds, rising to 152 pounds from her previous 142 pounds. More significantly, these weight gains have been larger among people who were heavier to begin with. As a result, obesity in America has more than doubled over this period: Over 30 percent of Americans now have a body mass index (BMI, a measure of weight relative to height) in excess of 30, the level at which doctors say a person passes from overweight to obese.[1] What explains these developments? Not surprisingly, economics has a lot to say on this question; in fact, some fairly simple changes in demand and supply explain why waistlines in America and elsewhere in the world have been expanding so quickly.

Actually, Americans put weight on throughout all of the twentieth century, largely as a result of two key factors. First, wages in sedentary occupations (those relying on brains rather than brawn) rose relative to those in active occupations. People responded by leaving jobs in manufacturing and agriculture and starting work in service and management jobs. This occupational switch reduced their calorie expenditures on the job and helped push up average

---

[1] In terms of the metric system, $BMI = K/M^2$, where K is weight in kilograms, and M is height in meters. Using the English measurement system, $BMI = (704.5)(W/H^2)$, where W is weight in pounds, and H is height in inches. BMIs in the range of 20–25 are considered healthy. Below 20 is thin, 25–30 is overweight, and 30 and above is obese—the range in which significant adverse health effects (ranging from diabetes to heart disease) begin to show up.

weights. The second force at work was the decline in the relative price of food during the twentieth century; as predicted by the **law of demand,** this price decline induced people to eat more, pushing up their caloric intake and their body weights. Between about 1900 and 1960, the weight of the average male rose 16 pounds, with similar but slightly smaller gains for the average female.

As it turns out, these weight gains during the first part of the twentieth century were probably a good thing from a health standpoint: many Americans at the beginning of the century were actually malnourished, and the added poundage led to better health outcomes for them. The excess weight we added during the last 35 years or so is an entirely different matter, however. By the 1960s, average BMI in the United States was already at the high end of the healthy range of 20–25, so those extra pounds since then have pushed us further into the unhealthy categories of overweight and even obese.

How can we explain this recent surge in poundage? There are three key components. First, levels of physical activity have declined, although not nearly as much as many popular commentators would have us believe. The big move from active to sedentary employments took place before 1970, so it cannot explain the last 30 years of weight gains. Still, caloric energy expenditures by both men and women in the United States have been falling. Americans are spending less time at work and less time on household chores, and more time watching TV, looking at computer monitors, and talking on the phone. Overall, per capita caloric energy expenditures have dropped a bit more than 25 percent since the 1960s. This is only a small part of the story, however; indeed, it can explain only a couple of the pounds Americans have added over the last 30 years. The rest comes from higher caloric intake.

By far the most important reason for this higher caloric intake appears to be a change in the way food is prepared: Due to major changes in food processing technology, the "time cost" involved in preparing meals has fallen dramatically. Consequently, the **full cost** (money plus time cost) of food has dropped, leading to the consumption of significantly more calories. The result has been expanding waistlines.

In the 1960s, food was prepared in the home by family members and eaten there. Since then, there have been a series of technological innovations in food processing:

- vacuum packing,
- flash freezing,
- improved preservatives and flavorings, and, of course,
- the microwave.

As a result, much food preparation now is done outside the home by manufacturers who specialize in that activity and then ship the packaged, prepared food to the consumer to be eaten at home. The result is that over the last 35 years, the amount of time spent on food preparation and cleanup in the home has fallen in half. In addition, outside the home convenient, tasty prepackaged foods are now merely a few steps away in a vending machine, rather than being 10 to 20 minutes away in the nearest store. On both counts, the full cost of consuming food has declined, and people are consuming more calories. Moreover, they are doing it not by eating more calories at each meal, but rather by eating more "meals" (actually snacks) during the day: caloric intake during the traditional meals of breakfast, lunch, and dinner has remained nearly constant at about 1800 per day for men and 1400 per day for women. But both sexes have nearly doubled their intake of calories from snacks. Overall, caloric intake has risen 15 percent for men and 10 percent for women.

A few questions remain. First, are the additional calories that Americans are consuming each day—the equivalent of a Coke or a few cookies—really enough to account for the poundage we have been accumulating? The answer is "yes." An extra 150 calories per day for men of average weight and activity levels will eventually lead to 11 pounds of excess waistline baggage. For women, the same 150 calories per day would eventually amount to an extra 13 pounds. (The weight gain from these extra calories eventually levels off, because as people get heavier they burn more calories just doing the things they usually do.)

The second question is, what started the revolution in food processing that made these extra calories cheaper? Although the answer to this is not completely settled, the most likely source may be found in the workforce decisions of women. Beginning about 35 years ago, women began entering the workforce in unprecedented numbers; indeed, the **labor force**

participation rate of women doubled over this period. Moreover, they have been moving into occupations and professions—such as medicine, law, and the upper ranks of business—in which annual earnings are much higher than in the traditional fields of female employment, such as teaching and nursing. On both counts, the **opportunity cost** of women's time has been rising, thus increasing the demand for laborsaving conveniences, such as prepared foods. The food industry has responded just as economics would predict.

A third question being asked by some people is this: Are Americans really better off due to the lower cost of food? Ordinarily, economists would argue that a technological improvement that lowers the costs of a good definitely will improve the lot of consumers. But in the present case, with more people becoming obese, the adverse health effects of the extra calories are becoming significant. The incidence of diabetes is rising, as is the number of people who are disabled due to obesity-related injuries or other health problems.

Indeed, some analysts have noted that people who were heavy to begin with are the ones most likely to have put on the most extra pounds. As the poundage has piled up across the country, so too have the sales of diet books, as well as the rates of expensive bariatric surgery (in which part of the stomach is stapled shut to reduce caloric intake and absorption). All in all, some analysts have suggested, maybe the lower cost of food has made people *worse* off, by inducing them to do something that they would rather not do—put on weight. This might be particularly the case for people who are said to have little self-control as to the amount they eat. While there may be something to this argument, we can consider a counter-argument expressed in the following analogy: People who live in cold-weather climates, such as Montana, the Dakotas, and Minnesota, routinely complain about the weather in the winter. People in such climes also spend far more than the average person on clothes to offset the adverse effects of the cold weather. Surely we would not want to argue that such people are worse off for having chosen to live where they do rather than in warmer locales. Similarly, in the case of people who are said to lack control over the amount they eat, just who is it that should decide—and enforce—their caloric intake?

There is one final point to our story, one that illustrates amply the fact that even the best of intentions sometimes result in unintended consequences. Over the same period that Americans have been packing on the pounds, the taxes on cigarettes have risen sharply, even while the number of places where it is lawful to smoke has shrunk significantly. On both counts, the full cost of smoking (price per pack, plus the hassle) has been rising, with the consequence that smoking has been on the decline in the United States. It is well known that people have a tendency to eat more when they stop smoking, and this very fact seems to be showing up in the national statistics on excess poundage. Where the full cost of smoking has risen the greatest, so too has the incidence of obesity. In effect, people are being induced to substitute eating for smoking. Despite the adverse health effects of the resulting weight gains, the *net* health trade-offs here are likely positive, given the highly lethal effects of smoking. Still, this development reminds us that although people's behavior can easily be understood by examining the incentives they face, some of those incentives are difficult to forecast in advance.

DISCUSSION QUESTIONS

1. The technological changes in food preparation seem to have had the greatest effect on the time costs of a "meal," rather than affecting the time cost of consuming extra calories during any given meal. What does economics predict about the number of meals consumed each day compared to the number of calories consumed per meal?

2. The change in food preparation technologies over the last 30–40 years caused the biggest reduction in time costs for married women. What does economics predict should have happened to the weight of married women relative to other people?

3. During the twentieth century the cost of the automobile fell drastically, leading to a dramatic rise in the number of miles driven. But all of this driving also led to more automobile accidents, which now kill more than 40,000 people each year and

maim hundreds of thousands more. Is it possible that the fall in the price of the automobile actually made Americans worse off? How much would your answer depend on whether those fatalities were among the people driving the cars as opposed to innocent bystanders, such as pedestrians and children? (Hint: Take a look at the chapters in Part Six, "Property Rights and the Environment.")

7

Is Water Different?

Mono Lake has gotten a reprieve. Over a 50-year period, this California lake—our country's oldest lake and one of its most beautiful—shrank from more than 80 square miles in area to about 60. Why? Because in 1941, most of the eastern Sierra mountain water that once fed Mono Lake began disappearing down a 275-mile-long aqueduct, south to Los Angeles, where it was used to wash cars, sprinkle lawns, and otherwise lubricate the lifestyle of southern California. Environmentalists cried out that the diversion of water from Mono Lake must stop. Los Angelenos, who pay $350 per acre-foot for the water, claimed there were no viable alternative sources. Central California farmers, who pay but $12.50 per acre-foot for subsidized water from the western side of the Sierras, feared that diverting their own "liquid gold" to save Mono Lake would dry up their livelihood. Meanwhile, this migratory rest stop for hundreds of thousands of birds was disappearing.

Finally, prodded by the California Water Resources Control Board and aided by special funds voted by the state legislature, the City of Los Angeles agreed to drastically curtail its usage of Mono Lake water. Under the water-trading plan agreed to, Los Angeles will cut its usage of Mono Lake water by more than 80 percent until the lake's water level has risen 16 feet. Even after that elevation has been reached, the city will limit its usage of Mono Lake water to less than half of its long-term average usage. To replace the water it is losing, Los Angeles will buy water from elsewhere, using state funds appropriated for this purpose.

The issues that have arisen over the future of Mono Lake are surfacing in hundreds of locations throughout the United States.

Conservationists are increasingly concerned about the toxic contamination of our water supply and the depletion of our underground water sources. Extensive irrigation projects in the western states use more than 150 *billion* gallons of water a day—seven times as much water as all the nation's city water systems combined. The Ogallala aquifer (a 20-million-acre lake beneath the beef-and-breadbasket states of Colorado, Kansas, Nebraska, New Mexico, Oklahoma, and Texas) has been dropping by three feet per year because 150,000 wells are pumping water out faster than nature can replenish it.

Water problems are not confined to the United States. In China, water is being siphoned away from farmlands surrounding Beijing in order to meet rising urban and industrial demands, and some 400 Chinese cities are now estimated to face water **shortages.** In the arid Middle East, water is a constant source of friction, and schemes to add to the region's supplies have included floating plastic bags of water southward across the Mediterranean, and stirring the sea in the summer in the hopes of causing more rain to fall in the winter. In the island city-state of Singapore, half of the total land area of 247 square miles is set aside for collecting and storing water. Because there is no more room for additional reservoirs, Singapore has built desalination plants to convert seawater into drinking water. The result is more water, but the cost of fresh water produced in such a manner is seven to eight times higher than the current cost of treated water.

The common view of water is that it is an overused, precious resource and that we are running out of it. The economic analysis of the water "problem," however, is not quite so pessimistic, nor so tied to the physical quantities of water that exist on our earth and in the atmosphere. Rather, an economic analysis of water is similar to an analysis of any other scarce resource, revealing that water is fundamentally no different from other scarce resources.

The water industry is one of the oldest and largest in the United States, and the philosophy surrounding it merits examination. Many commentators believe that water is unique and that it should not be treated as an **economic good,** that is, a scarce good. Engineering studies that concern themselves with demand for residential water typically use a so-called requirements approach. The forecaster simply predicts population changes and then multiplies those estimates by data showing the average amount of water currently used per person. The underlying assumption of such a forecast is that, regardless of the price charged for water in the future, the same quantity will be demanded per person. Implicitly, then, both the short- and long-run price elasticities of demand are assumed to be zero.

But is this really the case? Perhaps not. To see why, let's look at a study of water prices in Boulder, Colorado, conducted by economist Steve Hanke. Boulder was selected by Hanke because a number of years ago the water utility in that city installed water meters in every home and business that it supplied. Prior to that time, Boulder, like many other municipalities in the United States, had charged a flat monthly rate for water. Each household paid a specified amount per month no matter how much (or how little) water was used. In essence, the previous flat-fee system meant that a zero price was being charged at the margin (for any incremental use of water). The introduction of usage meters meant that a positive price for the marginal unit of water was now imposed.

Hanke looked at the quantity of water demanded both before and after the meters were installed in Boulder. He began by computing an index of water usage, relative to what he called the "ideal" use of water. (The term *ideal* implies nothing from an economic point of view. It merely indicates the minimum quantity of water required to maintain the aesthetic quality of each resident's lawn, taking into account such factors as average temperature, the effect of rainfall, and so forth.) An index value of 100 meant that usage was exactly equal to the hypothetical ideal. A value of, say, 150 meant that residents were using 50 percent more than the ideal, whereas an index of 75 meant that usage was 25 percent less than Hanke's ideal figure of 100.

From the data in Table 7–1, which compares water usage in Boulder with and without metering, we find that individuals used much more water under the flat-rate system than they did under the metered-rate system. Column 1 shows the meter route numbers of the eight routes studied by Hanke. Column 2 shows the index of water usage for each of the routes during the unmetered period when a flat rate was charged for water usage. The data in column 3 show water usage on each route for the one-year period after the metering system was put into effect. Note that under the flat-rate system every route used substantially more than the ideal amount of water, whereas under the metered system, six of the eight routes used less than the hypothetical ideal. Moreover, water usage dropped substantially on every route when metering was

TABLE 7-1   Water Usage with and without Metering

(1) Meter Routes	(2) Index of Water Usage (Flat-Rate Period)	(3) Index of Water Usage (Metered-Rate Period)
1	128	78
2	175	72
3	156	72
4	177	63
5	175	97
6	175	102
7	176	105
8	157	86

Source: Adapted from Steve Hanke, "Demand for Water Under Dynamic Conditions," *Water Resources Research*, vol. 6, no. 5, October 1970.

introduced, at which time each user was being charged for the actual amount of water used. Because less water is used in the presence of metering (which raises the price of incremental water), Hanke's data indicate that the quantity of water demanded is a function of the price charged for water. Hanke also found that for many years after the imposition of the metered-rate pricing system for water, the quantity of water demanded not only remained at a lower level than before metering but continued to fall slightly. That, of course, means that the long-run **price elasticity of demand** for water was greater than the short-run price elasticity of demand.

Would attaching a dollar sign to water help solve problems of recurring water shortages and endemic waste? Many economists feel it would. It is well known, for example, that much of the water supplied by federal irrigation projects is wasted by farmers and other users because they have no incentive to conserve water and curb overconsumption. The federal government, which has subsidized water projects since 1902, allots water to certain districts, communities, or farmers on the basis of previous usage "requirements." This means that if farmers in a certain irrigation district were to conserve on water usage by, say, upgrading their irrigation systems, their water allotment eventually would be reduced. As a result, a "use it or lose it" attitude has prevailed among users of federal water. Water supplied by federal water projects is also inexpensive. The Congressional Budget Office has estimated that users pay only about 19 percent of the total cost of the water they get.

One would think that with growing worldwide concern over water conservation, the federal government would be trying to do its part to reduce waste. Let's first consider toilets—or water closets, as they are often called in the industry—a major source of residential water usage. In 1992, Congress mandated that all new water closets installed in the United States be "low-flow" models, which discharge only 1.6 gallons per flush, about half the rate per flush of regular toilets. The idea, it was claimed, was that low-flow toilets would reduce the amount of water that people "wasted" when they flushed. There were some problems with congressional reasoning on this issue. First, the basic low-flow toilet simply doesn't work very well when attempting to dispose of some forms of waste, requiring that the user flush them twice or even three times to accomplish the task. This, of course, eliminates all of the supposed water-conservation advantages of the low-flow mode—and may also help explain why some people have taken to smuggling regular toilets in from Canada. Now, it is possible to reengineer toilets to make them work better with less water, including the addition of a compressed air-power assist. Such toilets cost up to ten times what regular water closets cost, however, and the power-assist models have one additional problem—their operation produces a noise level comparable to that of a loud vacuum cleaner. Just as importantly, Congress apparently failed to recognize that when water is flushed down the drain, it is not vaporized or sent into outer space. It is simply moved someplace else. The earth is a closed system, and flushing more water or more often simply moves water from one place to another more rapidly. Regular toilets may require that we devote more resources to treating waste water, but they don't destroy the water. Indeed, many (although not all) cities actually return the treated water to the lake or river from which it was originally drawn, and cleaner than it originally started.

The year after it gave us low-flow toilets, Congress authorized completion of the Central Utah Project (CUP). This project includes a series of dams, aqueducts, tunnels, and canals designed to collect water from the Colorado River drainage in Utah and transport it to the Great Basin. The cost of delivering this water to farmers for irrigation is estimated to be $400 per acre-foot. The water will be used to produce additional crops yielding enough revenue to make the water worth $30 per acre-foot to the Utah farmers who receive it. But these farmers will pay only $8 per acre-foot for the water—that is, only *2 percent* of the cost of delivering the water to them!

Economists have suggested that raising the price of federal water would lead to more efficient and less wasteful water consumption. For example, a study by B. Delworth Gardner, an economist now at Brigham Young University, concluded that a 10 percent rise in prices could reduce water use on some California farm crops by as much as 20 percent. Support for such a price increase is politically difficult, however, because federal law stipulates that ability to pay, as well as cost, must be considered when determining water prices.

An alternative solution involving the trading and sale of water rights held by existing federal water users has been proposed by some economists. Such a solution, it is felt, would benefit the economy overall because it could help curb water use, prevent water shortages, and lessen the pressure for costly new water projects. Trading and sales of water rights have already taken place in California, Oregon, and Utah. In addition, environmentalists were instrumental in helping to arrange the water trading plan for Mono Lake. Despite these modest successes, numerous federal and state laws have, to date, made such trading very difficult.

Until recent years, it had been thought that there was so much water we simply did not have to worry about it—there was always another river or another well to draw on if we ran short. Putting a price tag on water would require a substantial change in the way we have traditionally thought about water. Is this possible or even desirable? Well, events half a world away from Mono Lake may shed some light on this issue. In the Chinese capital of Beijing, an extended period of dry weather in a recent year caused the water levels in the city's reservoirs to drop sharply. The municipal State Council responded by raising the price of water for home use to $110 per acre-foot from its previous level of $80. For industrial and government users, the price hike was to $160 per acre-foot from the previous $125. Why were these actions taken? According to Liu Hangui, deputy director of the Beijing Water Conservancy Bureau, "the price adjustments were introduced to relieve the water shortage." Even communism, it would seem, is not enough to make water different.

DISCUSSION QUESTIONS

1. How much water does your neighbor "need"? Is your answer the same if you have to pay your neighbor's water bill?

2. Evaluate the following: "Although taxpayers foot the bill for federal water sold to farmers at subsidized prices, they also eat the crops grown with that water. Because the crops are cheaper due to the subsidized water, taxpayers get back exactly what they put in, so there is no waste from having subsidized water for farmers." Would you give the author of this quote an A or an F in economics?

3. During the drought that plagued California in the late 1980s and early 1990s, farmers in California were able to purchase subsidized water to irrigate their crops, even though many California homeowners had to pay large fines if they watered their lawns. Can you suggest an explanation for this difference in the treatment of two different groups of citizens within the state of California?

8

Slave Redemption in Sudan

Sudan is Africa's largest nation. Located immediately south of Egypt, it encompasses nearly 1 million square miles and is home to 36 million people. It is also home to poverty, disease, civil war—and the emergence of modern-day slavery. The slave trade, in turn, has given rise to a new humanitarian movement, whose adherents seek to alleviate Sudan's misery by buying freedom for its slaves. Well-intentioned though they are, these humanitarian efforts may be making things worse.

Slavery is a centuries-old practice in Sudan, one that colonial British rulers finally managed to halt during World War I. The Sudanese gained independence in 1956, but, despite ensuing periods of civil war, the slave trade initially remained a piece of history. This changed in 1989, when the National Islamic Front (NIF) took control of the government. The NIF quickly began arming the Muslim Baggara tribe in the northern part of the country to fight against the rebellious Christian tribes of the south. The Baggara previously had made a regular practice of enslaving members of the southern Dinka tribe, and once armed by the NIF the Baggara resumed the slave raids the British had suppressed. This activity was further aided by the government, which supplied horses to the Baggara and permitted slave markets to open in the cities controlled by the NIF. Perhaps as many as 20,000 Dinkas, mostly women and children, were enslaved and taken north, selling for as little as $15 each. The slaves were branded with the names of their owners and put to work as cooks, maids, field hands, and concubines.

Within a few years, word of the revived slave trade began filtering out of Sudan. In response, a variety of humanitarian groups from other nations began buying slaves in large batches and setting them free. The process is called "slave redemption," and its purpose—one hopes—is to reduce the number of people who are enslaved.

Raising money for slave redemption soon became big business, spreading rapidly among public schools and evangelical churches. A middle school in Oregon, for example, raised $2500 to be used for slave redemption. Even more impressive was an elementary school class in Colorado: After the children's efforts caught the media's eye, the class raised more than $50,000 for slave redemption.

The largest of the humanitarian groups involved in slave redemption is Christian Solidarity International (CSI). This group says it has freed 64,000 slaves since 1995, most at prices of about $50 each. Other groups have purchased the freedom of several thousand additional slaves, sometimes at prices of up to $100 each.

Per capita income in Sudan is about $500 per year, which makes slave prices of $50 to $100 apiece quite attractive to the Baggara slave raiders. This is particularly true when the redeemers are buying in the south, where the targeted Dinkas live, and prices in the north, the traditional market for slaves, are as low as $15 apiece. In fact, says one individual who used to be active in slave redemption, "We've made slave redemption more profitable than narcotics." What are the consequences of such profitability?

There have been two sets of responses. First, on the demand side, the higher prices for slaves make it more costly for owners in the north to hold slaves. So rather than own slaves, some of them have offered their slaves to the redeemers. This, of course, is exactly the effect the slave redemption movement has desired. But there is also a supply response: When the market value of slaves rises due to an increase in demand (the demand of the slave redeemers), we expect an increase in the quantity supplied. That is, we expect the raiders who produce slaves by capturing them to engage in more of that activity. This is exactly what has happened in Sudan.

Slave redemption began in earnest in 1995, and, according to local authorities, the number of slave raids grew sharply in response. Moreover, the size of a typical raiding party rose from roughly 400 attackers to more than 2500. Why the increase? Slaves used to be traded in relatively small batches, but the redeemers prefer to buy in large lots—1000 or more at a time. Collecting and assembling the number of slaves required to satisfy the redemption buyers thus requires considerably more manpower. Hence, the slave trade has been transformed from a cottage industry into a large-scale business enterprise. Overall, it is estimated that the number of slaves captured in raids each year is greater now than at the inception of slave redemption.

Initially, it is likely that the impact of slave redemption was chiefly on the demand side; that is, the first slaves redeemed were almost surely "freed from slavery" in the sense that we would normally use that terminology. But once the stock of slave holdings in the north had adjusted downward in response to the newly elevated equilibrium price, there was only one place for the slave traders to get the slaves demanded by the redemption buyers. This was from the raiders who were now taking slaves for one purpose only—sale to the redeemers. Thus, once the stock of slaves in the north is adjusted to its lower equilibrium level, *all* of the slaves subsequently "freed" by the redeemers are in fact individuals who never would have been enslaved had the redeemers not first made a market for them. In addition, because large numbers of new slaves now spend some time in captivity awaiting redemption, it is even possible that the total number of people in slavery at any point in time is actually *higher* because of the well-intentioned efforts of the slave redeemers.

As unpleasant as such reasoning is, it agrees with the opinions of people who observe the slave trade firsthand. As a local humanitarian worker says, "[G]iving money to the slave traders only encourages the trade. It is wrong and must stop. Where does the money go? It goes to the raiders to buy more guns, raid more villages. . . . It is a vicious circle." In a similar vein, the chief of one village that has been targeted by the slave raiders says, "Redemption is not the solution. It means you are encouraging the raiders."

In addition to encouraging the capture of new slaves, redemption also reduces any incentive for owners to set free their less productive slaves. Prior to 1995, about 10 percent of all slaves, chiefly older women and young children, were allowed to escape or even told to go home, because the costs of feeding, clothing, and housing them exceeded their value to their owners. Now slaves who would have been freed on their own are instead held in captivity until a trader can be found to haul them south for sale to the redeemers.

The final effect of redemption has been to create a trade in fictitious slaves—individuals who are paid to pose as slaves for the purposes of redemption, and who are then given a cut of the redemption price after they are "freed." Although redemption groups obviously try to avoid participating in such deals, observers familiar with the trade consider them a regular part of the redemption business.

Is there another way to combat slavery in Sudan? On the demand side, the U.S. government has long refused to negotiate with terrorists or pay ransom to kidnappers, because it believes that such tactics encourage terrorism and kidnapping. It recognizes that paying a ransom increases the profits of kidnapping, thus enticing more individuals into the trade.

On the supply side, the British were originally successful in ending the slave trade in Sudan and elsewhere in their empire by dispatching soldiers to kill or disarm slave raiders, and by sending warships to close off maritime slave-trading routes. Sudan, of course, is an independent sovereign nation today; both the United Nations and the British electorate would likely oppose unilateral military action by the British government against Sudanese slave raiders. Yet even the people who used to be subject to British colonial rule have mixed feelings. When asked to compare the colonial British policies to the redeemers' policies of today, a schoolmaster in the affected area remarked, "If the colonial government were standing for election, I would vote for them." So too might the victims of the slave trade in Sudan.

DISCUSSION QUESTIONS

1. Is there anything in the historical British experience with the slave trade that suggests how the international community of today could reduce slavery in Sudan?

2. It appears that the actions of the slave redeemers have raised the equilibrium price of slaves. What does this imply about the number of slaves held by private owners in northern Sudan—as long as the demand for slaves is downward sloping? What does the higher profitability and volume of slave trading today

imply about the number of slaves held in inventory in the south for trading purposes, compared to the number that used to be held there?

3. How does the cost of "backhauling" a slave from the north down to the south, where the redeemers are purchasing, affect the extent to which the efforts of the redeemers cause slaves to be released from the existing stock in the north, compared to causing new slaves to be produced in the south?

4. Suppose the redeemers had succeeded in buying slaves without causing the equilibrium price of slaves to change at all. What would this imply about the elasticity of supply of new slaves? What would it imply about the number of slaves actually released from slavery in the north?

9

Choice and Life

All three branches of the federal government are in the abortion business. For 16 years the 1973 *Roe v. Wade* Supreme Court decision legalizing abortion was the law of the land. But in 1989, in *Webster v. Reproductive Health Services,* the Court upheld the constitutionality of a Missouri law restricting, but not eliminating, a woman's right to have an abortion. Then, in a 1992 case, *Planned Parenthood v. Casey,* the Supreme Court upheld most of a Pennsylvania law that discourages, but does not prohibit, abortion. Since the *Webster* decision, citizens on both sides of the abortion issue have engaged in legislative battles and sometimes violent public protests over the issue of a woman's right to choose versus a fetus's right to live. Thus far most of the legislative battles have been won by the proponents of legal abortions, but in 2003 Congress passed, and the president signed, legislation banning a form of late-term abortion sometimes referred to as "partial birth abortion." Because this federal law is similar to a Nebraska law struck down by the Supreme Court in 2000, it is perhaps no surprise that opponents of the new legislation filed lawsuits challenging it even before the president signed the bill. It thus seems certain that one or more branches of the federal government will be in the abortion business long after you have finished reading this book.

Very few of the major issues of our time are purely economic, and abortion is no exception. Economics cannot answer the question of whether life begins at conception, at 24 weeks, or at birth, nor can economics determine whether abortion should be permitted or proscribed. Economics cannot (as yet) even predict how the branches of government will come down on these issues. What economics can do, however, is demonstrate the striking and sometimes surprising implications of government decisions on abortion—whatever those decisions may be.

Pregnancy termination has been practiced since ancient times, and any legal bars to abortion seem to have been based on the father's right to his offspring. English common law allowed abortion before quickening (when fetal movement is first evident), and there is some doubt whether abortion even after quickening was considered a crime. The American colonies retained the tradition of English common law until the changeover to state statutes at the adoption of the Constitution. In 1828, New York enacted an antiabortion statute that became a model for most other states. The statute declared that abortion before quickening was a misdemeanor and abortion after quickening, second-degree manslaughter. In the late nineteenth century, the quickening distinction disappeared, and the penalties for all abortions were increased.

Except under extreme circumstances (such as to protect the life of the mother), abortion remained illegal in this country until about 1960, when a few states began to ease the conditions under which it was legal to perform an abortion. The gradual process of liberalization that state legislatures seemed to be following was suddenly disrupted in 1973 with the landmark Supreme Court decision in *Roe v. Wade*, which overruled all state laws prohibiting abortion before the last three months of pregnancy. In effect, the Court ruled that a woman's right to an abortion was constitutionally protected except during the last stages of pregnancy. There matters stood until the Supreme Court's 1989 decision in *Webster v. Reproductive Health Services*.

Strictly speaking, the Court's decision in *Webster* was narrowly focused; its direct impact has been to permit states to restrict the circumstances under which abortion is legal. Although the *Webster* decision stops far short of overturning *Roe v. Wade*, both the subsequent *Planned Parenthood* decision, numerous legislative actions at the state level, and the 2003 federal law noted earlier have further restricted abortion. Examination of the market for abortions during the period prior to *Roe v. Wade* will help clarify the economic consequences of these developments.

Consider first the factors of cost and risk. During the early 1970s, an illegal but otherwise routine abortion by a reputable physician in the United States typically cost a minimum of $3500 (in 2005 dollars) and could run $5000 in a major East Coast City.[1]

---

[1] All of the dollar amounts mentioned in this chapter are adjusted for **inflation** and expressed in terms of 2005 dollars, for purposes of comparison.

Following *Roe v. Wade,* these prices dropped sharply, and by the time of *Webster,* a routine legal abortion performed during the first three months of pregnancy cost only about $350.[2] Prior to the legalization of abortion, more than 350,000 women were admitted annually to American hospitals with complications resulting from abortions, and it is estimated that more than 1000 women per year died from improperly performed pregnancy terminations. Following the Court's 1973 decision, complications and deaths from pregnancy termination dropped sharply. In recent years, it is estimated that significant physical complications occur in less than 1 percent of all legal abortions, and deaths due to legal abortions are virtually unknown. In short, the legalization of abortion was associated with a drastic reduction in both the monetary costs and physical dangers of pregnancy termination. Why was such an association observed?

Let us begin by looking at who might be willing to perform an illegal abortion and the price at which she or he would be willing to perform it. A physician convicted of performing an illegal abortion faced not only criminal prosecution (and the associated costs of a legal defense) but also expulsion from the medical profession and the consequent lifetime loss of license and livelihood. In addition, the doctor might have had to endure ostracism by a community that regarded abortion as a criminal act. In short, the costs to a doctor of such a criminal conviction were enormous, and the greatest portion of the fee for an illegal abortion was simply compensation for bearing this potential cost.

It must be acknowledged, of course, that there were physicians who had strong moral convictions regarding a woman's right to abortion. Some were willing to absorb the risks of performing an illegal abortion at a substantially reduced fee. Nevertheless, such physicians were a small minority and not easy to find. Consequently, most women were faced with the choices of paying $3500 or more for an abortion, paying $700 to $900 to an unlicensed abortionist operating under unsanitary conditions, or simply doing without. For those choosing back-alley abortionists, the consequences could include infection, hospitalization, sterility, or death.

---

[2] More complicated abortions, performed as late as the fifth or sixth month of pregnancy, cost $1200 to $1400 if done on an outpatient basis in a clinic, and $1600 to $2000 if performed in a hospital.

The illegality of abortions, of course, increased the cost both of supplying and obtaining information about them; in turn, this made decisions about whether to have an abortion and who should perform it more difficult, and increased the chances of an undesirable outcome. Information is never free, even in legalized activities, because there are costs to acquaint potential buyers with the location, quality, and price of a good or service. But, as mentioned in Chapter 5, in the case of an illegal activity the provision of information is even more expensive. Abortionists could not advertise, and the more widely they let their availability be known, the more likely they were to be arrested. Although some doctors unwilling to perform abortions did refer patients to other, more willing physicians, the referral was itself illegal and therefore risky. Women seeking an abortionist thus were not able to inform themselves of all of the possibilities without spending large amounts of money and time; and even having done so, many were left facing enormous uncertainty about the best path. Some ended up spending too much money; others exposed themselves to unnecessary risks. Some might even have chosen not to have an abortion had they been fully informed of the potential risks.

The situation confronting women during the years prior to the legalization of abortion can be usefully categorized by considering three examples. Although the settings are stylized, they are representative of the nature of the choices involved and the costs and risks of each.

First, there is a wealthy entertainer who visits a travel agency that arranges a package tour of Japan. Included is round-trip airfare, an essentially risk-free abortion procedure in that country (where abortions are legal), and several days of subsequent sightseeing. The price tag: $7500.

Next, let's look at how a young attorney earning $48,000 per year resolves her dilemma. She goes to her physician, who on the quiet refers her to a doctor willing to perform an illegal abortion in his office for $3500. The expense forces the attorney and her husband to delay the purchase of their first home, but then so would the cost of having the baby.

Finally, there is a blue-collar couple making $24,000 a year. Surreptitiously asking around, the wife finds out from an acquaintance someone who will do the abortion in a back room for $900—aspirins, but not antibiotics, included.

For the wealthy entertainer, both the risk and the financial burden are negligible; to be sure, the money could have been spent on an expensive bauble, but at least there was a trip to Japan in return. For the young lawyer, the financial burden is considerable; if unpaid law school debts preclude either the physician-performed abortion or the cost of completing the pregnancy, the only alternative is the risk of the backroom abortionist. The blue-collar couple gets the worst of both worlds: The abortionist's fee pushes them over their already tight budget, and the woman risks hospitalization or worse.

The pattern suggested by these examples was borne out in the years preceding the legalization of abortion. Relatively few women had the resources permitting travel to a foreign country where abortion was both safe and legal, nor did many have access to the information needed to learn about and arrange such an undertaking. Somewhat more women had established relationships with physicians who either would perform abortions or could refer them to other, willing doctors; these women had the option of choosing between the higher expense of the physician or the greater risk of the unlicensed abortionist. For many women, however, the lack of readily available information about alternatives, combined with the high costs of a physician-performed abortion, meant that the backroom quack, with the attendant risks, was the only realistic means of terminating a pregnancy.

The statistics for New York City in the early 1960s support this argument. Private hospitals performed abortions on 1 pregnant patient in 250; municipal hospitals, 1 in 10,000. The rate for whites was five times that for nonwhites and thirty times that for Puerto Ricans. Lower-income women simply were not having as many abortions performed by qualified physicians in suitable surroundings as were upper-income women; as we noted earlier, the result was hundreds of thousands of abortion-related complications, plus more than 1000 deaths each year.

The legalization of abortion in 1973 brought a relatively swift end to such outcomes. No longer faced with the risk of losing liberty and livelihood, thousands of physicians became willing to perform abortions. Even those who, for moral or religious reasons, were unwilling to terminate pregnancies could refer patients to other physicians without legal risk to themselves. Within a short time, properly equipped abortion clinics were established, and even in states requiring that abortions be performed in hospitals, women found a greatly increased range of options. Legalization thus produced an enormous increase in the supply of pregnancy termination services, which in turn had several consequences.

As in any market in which there is an increase in supply, the price of abortions fell drastically; holding quality and safety constant, the price reduction was as much as 90 percent. The decline in the price of physician-supplied abortions to levels at or below those charged by back-alley abortionists quickly drove most of the quacks out of business. As a result, the safety of abortions increased dramatically; serious infections and deaths due to abortion are estimated to have declined by 50 percent within a year of *Roe v. Wade* and have since become quite rare. Information about abortions, once available only "on the sly" and at considerable trouble and expense, became openly available. A woman considering pregnancy termination could call her physician's office or simply look in the telephone book for information about local services. Moreover, not only was knowledge about the price, quality, and safety of abortion openly available, so too were counseling services about the potentially adverse psychological or emotional consequences of what, for many women, was a difficult and trying decision.

As would be expected, the lower price of abortion and the more widely available information about the procedure combined to bring about a large increase in the number of abortions performed in this country. During 1973, slightly over 700,000 legal abortions were performed in the United States, many of them in the aftermath of the Supreme Court's landmark decision. One early study concluded that of the legal abortions that took place in the year following *Roe v. Wade,* well over half—most likely between two-thirds and three-fourths—were replacements for illegal abortions. By 1981, 1.6 million legal abortions per year were being performed in the United States. After holding steady at that rate until 1988, the number of abortions performed each year began a slow decline, reaching about one million in 2000.

What, then, have been the consequences of the Court's decision in *Webster*? In the short run, not much. To be sure, abortions in public facilities in Missouri are now illegal, and women in the later stages of pregnancy must undergo costly and risky tests regarding fetal viability before having an abortion. Thus the Court's decision has increased the costs of pregnancy termination in Missouri. The result has been fewer abortions, perhaps some illegal abortions, and the selection of more effective means of (prepregnancy) birth control. Nevertheless, there are good (albeit more expensive) substitutes available—abortions in private facilities or in neighboring states—so the magnitude of these effects has been small. Of more significance is that the Court's decision, combined with growing public opposition to abortion, has encouraged numerous states to restrict abortions. For example, at least 17 states now have three or more abortion restrictions, up from three states in 1992. Indeed, in 1997 alone, states passed a record 55 abortion restrictions, ranging from parental consent laws to outright bans on certain forms of late-term abortions. When combined with the 2003 federal legislation, we see that conditions are gradually moving toward those that prevailed before 1973: Abortions are becoming more expensive, and more are probably being performed illegally and less safely. As was the case before 1973, the burden of these consequences will be borne largely by women in the middle- and lower-income brackets.

We emphasized at the beginning of this chapter that the issues raised by abortion go far beyond the economic consequences, and that economics cannot, in any event, determine whether abortion should be permitted or proscribed. What economics can do—as we hope we have shown—is illustrate some of the consequences of the decision between "choice" and "life." Whether an understanding of those consequences can—or even should—play a role in making that decision is a matter we can leave only to the reader.

DISCUSSION QUESTIONS

1. Suppose you wished to predict which states would impose more restrictive conditions on abortions. What factors—for example, per capita income and average age of the population—would you take into account in making your predictions?

2. Before 1973, legal penalties generally were imposed on suppliers of abortion rather than on demanders. How might the effects of prohibiting abortion have been different had legal penalties been imposed on demanders rather than on suppliers?

3. The discussion in this chapter focused solely on the economic consequences of prohibiting abortion. Do you think that legislatures base their decisions about abortion solely on the economic consequences? Can an understanding of the economic consequences of laws give us (and legislatures) any guidance about the "best" public policy on abortion?

4. Some people have argued that the federal government (perhaps through a constitutional amendment) should decide on a uniform national policy regarding all abortions. What are the advantages and disadvantages of having separate state policies rather than a uniform national policy?

10

Smoking and Smuggling

Cigarette taxes have been in the news lately, and for good reason: federal taxes per pack recently jumped a nickel to 39 cents, and a majority of the states either have instituted their own tax increases or have such hikes on the legislative agenda. Indeed, higher federal and state taxes have helped to more than double the average price of a pack of cigarettes in the United States since 1995.

A variety of motives is pushing the increase in tax rates. Partly, the higher taxes are an effort to reduce smoking, particularly among young people. Taxpayers often end up paying the tobacco-induced medical bills of smokers, through Medicare (for the elderly) and Medicaid (for the poor). Reducing the number of smokers, it is argued, will help cut these costs. In addition, given the current low state of public opinion about smoking, cigarette taxes are proving to be a politically palatable way of raising tax revenues. Sometimes (as in California) these receipts are used in part to fund antismoking advertising campaigns; other times cigarette tax receipts are seen as a source of funds for publicly provided health care initiatives.

Cigarette prices also have been pushed up by a second force. Several years ago, the major tobacco companies settled a series of lawsuits filed by state governments. The companies agreed to pay $246 billion over 25 years into a fund to be distributed to the states. The purpose of the fund was said to be to help states promote antismoking campaigns. In fact, thus far most of the states have spent most of the money on almost anything *but* antismoking campaigns. Roads have been paved, college scholarships funded, and—in the latest economic downturn—budgetary shortfalls have been made up. Nevertheless, the settlement has had an antismoking impact along a different dimension. In the aftermath of the settlement, cigarette companies hiked their wholesale prices by up to $1.00 per pack. When added to state taxes that now range up to $1.50 (in the state of New York), this helped push retail cigarette prices past $5.00 per pack in some places. Many smokers have responded by becoming ex-smokers.

There is little doubt that, despite the addictive attributes of nicotine, higher cigarette prices make inroads on smoking—after all, the demand curve for cigarettes, like the demand curve for any other good, is downward sloping. For each 10 percent that taxes push up the retail price, the number of packs sold drops by 4 to 8 percent. Interestingly, however, although smokers respond to higher taxes by smoking fewer cigarettes, they also tend to smoke cigarettes that are longer and have higher nicotine and tar content. This effect is so pronounced among people aged 18 to 24 that the average daily tar intake among the young people who continue to smoke is actually higher when the tax rate is higher. Because tar is believed to be the principal carcinogenic substance in cigarettes, higher taxes probably lead to *more* adverse health consequences among young smokers.

Smoking tends to be concentrated among lower-income individuals, which means that the burden of cigarette taxes also tends to be concentrated in this segment of the population. For example, one survey several years ago revealed that only 19 percent of people earning more than $50,000 per year smoked, whereas 32 percent of those earning less than $10,000 smoked. As a result, cigarette taxes consumed 0.4 percent of the income of smokers in the high-income group but an amazing 5.1 percent of the income of the low-income smokers. Indeed, it is estimated that more than half of the latest increases in federal taxes will be borne by people earning less than $25,000 per year.

Perhaps the most interesting consequence of changes in cigarette taxes, however, is the change in distribution channels that results. Cigarettes are both light and compact relative to their market value, and this becomes increasingly important when the taxes on them are raised. Thus, cigarettes are prime candidates for smuggling—and taxes are a prime stimulus to such smuggling. Worldwide, of the 1 trillion cigarettes exported from producing nations, it is estimated that roughly 300 billion were sold by smugglers, up from 100 billion 15 years ago. The chief reason for this smuggling is that cigarette taxes vary enormously around the world, creating price differences across nations of several dollars per pack.

For example, in Britain, where cigarettes cost about $6.00 per pack, it is estimated that one-half of all British smokers consume at least some smuggled cigarettes each year. About one in four cigarettes consumed in Spain are illegal, 20 percent of Italian cigarettes are black-market, and perhaps 40 percent of all cigarettes consumed in Hong Kong are contraband. In low-tax Luxembourg, it is estimated that only 15 percent of tobacco purchased is consumed in-country—with the rest being moved covertly to higher-tax locales elsewhere in Europe.

In 1991 the Canadian federal government raised cigarette taxes by 146 percent, yielding a price per pack of $3.50, compared to an average U.S. price of $1.00 at the time. Provincial governments soon followed suit with higher cigarette taxes of their own. By 1994, black-market cigarette consumption in Canada had jumped to 25 percent of total consumption, up from about 2 percent. How did this happen? When Canadian cigarettes are exported, they are exempt from Canadian cigarette taxes. Soon after the higher federal and provincial taxes went into effect, there was a huge rise in (tax-exempt) exports to the United States, where the cigarettes were promptly—and illegally—reexported back to Canada. The federal and provincial goverments ultimately were forced to slash their taxes down to about what they had been before the smuggling outbreak.

How big are the potential cigarette smuggling stakes in the United States? With an average $1.00-per-pack hike in combined state and federal taxes, the potential net revenue to smugglers would be on the order of $3 billion to $6 billion per year, even if only a quarter of all smokers turned to the black market. And where would these smuggled cigarettes come from? Almost anywhere. Mexico, a transshipment point for much of America's illegal drug imports, is one place. Between 1989 and 1995, U.S. exports of cigarettes to Mexico went from 5 million packs a year to 150 million. Some of this surely was due to increased Mexican consumption, but a significant amount is believed to be due to reexports to California: In 1989 that state had raised cigarette taxes to 35 cents a pack from 10 cents a pack. In 2004 the federal government broke up a smuggling ring that had brought more than 100 million cigarettes into the United States from Mexico. Other likely sources of smuggled cigarettes are domestic U.S. military bases and Indian reservations, where cigarettes generally are tax-exempt. Both of these venues have been sources of bootleg cigarettes in the past, when combined federal and state taxes were far lower than they are now.

The potential problems facing states when they raise their cigarette taxes are magnified by the fact that other states represent potential sources of supply. Economists Daniel K. Benjamin and William R. Dougan have studied the role of bootleg cigarettes in shaping cigarette taxes around the country. They found that cigarette smuggling is highly sensitive to interstate tax differentials of only a few cents per pack, and that state governments are thus forced to consider the taxing behavior of other states or suffer the consequences. For example, the late 1940s saw an outbreak of smuggling when a significant number of states first began using cigarettes as a source of tax revenue. Another outbreak of smuggling occurred in the 1970s as states raised taxes to make up for other revenue losses caused by the recession of the early 1970s.

Recent experience in Michigan reveals that the latest round of state cigarette tax increases are producing yet another epidemic of interstate smuggling. In 1994 Michigan hiked its tax to 75 cents per pack from 25 cents. Within just over a year, 20 percent of the cigarettes consumed in Michigan were smuggled in, as smokers traveled to Ohio and Indiana to save more than $6.00 (about one-third) on the cost of a carton. There has been a sharp rise in organized, large-scale heists of cigarettes from convenience stores, and even a major law enforcement push against cigarette bootlegging seems unable to quell the onslaught of illegal imports.

None of these developments would be surprising to the British, who two centuries ago relied on import tariffs to fund much of their government spending and suffered the consequences. Between 1698 and 1758 the standard tariff rate went from 10 percent to 25 percent. After further increases in tariffs during the American Revolution, smuggled goods accounted for a full 20 percent of all imports to Britain. Tea was particularly popular and thus heavily taxed. Indeed, the tax rate reached 119 percent, and by 1784 it was estimated that two-thirds of all tea consumed in Britain was contraband. Given the direction that cigarette taxes are going, cigarette smuggling seems headed the same way.

DISCUSSION QUESTIONS

1. Various state and federal laws specify that a pack of cigarettes must contain 20 cigarettes, and that these cigarettes are limited in the total amount of tobacco they may contain. If such limits were not in place, when taxes per pack were raised, what would you expect to see happen to the number of cigarettes in a pack and the amount of tobacco in a cigarette?

2. In a world where transportation costs are positive, what effect would distance, from the point of production, be expected to have on the size of the tax that a state would find appropriate to levy on a pack of cigarettes?

3. In 1978, interstate trucking was deregulated in the United States, leading to greater competition in this industry and lower freight rates. In light of your answer to question 2, what effect would you expect trucking deregulation to have on the inter-state pattern of cigarette taxes? In particular, what would happen to taxes in states distant from the major point of production in North Carolina, relative to taxes in states closer to North Carolina?

4. Cigarettes that are smuggled from North Carolina to New York must pass through Virginia, Maryland, Delaware, and New Jersey along the way. Suppose that authorities in Delaware decide to raise taxes in the hope of discouraging smoking. What impact would this Delaware tax hike have on cigarette taxes in New York and New Jersey, compared to cigarette taxes in Maryland and Virginia?

Part Three

Alternative Rationing Systems

INTRODUCTION

Although monetary prices are the most commonly used instrument of rationing in a market economy, they are not the only means. A key productive feature of government is its role in defining and enforcing property rights so that market prices can perform their role in allocating scarce resources. But sometimes—for any of a variety of reasons—government seeks to prevent monetary prices from doing their job. We still live in a world of scarcity, however, so rationing must still take place. A variety of instruments may perform the rationing functioning, and in this section we examine many of them. Along the way we find that nonprice rationing is both more costly and more complex than most people ever imagined.

Our first look at nonprice rationing comes in Chapter 11, "Bankrupt Landlords, from Sea to Shining Sea." Here we examine the effects of **rent control**—a legal ceiling on the rent that landlords may charge for apartments. As with many of the issues we consider in this book, the effects of rent controls are more surprising, and costly, than you might think. We find, for example, that legal ceilings on rents have increased the extent of homelessness in the United States, have led to a rise in racial discrimination, and have caused the wholesale destruction of hundreds of thousands of dwelling units in our nation's major cities. We cannot escape one simple fact: Politicians may pass legislation, and bureaucrats may do their best to enforce it, but the laws of demand and supply ultimately rule the economy.

Perhaps not surprisingly, many of the same people who argue that rent controls should be used to ensure "affordable housing" also advocate that the government should guarantee access to "affordable health care." Unfortunately, these laudable goals, once again, are difficult to achieve. As we see in Chapter 12, "Rationing Health Care," in response to the high cost of medical care, many nations have tried to remove health care from the marketplace. Yet the fundamental problems of scarcity remain: producers must be rewarded for their efforts, and consumers' otherwise unlimited desires somehow must be rationed. In the market system, prices perform these functions. But under the systems of government-mandated, universal health care that now exist (or are likely to exist), suppliers are directed by government edict, and prices no longer ration demand. Instead, these systems rely on another method of rationing, called "rationing by waiting" because people are forced to wait—weeks or even months—for whatever level of medical care is offered to them. Under such a system, the costs of health care are clearly different than they are under a market system, but it is not clear that they are any lower.

A "living wage" is yet another social goal that proves to be surprisingly elusive. In Chapter 13, we examine "The Effects of the Minimum Wage" and find once again that the effects of government actions are not always what they seem, nor are they usually what their proponents claim for them. The chief losers in minimum wage hikes are often the very people who can least afford those losses, while those who claim to support the law on altruistic grounds are in fact likely to be the biggest winners. The message of this chapter may well be this simple piece of advice: When someone claims to be doing something *for* you, it is time to ask what that person is doing *to* you.

Our final foray into nonprice rationing takes place on the road—sitting somewhere in a traffic jam. Travel on most roads in the United States (and elsewhere in the world) is "free," in the sense that one does not have to pay a direct monetary price to commute to work or take a Sunday drive. Yet, as we see in Chapter 14, "Heavenly Highway," roads are in fact scarce goods, meaning that their usage ultimately must be rationed by something. In most places of the world, during parts of most days, the scarce space on roads is rationed by the valuable time of drivers, in the form of traffic congestion. Traffic jams not only yield economic losses that are avoidable, advancing technology is making it increasingly cheap to avoid those losses. Yet governments seem reluctant to take advantage of that technology. In examining the reasons for that reluctance, we also come to a better understanding of why, despite the great advantages of having prices ration scarce goods, we often chose instead to rely on nonprice rationing.

11

Bankrupt Landlords, from Sea to Shining Sea

Take a tour of Santa Monica, a beachfront enclave of Los Angeles, and you will find a city of bizarre contrasts. Pick a street at random, and you will likely find run-down rental units sitting in disrepair next to homes costing $500,000. Try another street, and you will find abandoned apartment buildings adjacent to luxury-car dealerships and trendy shops that sell high-fashion clothing to Hollywood stars. Sound strange? Not in Santa Monica—known locally as the People's Republic of Santa Monica—where stringent rent-control laws once routinely forced property owners to leave their buildings empty and decaying rather than even bothering to sell them.

Three thousand miles to the east, rent-control laws in New York City—known locally as the Big Apple—have forced landlords to abandon housing units because the owners no longer could afford the resulting financial losses. Largely as a result of such abandonments, the city government of New York owns thousands of derelict housing units—empty, except for rats and small-time cocaine dealers. Meanwhile, because the controls also discourage new construction, the city faces a housing gap of 200,000 rental units—apartments that easily could be filled at current controlled rental rates, if the units existed in habitable form.

From coast to coast, stories like these are commonplace in the 200 or so American cities and towns that practice some form of **rent control**—a system in which the local government tells building owners how much they can charge for rent. Time and again, the stories are the same: poorly maintained rental units, abandoned apartment

74

buildings, tenants trapped by housing gridlock in apartments no longer suitable for them, bureaucracies bloated with rent-control enforcers, and even homeless families that can find no one who will rent to them. Time and again, the reason for the stories is the same: legal limits on the rent that people may pay for a place to live.

Our story begins in 1943, when the federal government imposed rent control as a temporary wartime measure. Although the federal program ended after the war, New York City continued the controls on its own. Under New York's controls, a landlord generally could not raise rents on apartments as long as the tenants continued to renew their leases. Rent controls in Santa Monica are more recent. They were spurred by the inflation of the 1970s, which, combined with California's rapid population growth, pushed housing prices and rents to record levels. In 1979, the city of Santa Monica (where 80 percent of the residents were renters) ordered rents rolled back to the levels of the year before and stipulated that future rents could go up by only two-thirds as much as any increase in the overall price level. In both New York and Santa Monica, the objective of rent controls has been to keep rents below the levels that would be observed in freely competitive markets. Achieving this goal required that both cities impose extensive regulations to prevent landlord and tenant from evading the controls—regulations that are costly to enforce and that distort the normal operation of the market.

It is worth noting that the rent-control systems in New York and Santa Monica are slowly yielding to decontrol. For a number of years, some apartments in New York have been subject only to "rent stabilization" regulations, which are somewhat less stringent than absolute rent controls. In addition, New York apartments going for over $2000 per month are deregulated when a lease ends. In Santa Monica, the state of California mandated that, effective in 1999, rent for newly vacant apartments could increase. Even so, in both cities, much of the rental market is dominated by rent controls. Accordingly, in this chapter we focus on the consequences of those controls.

In general, the unfettered movement of rental prices in a freely competitive housing market performs three vital functions: (1) it allocates existing scarce housing among competing claimants; (2) it promotes the efficient maintenance of existing housing and stimulates the production of new housing, where appropriate; and (3) it rations usage of housing by demanders, thereby preventing waste of scarce housing. Rent control prevents rental prices from effectively performing these functions. Let's see how.

Rent control discourages the construction of new rental units. Developers and mortgage lenders are reluctant to get involved in building new rental properties because controls artificially depress the most important long-run determinant of profitability—rents. Thus, in one recent year, 11,000 new housing units were built in Dallas, a city with a 16 percent rental vacancy rate but no rent-control statute. In that same year, only 2000 units were built in San Francisco, a city with a 1.6 percent vacancy rate but stringent rent-control laws. In New York City, the only rental units being built are either exempt from controls or are heavily subsidized by the government. Private construction of new apartments in Santa Monica also dried up under controls, even though new office space and commercial developments—both exempt from rent control—were built at a record pace.

Rent control leads to the deterioration of the existing supply of rental housing. When rental prices are held below free market levels, property owners cannot recover through higher rents the costs of maintenance, repairs, and capital improvements. Thus such activities are sharply curtailed. Eventually, taxes, utilities, and the expenses of the most rudimentary repairs—such as replacing broken windows—overwhelm the depressed rental receipts; as a result, the buildings are abandoned. In New York, some owners have resorted to arson, hoping to collect the insurance on their empty rent-controlled buildings before the city claims them for back taxes. Under rent controls in Santa Monica, the city insisted that owners wishing to convert empty apartment buildings into other uses had to build new rental units to replace the units they no longer rented. At a cost of up to $50,000 per apartment, it is little wonder that few owners were willing to bear the burden, choosing instead to leave the buildings empty and graffiti-scarred.

Rent control impedes the process of rationing scarce housing. One consequence of this is that tenant mobility is sharply restricted. Even when a family's demand for living space changes—due, for example, to a new baby or a teenager's departure for college—there can be substantial costs in giving up a rent-controlled unit. In New York City, landlords often charge "key money" (a large, up-front cash payment) before a new tenant is allowed to move in. The high cost of moving means that large families often stay in cramped quarters whereas small families, or even single persons, reside in very large units. In New York, this phenomenon of nonmobility came to be known as *housing gridlock.* In Santa Monica, many homeowners rented out portions of their houses in response to soaring prices in the 1970s and then found themselves trapped by their tenants, whom they could not evict even if they wanted to sell their homes and move to a retirement community.

Not surprisingly, the distortions produced by rent control lead to efforts by both landlords and tenants to evade the rules. This in turn leads to the growth of cumbersome and expensive government bureaucracies whose job is to enforce the controls. In New York, where rents can be raised when tenancy changes hands, landlords have an incentive to make life unpleasant for tenants or to evict them on the slightest pretense. The city has responded by making evictions extremely costly for landlords. Even if a tenant blatantly and repeatedly violates the terms of a lease, the tenant cannot be evicted if the violations are corrected within a "reasonable" time period. If the violations are not corrected—despite several trips to court by the owners and their attorneys—eviction requires a tedious and expensive judicial proceeding. For their part, tenants routinely try to sublet all or part of their rent-controlled apartments at prices substantially above the rent they pay the owner. Because both the city and the landlords try to prohibit subletting, the parties often end up in the city's Housing Courts, an entire judicial system developed chiefly to deal with disputes over rent-controlled apartments.

Strict controls on monthly rents force landlords to use other means to discriminate among prospective tenants. Simply to ensure that the rent check comes every month, many landlords rent only to well-heeled professionals. As one commentator put it, "There is no disputing that Santa Monica became younger, whiter, and richer under rent control." The same pattern occurred under the rent-control laws of both Berkeley, California, and Cambridge, Massachusetts.

There is little doubt the bureaucracies that evolve to administer rent-control laws are cumbersome and expensive. Between 1988 and 1993 New York City spent $5.1 billion rehabilitating housing confiscated from private landlords. Even so, derelict buildings continued piling up at a record rate. The overflow and appeals from the city's Housing Courts clog the rest of New York's judicial system, impeding the prosecution of violent criminals and drug dealers. In Santa Monica, the Rent Control Board began with an annual budget of $745,000 and a staff of 20 people. By the early 1990s, the staff had tripled in size and the budget was pushing $5 million. Who picked up the tab? The landlords did, of course, with an annual special assessment of $200 per unit levied on them. And even though the 1999 state-mandated changes in the law meant that apartment rents in Santa Monica can be increased when a new tenant moves in, the new rent is then controlled by the city for the duration of the tenancy. Indeed, the Rent Control Board conveniently maintains a Web site where one can go to learn the Maximum Allowable Rent on any of the tens of thousands of rent-controlled residences throughout Santa Monica.

Ironically, the big losers from rent control—in addition to land-lords—are often low-income individuals, especially single mothers. Indeed, many observers believe that one significant cause of home-lessness in cities such as New York and Los Angeles is rent control. Often, poor individuals cannot assure the discriminating landlord that their rent will be paid on time—or paid at all—each month. Because controlled rents generally are well below free-market lev-els, there is little incentive for apartment owners to take a chance on low-income individuals as tenants. This is especially true if the prospective tenant's chief source of income is a welfare check. Indeed, a significant number of the tenants appearing in New York's Housing Courts have been low-income mothers who, due to emer-gency expenses or delayed welfare checks, have missed rent pay-ments. Often their appeals end in evictions and new homes in tem-porary public shelters or on the streets. Prior to the state-mandated easing of controls, some apartment owners in Santa Monica who used to rent one- and two-room units to welfare recipients and other low-income individuals simply abandoned their buildings, leaving them vacant rather than trying to collect artificially de-pressed rents that failed to cover operating costs. The disgusted owner of one empty and decaying eighteen-unit building had a friend spray-paint his feelings on the wall: "I want to tear this mess down, but Big Brother won't let me." Perhaps because the owner had escaped from a concentration camp in search of freedom in the United States, the friend added a personalized touch: a drawing of a large hammer and sickle, symbol of the former Soviet Union.

It is worth noting that the ravages of rent controls are not con-fined to capitalist nations. In a heavily publicized news conference several years ago, the foreign minister of Vietnam, Nguyen Co Thach, declared that a "romantic conception of socialism" had destroyed his country's economy after the Vietnam War. Mr. Thach stated that rent control had artificially encouraged demand and discouraged supply, and that all of the housing in Hanoi had fallen into disrepair as a result. Thach concluded by noting, "The Americans couldn't destroy Hanoi, but we have destroyed our city by very low rents. We realized it was stupid and that we must change policy."

Apparently, this same thinking was what induced the state of California to compel changes in Santa Monica's rent-control ordinance. The result of that policy change was an almost immediate jump in rents on newly vacant apartments, as well as a noticeable rise in the vacancy rate—both results being exactly what we would expect. Interestingly enough, however, prospective new tenants were less enthusiastic about the higher rents than many landlords had expected. The reason? Well, 20 years of rent controls had produced that many years of reduced upkeep, and thus apartments that were, well, less than pristine. As one renter noted, "The trouble is, most of this area . . . [is] basically falling apart." And another complained, "I don't want to move into a place that's depressing, with old brown carpet that smells like chicken soup." Higher rents are gradually changing both the ambiance and the aroma of Santa Monica apartments—but only at the same rate that the market is allowed to perform its functions.

DISCUSSION QUESTIONS

1. Why do you think governments frequently attempt to control apartment rents but not house prices?

2. What determines the size of the key-money payments that landlords demand (and tenants offer) for the right to rent a controlled apartment?

3. Who, other than the owners of rental units, loses as a result of rent controls? Who gains from rent controls? What effect would the imposition of rent controls have on the market price of an existing single-family house? What effect would rent controls have on the value of vacant land?

4. Why do the owners of rental units reduce their maintenance ex-
    penditures on the units when rent controls are imposed? Does
    their decision have anything to do with whether they can afford
    those expenditures?

12

Rationing Health Care

Americans spend a larger share of national income on health care—some 15 percent—than any other people in the world. Moreover, for almost every one of the last 25 years, the price index for medical care has increased more rapidly than the price index for all goods and services in general. With spending on health care at record high levels, it is little wonder that some political leaders have labeled health care in the United States a "crisis," arguing we should implement government-mandated universal health care coverage. It is thus instructive to look at what has happened in other countries that have adopted some form of a national health care system.

We obviously cannot cover every aspect of health care here, nor can we demonstrate that one system of health care delivery is better than another. What we can do, however, is note the consequences of this critical point: In a world of **scarcity,** some form of rationing is inevitable. In the market system, that rationing is done by prices. Under the systems of government-mandated universal health care that now exist (or are likely to exist in the future), prices are not permitted to ration demands. Instead, these systems rely on another system of rationing: It is called *rationing by waiting,* because people are forced to wait—for weeks or months—for whatever level of medical care is offered them.

The most common form of government-mandated universal health care coverage found in the world today is the single-payer health care system that in essence offers universal health care to consumers at a money price of zero. (The term *single-payer* is used because the government writes the checks for the medical bills.)

Britain offers a typical example. The British National Health Service (NHS) has been in existence since 1948. Once touted as one of the world's best national health care examples, the NHS has deteriorated dramatically. Consider hospital beds: in 1948 there were ten hospital beds per thousand people. Today there are about five per thousand people. Since 1948 about 50 percent of Britain's hospitals have been closed for "efficiency" reasons—meaning that the British government cannot or will not afford to keep them open. Britain now has fewer hospital beds per capita than every other Western European country except Portugal and Spain.

Because patients in Britain do not pay directly for the services they receive, some other means of rationing must be used. In Britain, the rationing device is waiting, and as the number of hospital beds and other medical facilities has been cut relative to the population, it is little surprise that waiting times have increased. Currently more than a million British patients are waiting for hospital admission. Many others do not show up on waiting lists because they simply do not apply, knowing that the wait is so long. In some London hospitals, individuals routinely spend more than 12 hours waiting to see a physician.

The total staff in the NHS has, in contrast, skyrocketed. Whereas in 1948 the staff-to-bed ratio was .73 to 1 for each hospital bed, today it is 3.1 to 1 for each hospital bed; even with the drop in beds per capita, there are now twice as many staff members for each patient as there were in 1948. One would expect this would enhance medical care. Unfortunately, however, the staff, for the most part, do not deal directly with the treatment of patients. Rather, they have become part of the NHS bureaucracy. This is because the government-run NHS adds a new department or committee for every new aspect of medicine that develops. The NHS consists of a bureaucratic network unknown in the decentralized medical system in the United States.

In fairness to the NHS, some of the changes in the system over the last 50 years have been mirrored in health care systems elsewhere. For example, improvements in surgical techniques and pharmaceuticals have shortened hospital stays in most nations, resulting in a reduced demand for hospital beds. This surely helps explain at least some of the sharp cuts in NHS beds per capita. Nevertheless, horror stories of bungled operations and patients left untended in hospital hallways have become a regular feature in British newspapers. Things got so bad by 2002 that Britain's Labor Party—the initial creator and steadfast supporter of the NHS—proposed that the poorest-performing NHS hospitals be handed over to the private sector.

The national health care system in Canada offers another example of the effects of nonprice rationing. In essence, under the Canadian system the government picks up the entire tab for all covered medical procedures. Currently, only 11 percent of Canada's national health care spending goes to administration, compared to 24 percent in the United States. Canada devotes 9.5 percent of its national income to health care, about a third less than in the United States. Perhaps because of the seemingly low cost of the Canadian system, many supporters of health care reform in the United States often point to Canada's system as one that the United States should emulate.

One impact of the lower level of spending in Canada is that their system does not provide the latest in medical technology. Although Canada ranks fifth highest among developed nations in health care spending as a share of income, it ranks in the bottom third of those countries in availability of technology. For example, compared to the United States, on a per capita basis Canada has far fewer computerized tomography (CT) and magnetic resonance imaging (MRI) machines, critical in performing sophisticated, difficult diagnostics. Similarly, Canadian medical facilities have almost none of the medical devices needed to remove kidney stones without painful and dangerous surgery. Moreover, operating rooms in Canada operate on strict financial budgets and are allowed to continue operating only if they are within those monthly budgets. What happens if an operating room exhausts its budget on, say, the 20th of the month? It shuts down until the beginning of the next monthly budget cycle.

The costs to the users of the Canadian system show up in other ways as well. Two Canadian economists, Cynthia Ramsay and Michael Walker of The Fraser Institute in British Columbia, have studied the waiting times across a variety of medical specialties. They discovered that many Canadians each year were not permitted to enter the hospital when they or their physician deemed best; instead they had to wait until facilities became available. Moreover, Canadians typically were not even able to get in to see their doctors when they wanted. Ramsay and Walker measured the delay from

TABLE 12–1   Median Waiting Time for Treatment by a Specialist in Canada

(In Weeks)

Specialty	Shortest Wait	Longest Wait	Canada Average
Orthopedics	24.9	63.4	32.2
Plastic Surgery	26.2	76.9	28.6
Ophthalmology	14.4	52.1	30
Gynecology	11.6	25.7	15.3
Otolaryngology	10.9	50.6	16.4
Urology	9.5	26.2	13
Neurosurgery	8.7	55.1	20.1
General Surgery	8	20.4	10.3
Internal Medicine	8.6	23.6	11.1
Cardiovascular	8.4	60.1	14.1

Source: The Fraser Institute, Vancouver, BC, Canada.

the time that a primary care physician referred a patient until a specialist actually treated the patient; they found that the demand for health care was rationed by waiting. Listed in Table 12–1 are the median waiting times in weeks for the services of various medical specialists. The three columns show the waiting times for Canada as a whole and the waiting times in individual Canadian provinces that had, respectively, the shortest and longest waiting times.

Two facts are apparent from the table. First, it is commonplace for Canadians to have to wait three or four months to receive health care that is anything beyond that offered by a nurse or primary care physician. Second, the Canadian system produces huge inequalities in the way people are treated, not only across illnesses, but also across provinces for the same illness. These long waits, and the extent of unequal treatment, have produced a regular stream of Canadians who come to the United States and spend their own money for medical care here, rather than await their fate at home. The waiting in Canada has gotten so bad that some provincial governments ship heart-bypass patients and cancer patients need-ing radiation over the U.S. border to receive treatment. Although this practice is frowned on by the Canadian federal government, the alternative, it seems, is to let the patients die at home, waiting.

Another example of government-controlled health care involves the Netherlands. The government there decides on global budgets to control hospital expenditures. It also limits the number of doctors who may specialize in a given area and caps the number of patients they may see. In addition, the government controls physician fees. To help the government meet its budgets, many medical specialists have simply stopped working as much as they used to work. It is common-place for highly trained surgeons to work only half-days or to take weeks off at the end of the year. The result is that typically there is about a three-month waiting list for coronary bypass surgery. Over 15 percent of the patients on the waiting list die before the operation can be performed. Diabetics wait an average of three months to ob-tain laser treatment for retinal hemorrhaging—and risk blindness in the process. The average wait for removal of gallbladder stones and repairs of hernias is from four to eight weeks. Some forms of recon-structive surgery require waits of up to four years.

Under Dutch law, companies must pay employees' salaries for the first two to six weeks of an illness, depending on the size of the company. This has generated an interesting incentive: The compa-nies have discovered that they can reduce their costs by renting hospital rooms that they keep open for their employees. The com-panies thus do not have to pay employee salaries while those em-ployees wait—disabled—for treatment. Although the Dutch sys-tem is supposed to provide equal treatment for all, treatment in fact has come to depend on the size and influence of the company for which a person works.

Although our analyses have involved three foreign countries, we need go no further than our own Veterans Administration (VA) to find similar examples. The VA operates a 100 percent gov-ernment-owned and government-financed health care system. It is the largest health care system in our country and one of the largest in the world, with 163 medical centers housing more than 80,000 beds. It operates 362 outpatient and community clinics that re-ceive 43 million patient visits a year. In addition, it has 137 nursing homes with over 87,000 patients. All of the states, plus the District of Columbia and Puerto Rico, have at least one VA medical center, and the VA boasts almost 250,000 employees nationwide.

The General Accounting Office (GAO) did a study of the VA a few years ago, concluding that the VA system faces a growing demand for "free" medical services. Herein lies the rub: The quantity demanded of most services at a zero price will almost always exceed the quantity supplied. Consequently, because price is not used as a rationing device, some other method must be used to ration the scarce resources. Fifty-five percent of the patients who use the VA for routine medical problems wait three hours or longer and sometimes an entire day in order to be seen for a few minutes by a VA primary care physician. Even among patients requiring urgent medical care, one in nine must wait at least three hours. Patients in need of specialized care cannot even be *seen* by a specialist for 60 to 90 days. They wait months more if surgery or other special procedures are required.

Whether the location is Britain, Canada, Holland, or even the U.S. Veterans Administration, when prices are prevented from clearing the market for medical care, waiting time is the most commonly used means of rationing demand. As one unidentified U.S. veteran told the GAO, "I pack a lunch and take a book." Another veteran, retired 69-year-old Army Major Elmer Erickson, stated, "Be prepared to spend the day there. You will eventually see a doctor."

DISCUSSION QUESTIONS

1. Suppose we had government-mandated universal access to food. How would the outcome likely differ from what is observed with health care systems of this type?

2. Under the Canadian system, those who are unhappy with the health care they receive can come to the United States for medical care if they can afford it. If the United States adopted a system similar to Canada's, where could Americans go if they were not satisfied with the medical care they were receiving?

3. Under the current U.S. health care system, insurance companies often perform the role performed by government agencies

under the British, Canadian, and Dutch systems. That is, they pay the bills, and they limit the care that people are able to consume. Why might health insurance companies be expected to do a better job in performing these functions than a government agency?

4. How much health care do people "need"? Does this amount depend on the cost of providing it?

13

The Effects of the Minimum Wage

Ask workers if they would like a raise and the answer is likely to be a resounding yes. But ask them if they would like to be fired or have their hours of work reduced and they would probably tell you no. The effects of the minimum wage are centered on exactly these points.

Proponents of the **minimum wage**—the lowest hourly wage firms legally may pay their workers—argue that low-income workers are underpaid and therefore unable to support themselves or their families. The minimum wage, they say, raises earnings at the bottom of the wage distribution, with little disruption to workers or businesses. Opponents claim that most low-wage workers are low-skilled youths without families to support. The minimum wage, they say, merely enriches a few teenagers at the far greater expense of many others, who can't get jobs. Most important, opponents argue, many individuals at the bottom of the economic ladder lack the skills needed for employers to hire them at the federal minimum. Willing to work but unable to find jobs, these people never learn the basic job skills needed to move up the economic ladder to higher-paying jobs. The issues are clear—but what are the facts?

The federal minimum wage was instituted in 1938 as a provision of the Fair Labor Standards Act (FLSA). It was originally set at $0.25 per hour, about 40 percent of the average manufacturing wage at the time. Over the next 40 years, the legal minimum was raised periodically, roughly in accord with the movement of market wages throughout the economy. Typically, its level has averaged between 40 percent and 50 percent of average manufacturing wages.

In response to the high inflation of the late 1970s, the minimum wage was hiked seven times between 1974 and 1981, reaching $3.35 per hour—about 42 percent of manufacturing wages. Ronald Reagan vowed to keep a lid on the minimum wage, and by the time he stepped down as president, the minimum's unchanged level left it at 31 percent of average wages. Legislation passed in 1989 raised the minimum to $3.80 in 1990 and $4.25 in 1991. Five years later, at the urging of President Clinton, Congress raised it in two steps to $5.15 per hour. By the time you read this, it is likely that the minimum wage will have been increased again.

Nearly 600,000 workers earn the minimum wage; another 1.6 million or so take home even less because the law doesn't cover them. Supporters of the minimum wage claim that it prevents exploitation of employees and helps people earn enough to support their families and themselves. Even so, at $5.15 per hour, a full-time worker earns less than 60 percent of what the government considers enough to keep a family of four out of poverty. In fact, to get a family of four with one wage earner up to the poverty line, the minimum wage would have to be over $9.00 per hour.

Yet those who oppose the minimum wage argue that such calculations are irrelevant. For example, two-thirds of the workers earning the minimum wage are single, and they earn enough to put them above the poverty cutoff. Moreover, about half of these single workers are teenagers, most of whom have no financial obligations, except possibly for their clothing and car insurance expenditures. Thus opponents argue that the minimum wage chiefly benefits upper-middle class teens who are least in need of assistance at the same time that it costs the jobs of thousands of disadvantaged minority youths.

The debate over the minimum wage intensified a few years ago when research by David Card and Alan Krueger suggested that a change in the New Jersey minimum wage had no adverse short-run impact on employment. Further research by other scholars focusing on Canada reveals more clearly what happens when the minimum wage is hiked. In Canada there are important differences in minimum wages both over time and across different provinces. These differences enabled researchers to distinguish between the short-run and long-run effects of changes in minimum wages. The short-run effects are indeed negligible, as implied by Card and Krueger. But the

Canadian research shows that in the *long run* the adverse effects of a higher minimum wage are quite substantial. In the short run, it is true that firms do not cut their workforce by much, if at all, in response to a higher minimum. But over time, the higher costs due to a higher minimum wage force smaller firms out of business, and it is here that the drop in employment shows up clearly.

The Canadian results are consistent with the overwhelming bulk of the U.S. evidence on this issue, which points to a negative impact of the minimum wage on employment. After all, the number of workers demanded, like the quantity demanded for all goods, responds to price: the higher the price, the lower the number desired. There remains, however, debate over *how many* jobs are lost due to the minimum wage. For example, when the minimum wage was raised from $3.35 to $4.25, credible estimates of the number of potential job losses ranged from 50,000 all the way up to 400,000. When the minimum was hiked to $5.15, researchers suggested that at least 200,000 jobs were at stake. With a workforce of 150 million persons, numbers like these may not sound very large. But most of the people who don't have jobs as a result of the minimum wage are teenagers; they comprise only about 5 percent of the workforce but bear almost all of the burden of forgone employment alternatives.

Significantly, the youths most likely to lose work due to the minimum wage are disadvantaged teenagers, chiefly minorities. On average, these teens enter the workforce with the fewest job skills and the greatest need for on-the-job training. Until and unless these disadvantaged teenagers can acquire these skills, they are the most likely to be unemployed as a result of the minimum wage—and thus least likely to have the opportunity to move up the economic ladder. With a teen unemployment rate better than triple the overall rate, and unemployment among black youngsters hovering around 30 percent, critics argue that the minimum wage is a major impediment to long-term labor market success for minority youth.

Indeed, the minimum wage has an aspect that its supporters are not inclined to discuss: It can make employers more likely to discriminate on the basis of sex or race. When wages are set by market forces, employers who would discriminate face a reduced, and thus more expensive, pool of workers. But when the government mandates an above-market wage, a surplus of low-skilled workers results, and it becomes easier and cheaper to discriminate. As former U.S. Treasury Secretary Lawrence Summers noted, the minimum wage "removes the economic penalty to the employer. He can choose the one who's white with blond hair."

Critics of the minimum wage also argue that it makes firms less willing to train workers lacking basic skills. Instead, companies may choose to hire only experienced workers whose abilities justify the higher wage. Firms are also likely to become less generous with fringe benefits in an effort to hold down labor costs. The prospect of more discrimination, less job training for low-skilled workers, and fewer fringe benefits for entry-level workers leaves many observers uncomfortable. As economist Jacob Mincer of Columbia University notes, the minimum wage means "a loss of opportunity" for the hard-core unemployed.

The last time Congress and the president agreed to raise the minimum wage, it was only after a heated battle lasting months. Given the stakes involved—an improved standard of living for some, a loss of job opportunities for others—it is not surprising that discussions of the minimum wage soon turn to controversy. As one former high-level U.S. Department of Labor official said, "When it comes to the minimum wage, there are no easy positions to take. Either you are in favor of more jobs, less discrimination, and more on-the-job training, or you support better wages for workers. Whatever stance you choose, you are bound to get clobbered by the opposition." When the Congress and the president face this issue, one or both parties usually feel the same way.

DISCUSSION QUESTIONS

1. Are teenagers better off when a higher minimum wage enables some to get higher wages but causes others to lose their jobs?

2. Are there methods other than a higher minimum wage that could raise the incomes of low-wage workers without reducing employment among minority youngsters?

3. Why do you think organized labor groups, such as unions, are supporters of a higher minimum wage, even though their members all earn much more than the minimum wage?

4. Is it possible that a higher minimum wage could ever *raise* employment?

14

Heavenly Highway

If you've ever been caught in a rush-hour traffic jam you understand what happens when a scarce good has a price of zero. In this
case, the scarce good is highway travel, and when the money price
of travel is zero, something else must be used to ration the quantity of the good demanded. During rush hour (and much of the
rest of the day in places such as Los Angeles, New York, Seattle,
and Atlanta) the "something" that rations travel demand is time—
the time of the motorists caught in traffic.

Whenever a person drives a car, he or she generates a variety
of costs. First are the **private costs** of driving: fuel, oil, vehicular
wear and tear, and the value of the driver's time.[1] These are all
borne by the driver, so when deciding whether and how much
highway travel to consume, the driver weighs these costs against
the benefits of that travel. If these were the only costs of driving—
and on some roads at some times they are—this discussion would
end here. Drivers would bear the full cost of their activities, just as
the consumers of pizza do, and there would be no further issues to
consider. But in most places of the world, during parts of most
days, driving generates another cost—congestion—which is not
borne by the individuals responsible for it.

On any road, after traffic volume reaches some level, additional cars entering the road slow the flow of traffic. Once this
process of congestion occurs, every additional car slows traffic

---

[1] Ideally, the excise taxes on fuel, as well as automobile licensing fees, are set to accurately reflect the costs of maintaining and policing the road system. Hence drivers pay
not only for their vehicles and their time but also for roads and the police necessary to
keep them safe.

even more. Eventually, traffic may even come to a complete halt. Under these circumstances, each driver is implicitly using, without paying for it, a valuable resource that belongs to other people— the time of other drivers. Unless drivers are made to bear the **congestion costs** they create, we know two things must be true: first, the money price of traveling on the road is too low, and second, the value of motorists' time spent in traffic must be rationing the quantity of travel demanded.

Why do economists worry about congestion? Because its existence raises the possibility that the people using the road could actually be made *better off* if they were somehow charged a money price for using the road. This money price would induce fewer motorists to drive, because some would carpool, others would use public transit, and still others might telecommute rather than come into the office at all. The reduced driving would reduce congestion, and so conserve the valuable time of those people who continued to drive. In fact, it is even possible that by charging drivers a monetary fee or "toll" to drive on a road, *more* people would succeed in reaching their destination in any given time period. It is easiest to see this when traffic is so bad it comes to a grinding halt. The toll would discourage some people from entering the road, and so permit the remaining traffic to move, and thus reach its destination. But the general principle holds true even when traffic is just greatly slowed down by the congestion: road tolls can both improve traffic flow and make drivers better off— surely a heavenly combination for those sick of being stuck in traffic.

Why, then, do we not see more widespread use of tolls on highways? There are three reasons. First, toll collection is not free, and until recently the costs were often large enough to offset many of the benefits. If you've ever traveled on a toll road such as the Pennsylvania or New Jersey turnpikes, you have some notion of these costs. The toll booths there must be constructed and then manned 24 hours a day, and traffic must come to a halt to pay the toll. The result is that the tolls are *creating* some of the congestion they are supposed to relieve.

But over the last 15 years, electronic toll collection systems have been developed that reduce these costs substantially. Small, inexpensive electronic devices called transponders can be installed in cars that will be using the toll road. The transponders transmit identifying information to receivers at the toll stations, which are suspended above the roadway. (The toll stations are also equipped with cameras to record the license plate number of anyone passing through with a missing or malfunctioning transponder.) Cars need not even slow down from cruising speeds to have their identification recorded as they pass through. At the end of the month each motorist receives a bill in the mail for his toll charges (or a ticket if he's tried to avoid the toll). Clearly, such a system is designed for roads or bridges heavily trafficked by regular commuters, but in these circumstances, such as on the bridges in the New York City area, electronic toll collection has drastically lowered the costs of using monetary prices to ration roadway usage. The result has been reduced congestion and improved economic efficiency. Drivers are better off, and local governments have extra revenue to spend on other services.

The second impediment to pricing highway travel is the often radical and unpredictable consequences of changes in the cost of travel. Unlike a typical privately provided good, each road is part of a network of roads; a change in costs on one segment of the system can sometimes have striking and substantial consequences elsewhere—consequences that can largely or completely offset the benefits of the tolls.

The island nation of Singapore, for example, has some of the worst traffic in the world. As a result, its government has been experimenting with pricing roads since 1975, charging a special fee for vehicles entering the central business district during peak traffic periods. When combined with other traffic-control measures, the fee helped cut traffic in central Singapore by 45 percent during peak hours, enabling traffic speed to almost double, to about 22 miles per hour. But these positive effects in the central city between 7:30 AM and 9:30 AM were accompanied by deleterious effects elsewhere. For example, just outside the central city, traffic jams got worse as drivers sought routes they could use without paying. Moreover, on the roads leading into the central city, the drop in rush-hour traffic was nearly matched by a sharp increase in traffic just before 7:30 and after 9:30.

Tolls don't always have to have such adverse side effects, however, as illustrated by the success of London, England, in implementing them. Beginning in 2003 drivers entering the central area of London were charged a fee of £5 (about $9 at recent exchange rates), with fines ranging in excess of £200 if they failed to pay. The result has been a 20 percent reduction in traffic and about a 5 percent increase in average speeds—which doesn't sound like much, until you realize that average traffic speeds in London actually *fell* during the twentieth century, as cars first replaced horses and then simply got in each other's way. The big difference between Singapore and London seems to be the magnitude of the charge: London got it roughly right, but Singapore has tried to charge too much—a point to which we shall return.

Perhaps the biggest impediment to efficient pricing of roads is the fact that roads typically are operated by governments rather than by private-sector firms. Decisions to price roads must pass through the political process, which necessarily means that the efficiency concerns of the economist are likely to be outweighed by political concerns over who shall pay how much for what. Public-opinion polls from densely populated and heavily congested Hong Kong help us understand the consequences.

Although motorists and non-motorists in Hong Kong are almost identical in agreeing that traffic congestion is serious (84.5 percent and 82.0 percent, respectively), they differ sharply in what they think should be done about it. Motorists favor new road construction, presumably because this would shift to taxpaying non-motorists part of the cost of relieving congestion. In contrast, non-motorists believe that financial disincentives to driving (such as tolls and licensing fees) should be given the top priority, presumably because this would shift more of the burden to drivers. These divergences of public opinion have slowed the use of private-sector remedies for the congestion on publicly owned roads, just as they have elsewhere in the world. The result is too many roads on which monetary prices are too low (or nonexistent), and thus congestion is too high.

The nation of Japan offers us an illustration from the other end of the spectrum on the hazards of having politicians set prices. Unlike in the United States, where "freeways" are commonplace, all 4350 miles of expressways in Japan's national highway system are toll roads. The nation began building the expressways in 1956 with loans from the World Bank, imposing tolls to pay off the loans.

The loans are long-since paid off, but the tolls remain—generating $15 billion per year to help the national government pay off its $360 billion debt for other public-works projects. Yet the government is so addicted to tolls as a revenue source that many of its citizens think it has gone off the deep end. Tolls are so high that if you were to drive the length of Japan (a nation smaller than California), you would rack up $330 in tolls. Just making the 10-minute trip across Tokyo Bay from the airport will set you back $25, which is actually an *improvement* over the $42 that drivers used to pay. With fees like this, you can imagine the response: people buy airline tickets rather than drive when making trips of 200 miles, and trucking companies devise elaborate routing schemes for their trucks to keep toll costs down. And how's traffic? Well, along many of the pricier portions of the Japanese highway system, you may find yourself alone on the road.

The message of our story is quite simple. For a variety of reasons, highways, unlike hamburgers, are tricky things to price correctly. More often than not, the price is too low, but sometimes it is too high. So if you are out there looking for that heavenly combination of speedy travel and low money prices, you may be on the road quite a while.

DISCUSSION QUESTIONS

1. Rather than use tolls, some localities use other means to reduce congestion on major routes—for example, access-limiting traffic lights at freeway on-ramps. From an economist's perspective, what are the disadvantages of such a system?

2. If the purpose of a toll is to bring the private costs of a driver's actions into equality with the social costs, should the size of the toll depend on how many passengers are in the car? Should it depend on the size of the car (or differ between cars, trucks, and buses)? Should it depend on the time of day that it is collected?

3. Suppose that when you ate a pizza you had to pay only for the crust, not the toppings. What would happen to (i) the number of pizzas you ate, and (ii) the amount and quality of the top-

pings on each one? If you faced a price of zero for toppings, after you had fully adjusted to this new pricing, what would be the marginal value to you of the last topping consumed? (You can give an exact number.) Does this equal the marginal cost of the last topping, assuming that toppings are a scarce good? Are you consuming the efficient number of toppings? Of pizzas?

Part Four

Market Structures

INTRODUCTION

The competitive model employed in our discussion of demand and supply assumes that firms on both sides of the market satisfy the conditions of **pure competition.** For sellers of goods, this means the demand curve they face is **perfectly elastic:** suppliers must take the market price as given, because any attempt by them to raise their price above the market price will result in the loss of all of their sales. Similarly, purchasers in the competitive model face a supply curve that is also perfectly elastic. The market price is given, and any attempt by them to purchase at less than that price will be unsuccessful—no one will sell to them.

The conditions of pure competition imply that buyers and sellers have no effect individually on market prices. Even a casual glance at the world suggests that the conditions of pure competition are not always met. Sometimes, as is the case for major corporations, the firms are large enough relative to the market that significant changes in their purchase or sale decisions clearly must have an effect on prices. In other cases, buyers or sellers are somehow "unique," in that no other buyer or seller offers exactly what they do. (Classic examples include the superstars of sports and entertainment, who will sell less of their services if they raise their prices, but will still sell some.) Sometimes firms that otherwise would be pure competitors join to form a **cartel,** acting as a single decision-making unit whose collective output decisions affect the market price.

When a seller's decisions affect the price of a good, economists usually call the firm a **monopoly.** Literally, this means "single seller," but what is actually meant is that the firm faces a downward-sloping demand curve for its output, so that its decisions affect the price at which its output is sold. When a buyer's decisions affect the market price, we term the firm a **monopsony,** or "single buyer." This just means that the firm faces a positively sloped supply curve, so that its purchasing decisions affect the price at which it buys goods. (Some economists use the term **price searcher** to mean any firm, buyer or seller, whose decisions affect market prices, and who must therefore search for (or decide on) the price that maximizes the firm's profits. Following this terminology, a pure competitor would be called a **price taker,** for such a firm takes the market price as given.)

The starting point for our examination of different market structures, Chapter 15, "Give Me MP3 or Give Me Death," provides a look at some implications of our increasingly digital world. Digital information has the great advantage that it can be copied and transmitted at almost zero cost. Unfortunately for record companies, many recording artists, and Hollywood studios, this is also the great *disadvantage* of digital information. Recent years have witnessed an explosion in the piracy of music and movies, as individuals have used **peer-to-peer (P2P) networking** to engage in **file sharing.** Some people justify this piracy on the grounds that copyrights, trademarks and the like each create a monopoly for their owners, because the owners are the only ones who can sell the resulting goods. Technically, this is true, but so too is the fact that *you* have a monopoly on the labor you sell: no one else but you can sell your services. You, like record companies, face lots of competition, which limits the ability to price what you and they sell above marginal cost. Clearly, the amount of competition varies from case to case, but the presence of that competition is inescapable. If you are prevented from capturing, say, the return on your investment in education, you are less likely to make that investment. The same is true for record companies when it comes to music. The moral of this story is that illegal downloading of copyrighted music (and movies) is not only a crime but also will have *long-run* consequences for those who like to listen to music, including less investment in new artists by the music industry and less new music.

As we see in Chapter 16, "Contracts, Combinations, and Conspiracies," the rigors (and low profits) of competition are such that firms often try to devise ways to avoid competing. One of the most popular is the **cartel,** which is simply a collective agreement by many or all firms in an industry to reduce total output so that the price of the product—and thus the profits of the cartel's members—can be raised. Cartels generally are illegal in the United States, but the National Collegiate Athletic Association (NCAA) is a cartel that is both legal and flourishing in the United States. Cartels more commonly are observed in international markets. Here we examine three international cartels, in the markets for oil, diamonds, and caviar. In each case we find that although the incentives to form cartels are great, even greater are the incentives to cheat on the cartels, almost as soon as they are formed. The overriding message of this chapter is that, despite their enormous profit potential, competitive pressures make cartels inherently unstable, and thus generally short-lived.

Whatever the degree of competition, firms are always seeking ways to raise profits. Often this means developing new products and striving to offer superior service. But sometimes, as we see in Chapter 17, "Coffee, Tea, or Tuition-Free?", it simply means adjusting prices on existing products. The practice of charging prices that differ across customers in ways not due to differences in the marginal costs of supplying them is called **price discrimination.** Although technically illegal in the United States, it is routinely observed in markets ranging from airline travel to college financial aid. In the case of air travel, you are almost certainly the beneficiary of price discrimination, paying a lower price than you would if price discrimination were completely eliminated. But don't feel too smug: by the time you start traveling for business rather than pleasure, you are likely to be on the wrong end of the price discrimination, paying plenty so that the college kid in the seat next to can enjoy spring break in a sunny clime.

As we see in Chapter 18, "Keeping the Competition Out," enlisting the government to hamstring or exclude competitors is probably the most reliable means of ensuring that you are protected from the rigors of competition. Perhaps for this reason, the array of markets in which the government stifles competition is nothing short of remarkable. Here we examine just a handful, ranging from taxicabs to hair braiding, but the list could have gone on and on. In each case, the method is the same: usually under the guise of "consumer protection," the government prevents entry by some firms into a market, thereby reducing supply in that market. The effect is much the same as that produced by a fully enforced cartel. Firms thus protected by the government enjoy both a higher price for their product and a larger market share. The consumers, supposedly "protected" by their government, are usually the big losers due to higher product prices and reduced selection among suppliers.

Yet another way that firms try to enhance profits is **product differentiation**—that is, developing new products or styles that catch the fancy of customers and pull business away from one's rivals. The story of product differentiation is usually told as a tale of great financial gain to the firms that do it, inflicted at sizable cost on consumers, who don't really "need" the new products. In fact, as we see in Chapter 19, "The Perils of Product Differentiation," a careful look at the record suggests that the practice is neither so easy nor so profitable as it might seem at first glance. Instead, it appears that consumers are considerably more discriminating than they are usually given credit for. Moreover, if they are not interested in what is being offered, they'll reject it—at great cost to the firm that tries to inflict it upon them. Consequently, product differentiation is a risky business, fraught with potential losses and likely to succeed only if the firms doing it have something that is truly of value to consumers. Thus, product differentiation seems to be much like any other business venture in that it is likely to be successful only if the product is valued by the consumer and on average is an activity that can be expected to yield only the competitive rate of return.

15

Give Me MP3
or Give Me Death

The music industry is frightened, so much so that it has been suing music "pirates" for theft. Some of the hundreds of people who have been sued are as young as 13 and others as old as 70. The Recording Industry Association of America (RIAA) also has sent subpoenas to Internet service providers (ISPs) asking for the names of their most flagrant **file-sharing** customers, under the assumption that Internet users who download big files are doing something illegal.

Before we look at the details of the current legal and economic battles over music transferred over the Internet via file sharing, it is worth looking at how we got to the point that 13-year-old Internet users are receiving subpoenas. Back in 1987, the Moving Picture Experts Group set a standard file format for the storage of audio recordings in a digital format. They called it MPEG-3, abbreviated as "MP3." Digital MP3 files are created through a process called "ripping." Ripping software allows a computer owner to copy an audio compact disc (CD) directly onto the computer's hard drive by compressing the audio information on the CD into the MP3 format. The MP3's compressed format allows for rapid transmission of digital audio files from one computer to another by e-mail or by using **file transfer protocol (FTP)** software.

Not surprisingly, as the ripping of existing prerecorded audio CDs became more and more popular (and less and less expensive as both computers and Internet access became cheaper), the volume of *blank,* recordable CDs sold in North America skyrocketed, as revealed in the middle column of Table 15–1. Note also

TABLE 15–1   As Sales of Prerecorded CDs Fall, Sales of Blank CDs Increase

Year	Volume of Blank, Recordable CDs Sold in North America in Millions	Volume of Prerecorded CDs Made in North America in Millions
1999	490	1800
2000	720	1720
2001	1540	1611
2002	2010	1600
2003	2030	1540

that, as the sales of blank CDs increased, the sales of prerecorded audio CDs fell—a point to which we shall return.

As just about everybody knows today, the ability to compress music (and now video) files, send them through the Internet, and then decompress them has led to a boom in the exchange of MP3 files. Most systems for exchanging MP3 files, particularly those that are illegal, involve **peer-to-peer (P2P) networking.**

Not that many years ago, most college students had heard of Napster's Web site (at http://www.napster.com), which used a file-sharing system invented by a New Jersey teenager named Shawn Fanning. Although the software he developed was complex, the concept was simple. No large servers or mainframe computers were involved. Rather, individuals who had downloaded the Napster program (over 40 million, according to Napster before it was effectively shut down due to legal actions) could share files, particularly music files, with anybody else who had downloaded the program. Those who shared their existing files of music with others had to, of course, leave their computers on. The reason this process is called peer-to-peer file sharing is that all of the participants are peers: individuals using personal PCs to share with one another on an equal basis.

The problem with this arrangement—at least as far as the record companies were concerned—was that all but one of the peers got the music without paying for it. Finally, the record companies had "had enough." They got together and filed suit against Napster, alleging **copyright infringement,** because the company had allegedly aided consumers in sharing files with one another. The federal court issued a **preliminary injunction,** which eventually became permanent. Napster soon went out of business as a free peer-to-peer system and reinvented itself as a for-fee music download system, similar to iTunes from Apple, Jukebox from Dell, and other competing for-fee music download systems.

To understand fully the issues involved in peer-to-peer networking, illegal music pirating, and the like, you have to have some notion of what we call **intellectual property,** or IP, as the lawyers call it. IP consists of the products that result from intellectual creative processes. Although intellectual property is an abstract term for an abstract concept, it is nonetheless wholly familiar to just about everyone. Trademarks, copyrights, and patents are all forms of intellectual property. The book you are reading is copyrighted. The personal computer you use is trademarked. The software you use, the movies you see, and the music you listen to are all forms of intellectual property. In each case you cannot legally use the property without the permission of the property's owner—just as you cannot legally use an automobile without the permission of the car's owner.

Intellectual property has taken on increasing significance not only in the United States, but globally as well. Today the value of the world's intellectual property exceeds the value of physical property such as machines and houses. For U.S. companies, ownership rights in intellectual property are often more important to their prosperity than their **tangible assets.**

For all types of investment, the higher the expected rate of return, the more investment there will be. Record companies are no different than other businesses in this respect. A record label has to invest in its recording artists, particularly if it wants to popularize a new group. This investment consists of recording time, publicity, and the like. There is also the cost of producing CDs and distributing them to the various retail outlets. Consider two scenarios. The first one is the way things "used to be in the good old times," before peer-to-peer networking. When a record label signed a new artist, say Sheryl Crow, it was generally secure in its belief that it alone could distribute her songs. Hence, it gradually increased its investment as her records started to sell more and more. The second scenario applies more recently, in the presence of file sharing. When a new group is signed, say OutKast, the record company faces the prospect that as soon as one CD is sold, thousands of unauthorized copies will appear, courtesy of numerous Web sites that offer free file-sharing software. Indeed, the available "illegal" peer-to-peer networking systems are many, including KaZaA, Scour, and WinMX. Clearly, in the second scenario, the *potential* total revenues and hence profits from the sales of OutKast CDs are much lower than they were for Sheryl Crow, who became popular before peer-to-peer networking was even understood by most music fans.

We know that music piracy is currently rampant. Boston-based Forrester Research Group has estimated that in one recent year, about 25 million music pirates did not buy almost 50 million CDs, costing the record industry anywhere from $800 million to a billion dollars in lost sales. Recording companies' sales and thus their profits have dropped dramatically. So, as a well-informed economist, you might predict the obvious here—a lower rate of return to investing in new music groups will lead to less investment in new music.

Some people argue that copyrights, trademarks, and the like each create a **monopoly** for their owners, because the owners are the only ones who can sell the resulting goods. Technically, this is true, but so too is the fact that *you* have a monopoly on the labor you sell: no one else but you can sell your services. You, like record companies and book publishers, face lots of competition, which limits your ability to price what you and they sell above marginal cost. Clearly, the amount of competition varies from case to case, but the presence of that competition is inescapable. If you are prevented from capturing, say, the return on your investment in education (including what you spent on this book!), you are less likely to make that investment. The same is true for record companies when it comes to music.

The moral of this story is not merely that illegal downloading of copyrighted music (and movies) is in fact a crime, but that it also will have *long-run* consequences for those who like to listen to music. Those consequences will, at a minimum, be less investment in new artists by the music industry. In other words, as with all economic situations involving scarcity, "there is no free lunch." Those who proclaim that the downloading of pirated MP3 files should be legally unrestricted are ignoring the long-run costs to society and to music lovers in general.

The same analysis can be applied to other economic areas in which intellectual property rights are at stake. Consider the pharmaceutical industry. Just as the music industry invests in new talent, the pharmaceutical industry invests in new drugs. A typical new drug costs roughly $800 million in investment to bring it to market. When foreign countries pass laws restricting the prices that pharmaceutical companies can charge for those drugs abroad, those countries are, in effect, usurping part of the expected rate of return on those hundreds of millions of dollars of investment in the new drugs.

In some cases, such laws are passed in impoverished developing countries, who argue that without the laws their citizens could not afford the medicine. But many of these laws—which result in artificially lower prices—have been passed in rich countries in Europe, such as France and Germany, as well as in Japan and Canada. In essence, these countries are engaged in a type of piracy, not dissimilar to the illegal downloading of music files. As the head of the Food and Drug Administration, Mark McClellan, pointed out, "The economic consequences of overly strict price controls on drugs are no different than violating the patent directly. . . ."

The most extreme case of this transfer of wealth from the shareholders of U.S. pharmaceuticals to foreigners occurs when (as a result of political pressure) drugs are given away free of charge. For example, some U.S. pharmaceutical companies have been providing "free" AIDS drugs to victims in Africa, apparently fearing that if they do not do so they will ultimately face laws requiring such actions. In the short run, low-income people get drugs they otherwise might not be able to afford. This is the good news. But the bad news is that the long-run consequences are *fewer* drugs for them and everyone else, because reduced revenue from drug sales means less incentive to invest in research and development of more and better drugs to cure that terrible disease in the future.

Let's return to the original subject of this chapter, music piracy. In addition to suing alleged pirates, the music industry has undertaken two additional measures to fight back. One involves testing the **price elasticity of demand.** In 2003, Universal Music Group cut the suggested retail price of nearly all of its CDs to $12.95, which represented about a 30 percent drop. In practice, many of its CDs have sold since then for $9.99. In effect, this amounted to cutting the **constant-dollar price** of CDs back to the level it had been in 1997. Whether the price elasticity of demand is great enough in the long run to increase revenues (and perhaps, profits) for Universal remains to be seen.

The second way in which record companies are combating music piracy is by offering easy-to-use legal for-fee music file download systems. The first to get the ball rolling was Steve Jobs' Apple Computer Company. Apple created the iPod, which has now sold over a million units since it came out a few years ago. The iPod coupled with its iTunes system has been wildly successful. Although the "library" of music is only five or six hundred thousand songs strong right now, it is destined to grow. The typical price of a song is 99¢. The user can download a song to three different computers and one iPod. Other companies that have followed suit include Real, Dell, iRiver, Rio, Creative Nomad, and Gateway. Legal downloading of MP3 music files is definitely a growing business. Currently, no one company is making any true profits on the process, but that situation may change in the future. Apple, the leader in the field, says it makes virtually nothing on the downloading of music files, but it is making a handsome profit on the sale of its music player, the iPod.

Technology creates numerous new business opportunities. Technology also creates problems for existing businesses. A combination of the Internet, cheaper communication, high-speed broadband access proliferation, MP3 compression and decompression software, and peer-to-peer networking has clearly created a host of potential profits for business and also many problems. As with all other innovations in our past, some company will figure out the correct formula for making solid long-run profits, and other companies will emulate it.

DISCUSSION QUESTIONS

1. If you were the economist for Universal Music Group, how would you have presented the argument in favor of the firm's decision to lower prices by 30 percent in 2003?

2. Why do you think that prosecuting individual copyright violators—music pirates—might turn out to be a futile effort by the record industry? Or, alternatively, is it possible that such prosecution could work in the long run and, if so, under what circumstances?

3. How might the proliferation of music file sharing on the Internet be responsible for the trend toward fewer and fewer major live-music concerts in large venues, such as football stadiums? (You should be aware that in the 1960s, 1970s, and 1980s, numerous music groups toured the United States and, indeed, the world frequently and sold out football stadiums and other venues that held tens of thousands of screaming fans.)

16

Contracts, Combinations, and Conspiracies

The Sherman Act of 1890 outlaws any "contract, combination, . . . or conspiracy, in restraint of trade or commerce" in the United States. Translated from the legalese, this means that firms in America cannot lawfully join with competitors to form a **cartel** to raise prices above the competitive level.[1] Because successful cartels have the potential for great profits, there are strong incentives to form them. Usually, however, if the government discourages them, or even if it does not actively encourage them, cartels are difficult to keep together. This is because a cartel must meet four requirements if it is to be successful:

1. *Share*. It must control a large share of actual and potential output, so that other producers of the good it sells will not be able to depress prices by expanding output significantly.
2. *Substitutes*. Consumers must regard alternatives to the cartel's product as being relatively poor substitutes, and these substitutes must be few in number and relatively inelastic in supply; such factors all reduce the elasticity of demand facing the cartel, helping it to raise prices.
3. *Stability*. There must be very few outside factors that tend to disturb cost or demand conditions in the industry, so that the

---

[1] Despite this, many American agricultural producers are legally permitted to collectively agree to raise their prices on products ranging from almonds to oranges. They do so under the umbrella of "marketing orders," which effectively are cartels approved and enforced by the U.S. Department of Agriculture.

cartel is not continually having to make new price and output decisions in response to changing conditions.
4. *Solidarity*. It must be relatively easy for the cartel to maintain solidarity by identifying and punishing members who cheat on the cartel agreement with price cuts.

All successful cartels have been able to meet these requirements to some extent. Conversely, it has been a breakdown in one or more of these factors that has been the downfall of each of them that has failed. In general, successful cartels are international in character. They are either effectively beyond (or exempt from) national laws forbidding them, or are encouraged by, or comprised of, governments themselves.

One of the most famous and successful cartels has been the Organization of Petroleum Exporting Countries (OPEC). Formed in 1960, its members have included many major oil producing countries, such as Algeria, Indonesia, Iran, Iraq, Kuwait, Libya, Nigeria, Saudi Arabia, and Venezuela. OPEC had little impact on the price of oil until the outbreak of the Middle East war in 1973 provided the impetus for cohesive action. Saudi Arabia, Kuwait, and several other Arab nations sharply reduced their production of oil; because the demand curve for oil is downward sloping, this reduction in supply pushed oil prices—and thus the profits of OPEC members—up sharply. On January 1, 1973, one could buy Saudi Arabian crude oil at $2.12 per barrel. Within one year, the price of crude had risen to $7.61 per barrel; by 1975, to $10.50; and by the end of the decade, the price of oil was $35 per barrel and rising.

Several forces combined to send oil prices in the opposite direction by the mid-1980s. At least partly in response to the high prices charged by OPEC, worldwide output of oil from other sources began to grow, led by rising production on Alaska's North Slope and by aggressive marketing of the oil flowing out of the Norwegian and British fields located in the North Sea. Eventually, this additional production significantly reduced the market share controlled by OPEC members and thus helped reduce their stranglehold on price.

The most important problem for OPEC, however, as for so many cartels, has been cheating on the cartel agreement by its members. Whenever there are numerous firms or countries in a cartel arrangement, there will always be some that are unhappy with the situation, perhaps because they think they are not getting enough of the profits. They cheat by charging a slightly lower price than the one stipulated by the cartel, a move that will result in a very large increase in the cheater's revenues (and thus profits). The potential for cheating is a constant threat to a cartel's existence, and when enough of a cartel's members try to cheat, the cartel breaks up.

In the case of OPEC, war between the member nations of Iran and Iraq during the 1980s precipitated a major outbreak of cheating, as those two nations expanded production beyond their quotas, using the extra sales to finance heavy military expenditures. The price of crude oil plunged to $10 per barrel in 1986, when cheating on output quotas spread throughout the cartel. OPEC member Saudi Arabia, the world's largest producer of crude, finally restored order when it threatened to double its output if other OPEC members did not adhere to quotas. Although there have been short-lived price spikes since then, crude oil prices typically have hovered around $25-30 per barrel; after adjusting for inflation, this is 60 percent cheaper than in 1980.

The perils faced by cartels are also illustrated in the diamond market, where DeBeers Consolidated Mines, the famous diamond company, controls 65 percent of the world supply. Although DeBeers itself produces only about 35 percent of the world's diamond output, it typically has directed the marketing of another 30 percent through a cartel called the Diamond Trading Company, or DTC. (The cartel was for many years known as the Central Selling Organization.) The DTC has long restricted the sale of rough-cut diamonds to keep their prices at levels that maximize the profits of its members. After many years of profitable success, however, the diamond cartel hit rough times. Cartel profits spurred searches for new sources of supply, and major discoveries were made in Australia and Canada. Moreover, Russia, which accounted for about one-fourth of DTC's output, became a chronic cheater on DTC rules by permitting diamonds to "leak" into international markets. The combined effect of these forces has been substantial. In 1980, the wholesale price of investment-grade D-flawless diamonds—considered the most reliable measure of market conditions in the industry—was about $75,000 per carat. After adjusting for inflation, D-flawless diamonds recently have been worth less than half that amount.

Russians have had troubles with their own historically success-ful cartel, the one that controls—or controlled—the supply of fine caviar. The principal source of some of the world's best caviar is the Volga River Delta, where Kazakhstan and Russia (both for-mer members of the Soviet Union) share a border at the northern end of the Caspian Sea. Both the temperature and salinity of the water in the Delta make it the ideal spawning ground for sturgeon, the long-nosed prehistoric fish whose eggs have for centuries been viewed as the world's finest caviar. Originally, the Russian czars and czarinas ran the show, eating what they wanted of the harvest, and then controlling the remaining supplies to their advantage.

Once the Bolsheviks disposed of the Romanovs in 1917, they quickly saw the potential profits to be had from cornering the market on caviar. Thus, for the next 75 years or so, a Soviet state-dominated cartel controlled the nation's caviar business from top to bottom. Although the Soviet sturgeon were considerate enough to produce an annual catch of some 2,000 tons of caviar, the com-munist cartel allowed only 150 tons out of the country. As a result, a state-supplied kilogram (2.2 pounds) of top-grade black caviar costing $5 or less on the Moscow black market, commanded $1000 or more in New York.

The demise of the Soviet Union spawned trouble, however, for competition reared its ugly head. As it turns out, the largest stur-geon fisheries fell under the jurisdictions of two different au-tonomous republics—Russia and Kazakhstan—each of which wanted to own and operate its own lucrative caviar business. Moreover, a variety of individuals, including enterprising Caspian Sea fishermen from these republics, staked private claims, and in some cases set up their own export channels (behavior officially termed "black market piracy"). The effect of this capitalist behavior was a 20-percent drop in the official caviar export price during the first year of autonomy, plus an escalation of competition since then.

Caviar consumers were pleased at this turn of events, but old-line suppliers were not quite so happy. "We don't need this kind of competition," complained one. "All of these small rivals mean that prices will fall and the market will be ripped apart. This is a deli-cacy—we need to keep it elite." Recent years have seen a sharp upswing in world caviar prices, although not because Russia and Kazakhstan have managed to get competition under control.

Instead, it turns out that pollution from leftover Soviet industry in the area has helped to sharply reduce the region's sturgeon population. The resulting decline in the amount of harvestable caviar drove costs and prices up, and profits even lower. Adding insult to injury, firms in America (whose costs are not affected by the Soviet pollution) have entered the caviar market in response to the higher prices, intensifying the price-cost squeeze that the former Soviet republics are suffering. And so, just as Soviet citizens found that communism wasn't all that it was cracked up to be, it appears some of them are now learning that capitalism may be more than they bargained for—but perhaps no less than Karl Marx warned them about.

Oddly enough, despite the Sherman Act and other tough antitrust laws, one of the longest-running cartels can be found right here in the United States. The National Collegiate Athletic Association (NCAA), which operates under a special exemption from the antitrust laws, sets the rules not only for how intercollegiate sports competition takes place but also for how athletes are recruited and paid. And under NCAA rules, college athletes are not paid much. Indeed, as a practical matter, compensation for collegiate athletes is limited to the cost of room, board, books, and tuition at their university or college, an amount that typically ranges from $20,000 to $40,000 per year. Now, this might sound like pretty good pay to you, and, indeed, for a field hockey player or college wrestler, it probably is. But for the so-called "revenue sports" of college athletics, most notably football and basketball, such sums amount to a pittance compared to what these athletes would bring on the open market. (This, of course, is exactly the point: universities are joined together in the NCAA in part simply to keep down the costs of college athletics.) In the case of football, this issue has been studied quite intensively, so we actually have a good idea of what top college players are worth. Over a four-year college career, a player who ends up getting drafted by a professional team is underpaid by about $2 million. And while lesser players are underpaid by lesser amounts, numbers like these make it clear that, despite encouraging open competition on college playing fields, when it comes to competition in the marketplace, the NCAA is guilty of unsportsmanlike conduct.

DISCUSSION QUESTIONS

1. Why are all cartels inherently unstable?

2. Would it be easier to form a cartel in a market with many producers or one with very few producers?

3. What happens to the producers of caviar made from other types of fish eggs (such as salmon, whitefish, and trout) when the price of the finest sturgeon caviar changes? Would these firms ever have an incentive to help the governments of Russia and Kazakhstan reestablish the caviar cartel?

4. If the members of your class were to attempt to form a study-reduction cartel in which everyone agreed to study less, which individuals would have the greatest to gain from the cartel? Which ones would have the greatest incentive to cheat on the cartel?

17

Coffee, Tea, or Tuition-Free?

A few years ago, Internet retailing giant Amazon.com received some unwanted publicity when it was revealed that the company was charging different prices for movies sold to different customers. Amazon insisted that the price differences were random and amounted to an effort to simply test the market. But some customers complained that Amazon was using the practice to tailor prices to customer characteristics, charging more to people who were likely to be willing to pay more. The flap over Amazon's "market test" soon died out, but as time passes, Internet firms will find it almost irresistible to regularly charge different prices to different customers. The reason is simple: by tracking past buying habits, other sites visited, and so forth, firms can get a pretty good idea of how to engage in **price discrimination** among their customers, and thus increase their profits.

Now, price discrimination not only sounds like something that should be illegal, it *is* illegal, at least under some circumstances. Despite that, it is routinely practiced by businesses of all descriptions—and perhaps even by the college you attend. Interestingly, although price discrimination definitely benefits the firms (or colleges) that engage in it, you too may benefit. Let's see how.

First things first: Price discrimination is defined as the existence of price differences across customers for the same good that are not due to differences in the marginal costs of supplying the customers. Thus, price discrimination can occur when marginal costs are the same across customers, but prices are different, or when prices are the same, despite differences in marginal costs. An example of the former occurs when pharmacies or movie theaters charge lower prices to "senior citizens" than to other customers. An example of the latter can be found at "all-you-can-eat" buffets, where the price is the same to all diners, even though some eat much more food than others.

There are three conditions that must exist for a firm to engage in price discrimination. First, the firm must be, at least to some extent, a **price searcher**—that is, it must be able to raise price above marginal cost without losing all of its sales to rivals. Second, there must be identifiable differences across customers in their willingness (or ability) to pay different prices for the same good. Third, the firm must be able to prevent customers who pay lower prices from reselling the good to customers who otherwise would be charged higher prices—or else customers eligible for the lowest price will buy on behalf of all customers.

The objective of price discrimination is, of course, higher profits for the firm that engages in it. To see how this might work, consider a firm selling to two identifiable groups of customers, say, retirees and working people. Also suppose that the retirees have lower income, and so perhaps have a higher **price elasticity of demand** for the good; that is, they tend to be more sensitive to changes in price. In this case, it may be possible for the firm to reallocate sales among customer groups, lowering prices slightly to retirees and raising them somewhat to working people, thereby getting more revenue at the same costs, and so earning higher profits. Of course, to be able to accomplish this, the firm must be able to distinguish between the two groups. (This ability is often approximated by offering the lower prices only to persons who can prove they are older and thus more likely to be retired.) Moreover, the firm must be able to prevent resale from low-price buyers to other customers; in the case of prescription medicines, pharmacies are aided by federal and state laws that forbid such resale, while in the case of movie theaters, the person getting the lower price generally must attend the movie personally to get the lower price. (This helps explain why movie rental companies like Blockbuster are less likely to offer senior-citizen discounts than are movie theaters: it would be too easy for seniors to rent movies on behalf of other people who wish to avoid the higher prices applicable to them.)

If you have ever traveled on an airplane, you are likely to have been a beneficiary of price discrimination (although your parents—or their employers—may have been the victim of such discrimination if they fly on short-notice business trips). Prior to 1978, the fares charged by airlines in the United States were regulated by the federal government, so all airlines offered the same government-approved fares; discounts were rare beyond late-night ("red-eye") or weekend flights.[1] Once deregulation occurred, airlines quickly discovered there were large differences in the price elasticity of demand across customers. Business travelers typically had a lower price elasticity of demand, and thus were willing to pay higher fares, than leisure travelers. Fares charged business travelers are now higher than they used to be, even though leisure fares are significantly lower than they were in the days of government regulation.

The precision and effectiveness with which the airlines engage in price discrimination have been rising steadily over time, thanks to a process known as "yield management." Combining sophisticated statistical techniques and massive historical databases, together with computerized up-to-the-minute bookings, the airlines can predict with almost pinpoint accuracy how many business customers will want seats on a given flight—and how much they'll be willing to pay. As a result, says one industry insider, "high fares get higher and low fares get lower."

The process begins months before a flight ever departs, as the airline divides the seats on a plane into as many as seven or more different fare classes, or categories. Initial fares on a flight are established for each of the categories, and the yield-management computers begin the process of monitoring the reservations, comparing them to historical patterns. If advance bookings are slow, the airline will move seats to low-fare categories. But if business travelers buy higher-priced, unrestricted tickets sooner than expected, the yield-management computer removes seats from

[1] Those fares were also considerably higher on average than they are today, because the federal government agency responsible for regulating the airlines also prevented them from competing with one another on the basis of price.

discount categories and holds them for last-minute business passengers that are predicted to show up.

A host of techniques are utilized to optimize the blend between filling the seats on a plane and getting the highest possible fare for each seat. In the weeks leading up to a flight, the level of fares assigned to each category may be adjusted up or down based on the latest moves by competitors, and as the flight date approaches, lower-priced categories are likely to be closed out altogether. Moreover, some people seeking reservations may be told a given flight is "sold out" even though passengers using that flight as a connector to another of the airline's routes may find ample seating—for a price, of course. The result of all this fine-tuning is that passengers on the same flight from, say, Chicago to Phoenix, may pay round trip fares that vary by a factor of *five*—ranging, say, from $240 for the lowest-priced seats to $1400 for the top fares.

Interestingly, the same yield-management techniques refined by the airlines are now being used by universities when they decide on financial-aid packages offered to students. After all, given the nominal tuition at a university, a more generous financial-aid offer can be thought of as a lower price, and students, like everyone else, behave according to the **law of demand.** Universities have found, for example, that they can offer less generous aid packages to students who apply for early admission, because such students are more anxious to attend; as one financial-aid consultant notes, "Those who have the most interest in the school are going to be less price sensitive." In a similar vein, some colleges have found that people who come for campus interviews are more interested in attending; the response has been to offer slightly less generous aid packages to such students, even though the colleges routinely recommend that students come for interviews.

In addition to these regular features of price discrimination in financial-aid offers, universities also monitor their enrollment figures each year, just as the airlines watch bookings by fare category. If a school is getting, say, too many pre-med students and not enough in the humanities, financial-aid offers will be adjusted accordingly, with bigger than usual aid offers being made to the students the school is trying to attract. Schools that are noted for excellence in one area but are trying to maintain a balanced mix of majors have become particularly adept at the financial-aid game.

As the enrollment vice president for Carnegie Mellon University notes, without sophisticated adjustments to the blend of aid packages offered, "I'd have an institution full of engineers and computer scientists and I wouldn't have anybody in arts and design." Carnegie Mellon also recognizes the importance of competition in determining the prices it charges: After admitted students are notified of their aid offers in the spring, they are invited to fax the school any better offers they receive from other colleges. Using money from a special fund set aside for the purpose, the university generally meets competing offers received by desirable students.

Price discrimination has also shown up in the news lately on the international front. Most major pharmaceutical companies price-discriminate based on the nationality of the people buying their drugs. Partly because incomes in other nations are lower than in the United States, people in other nations have higher elasticities of demand than do American citizens. Hence, pharmaceutical companies sell prescription drugs elsewhere at lower prices than they do in the United States. But one of these other nations is Canada, and American senior citizens have found that by getting on a bus (or even just visiting the Web site of a Canadian pharmacy) they can save a bundle on their prescriptions.[2] Although this practice is technically illegal, as of this writing not much has been done by the governments of either the United States or Canada to stop it. If cross-border reshipments of prescription drugs continue to mount, however, the Canadians may find that American pharmaceutical companies wishing to protect their profit margins are unwilling to sell to them at the low prices of the past.

Price discrimination certainly profits the firms that practice it, but there is an entirely different question—one that cannot be answered by economics—as to whether it is fair. Most college students who can stay over a Saturday night, or make reservations a month in advance, probably don't mind the lower fares made possible by price discrimination. But business travelers are far from

[2] Another reason for lower prices in Canada is that it has a nationalized health care system, therefore, the government buys drugs on behalf of all Canadians. This practice makes the Canadian government a **monopsonist** (literally, "single buyer"), with the power to force drug prices down below what they otherwise would be.

pleased with the high fares they must pay to get where they want, when they want to, usually on short notice. "They've got you, and they know it," says one executive. The flip side, of course, is that without the extra revenue generated by price discrimination, some companies or colleges would be hard-pressed to survive. Indeed, when asked about the equity of fine-tuning aid packages to willingness to attend rather than ability to pay, one financial-aid official noted he had little choice in the matter: "I could make it very fair—and be out of business."

DISCUSSION QUESTIONS

1. First-class passengers generally pay higher fares than coach-class passengers, even when they take advantage of advance-purchase discounts. Is this price discrimination? (Hint: Seats in first class are generally leather rather than fabric, and are about 50 percent wider than coach seats. Also, there are more flight attendants per passenger in the first-class section.)

2. Is it price discrimination when a professional football team charges, say, $150 per ticket for 50-yard line tickets in the lower deck and $30 per ticket for upper deck tickets overlooking the end zone?

3. What factors other than income are likely to affect willingness to pay? How will differences in these factors among its customers affect the likelihood that a firm will engage in price discrimination?

18

Keeping the Competition Out

Most competitors hate competition. And who can blame them? After all, if a firm can keep the competition out, profits are sure to rise. How high they will rise obviously varies by industry, but the lowly taxicab market gives some indication of what is at stake.

In New York City, the number of taxicabs is limited by law—limited, in fact, to one cab for every 600 people, in a town where many people don't own cars. To legally operate a taxi in New York, one must own a taxi medallion, a city-issued metal shield affixed to a cab's hood. After capping the number of medallions since 1937, the city offered 133 new ones for sale in 1996. Winning bidders paid about $175,000 for each medallion—that is, for the right to work 70-hour weeks, subject to robbery, rude customers, and the erratic driving habits of other cabbies. And lest you think New York taxi drivers are crazy to pay such sums, keep this in mind: because the city keeps the competition out, the taxi business is so lucrative that the medallions can be used as collateral to borrow money at favorable interest rates, and any cabby who wants to leave the business can immediately find a buyer for his medallion, usually at a price that will bring even more profit. And those new medallions that went for $175,000 in 1996? Well, by 1998 they had risen in value to over $250,000, but five years later their prices had dropped back to "only" $225,000.

In 2004 the city implemented two changes affecting the taxi market. First, it began to phase in a fare hike of about 25 percent, one that will bring fares to their highest inflation-adjusted level since the 1970s. Second, the city decided to start selling 900 new taxi medallions, to bring the total on the street to 13,087. Both of these measures will make it easier to get a cab in New York City. But here's another fact you can count on: Because the city gets to keep the revenues from the sale of the new medallions, it will be sure to time their sales so that the price of medallions is not adversely affected.

Keeping the competition out works this way: Reducing the number of firms in an industry decreases the supply of the good, thus driving up its price. Firms that remain thereby enjoy both a higher price for their product and a larger market share. Consumers lose, however, suffering not only from higher prices but also from fewer alternative sources of supply from which to choose. Another group of losers is comprised of the firms who are excluded. They are forced to go into lower-paying pursuits for which they are not as well suited. The higher profits enjoyed by the firms that are protected from competition thus come at the expense of consumers and excluded competitors; the net result is also an overall loss to society as a whole, because the limit on competition reduces the total extent of mutually beneficial exchange.

Note we said that the number of taxi medallions in New York is limited by the government. This is typical. Even though many government agencies (for example, the Federal Trade Commission and the Department of Justice at the federal level) are supposed to promote competition, the most effective way to *prevent* competition is usually to get the government involved. Consider telephones. It used to be that both long-distance and local telephone markets were regulated by the federal government. In 1984 the long-distance market was deregulated, and AT&T had to begin competing with MCI and Sprint for customers. The result was a 40 percent drop in inflation-adjusted long-distance rates. Local telephone service continued to be regulated by the Federal Communications Commission (FCC), however, and over the same period of time, local phone rates *rose* 40 percent in real terms— chiefly because the FCC has kept competition out of the local phone service market.

The government of Mexico has been even more successful in protecting phone giant Telmex from competition. Formerly a state-owned company, Telmex was privatized in 1990, with the understanding that the government would gradually but steadily end the firm's monopoly. The thought was nice, but the monopoly remains.

Telmex has effectively been permitted to prevent potential entrants to the Mexican phone market from connecting through its dominant switching equipment. The result has been sky-high connection charges and virtually no new connections. Hence, there are now only 10 telephones per 100 inhabitants of Mexico. In Poland, the fellow member of the Organization of Economic Cooperation and Development with the next fewest number of lines, there are 20 telephones per 100 inhabitants. In addition to poor service, the lack of competition also shows up in prices, which sharply hamper Mexican businesses. For example, a U.S. firm trying to drum up business in London would pay $5.40 to make five phone calls to Britain of four minutes each. Those same calls would cost its Mexican rival $25.40.

Many of the decision makers who work for the government agencies that limit competition are lawyers, so it is not surprising that competition among lawyers is limited. For example, in every state but one (California), the number of law schools is capped by state law, thereby restricting entry into the profession and driving up earnings. The high fees lawyers earn have in turn generated competition from lawyers' assistants, called paralegals. This competition—or rather, attempted competition—can be seen in the market for personal bankruptcies. Rising consumer debt, combined with less restrictive federal bankruptcy law, caused the number of people declaring bankruptcy to triple during the 1990s. A typical personal bankruptcy case costs about $750 when done by a lawyer, but the procedure is a simple one, requiring only that some standard paperwork be filled out and filed with the relevant authorities. Thus, in come the paralegals (who, if working for a lawyer, would be doing the paperwork anyway), offering to perform the same services for, say, $269. Faced with competition like this, the legal profession struck back, gaining passage of Section 110 of the Bankruptcy Reform Act. This statute gives judges the power to cap the fees paralegals can charge. Thus far, imposed caps have run from $50 to $100 per case, which is low enough to force most paralegals out. Paralegals who charge more than the legal limit are subject to fines of up to $500 for each violation of the law. Lawyers are free to charge what they like, sometimes as much as $1500, now that they don't have paralegals to worry about.

Sometimes the government gets involved in some unlikely markets in its efforts to prevent the ravages of competition from taking their toll. Consider hair braiding. Some African Americans like to have their hair straightened in beauty shops, a procedure that requires a touch-up every four weeks, for an average monthly cost (excluding cutting and styling) of about $100. An alternative is to get one's hair braided at a braiding salon. There are now about 10,000 of these salons across the country. Braids need maintenance only once every ten weeks, cutting the cost to $50 per month. The same low cost and convenience that make braiding salons attractive to consumers also make them threatening to the conventional beauty shops that straighten hair, especially in fashion-conscious California. Claiming that they are seeking to protect consumers, agents of the California Barbering & Cosmetology Board have begun raiding the salons of unlicensed hair braiders. Not surprisingly, the hair braiders think the state is actually trying to protect state-licensed cosmetologists at beauty shops, who must spend $6000 for 1600 hours of training to get their licenses. Indeed, one of the braiders, Ali Rasheed, argues that the marketplace is better than state licensing boards at protecting consumers. "It's simple," he says. "If I mess up your hair, you don't come back. You spread the word. And very quickly I'd be out of business." Perhaps so, but it looks like the state of California doesn't want to give consumers that option.

Back in New York, there is an example of the fact that the government likes to protect itself from competition, too. New York City is well known for its massive public transit system, comprising both subways and bus lines. What is not so well known is that mass transit in New York City started off as private enterprise. The first horsecars and elevated trains in the city were developed by private companies. Moreover, even though New York's first subway was partly financed by a loan from the city, it was otherwise a private operation, operated profitably at a fare of a nickel (the equivalent of less than a dollar today).

New York's politicians refused to allow fares to rise during the inflation of World War I, yielding financial losses for the private transit companies. Promising to show the private sector how to run a transit system efficiently, while simultaneously offering to protect the public from the "dictatorship" of the transit firms, the city took over the subway, merged it with the bus line, and promptly started raising fares. Despite fare increases double the inflation rate, however, costs have risen even faster, so that today, even though the basic fare is $1.50, the city *loses* $2 a passenger.

Enter the jitneys, privately owned vans that operate along regular routes, like buses, but charge only $1 a passenger and make detours for pick-ups and drop-offs on request. Actually, we should have said "attempted entry" by the jitneys, because the New York City Council—at the insistence of the public transit system—has denied operating permits to almost all jitney operators who have applied. The council says it is only seeking to prevent the vans from causing accidents and traffic problems, but even fully insured drivers who have met federal requirements for operating interstate van services are routinely denied permits. Thus most of the hundreds of jitneys operating in New York City do so illegally. Even the few jitneys that have managed to get licensed are forbidden from operating along public bus routes—all in the name of public safety, of course.

Transportation economists such as Daniel Klein of Santa Clara University have argued that public transit systems could once more be profitable—instead of losing sixty cents on the dollar—if the jitneys were given a chance. "Government has demonstrated that it has no more business producing transit than producing cornflakes. It should concentrate instead on establishing new rules to foster competition," says Klein. Unfortunately for the jitneys and their customers, however, that competition would come at the expense of New York's public transit system. Thus, for the foreseeable future, it seems the jitneys will have to compete only by breaking the laws, because, like most competitors, the New York City mass transit system just hates competition.

DISCUSSION QUESTIONS

1. Consider two different ways of beating your competition. One way is to offer your customers lower prices and better service. The other is to get a law passed that raises your competitors' costs—for example, by imposing special operating requirements

on them. Can you see any difference between these two methods, assuming that both succeed in keeping your competition out?

2. Although governments at all levels sometimes act to prevent some individuals from competing with others, the federal government is probably the most active in this role, state governments are less active, and local governments are the least active. Can you explain this pattern?

3. Is there any difference between prohibiting entry by a group of firms and levying a special tax on those firms?

19

The Perils of Product Differentiation

The story of **product differentiation** is usually told as a tale of great financial gain to the firms that do it, inflicted at sizable cost on consumers, who don't really "need" the new products. Whether it is fast food, soft drinks, clothing styles, or automobile models, the reasoning seems to be this: Develop a catchy name or theme, design a slick advertising campaign to clearly differentiate your product from others on the market, and presto—instant wealth.

At first blush, the story seems eminently plausible. After all, are "Tommy Jeans" really any better than Levi's? Is a Whopper fundamentally different from a Big Mac? And does anybody believe the Gateway cows make the company's computers any faster? In each case, the firms that differentiated their product from those of their rivals profited handsomely. And in each case, it is remarkably difficult to come up with any objective evidence that one product is much different from another—much less any *better*. Product differentiation, it seems, is the sure road to financial success: Gullible consumers will buy almost anything if it is just "positioned"—packaged and advertised—properly.

In fact, a careful look at the record suggests that product differentiation is neither so easy nor so profitable as it might seem at first glance. Instead, it appears that consumers are considerably more discriminating than they are usually given credit for. Moreover, if they are not interested in what is being offered, they'll reject it—at great cost to the firm that tries to inflict it upon them. Because of this, product differentiation is a risky business, fraught with potential losses and likely to succeed only if the firms doing it have something that is truly of value to consumers. The fact is that most new products fail—often spectacularly. Thus, product differentiation seems to be much like any other business venture in that it is likely to be successful only if the product is valued by the consumer, and on average it is an activity that can be expected to yield only the competitive rate of return. A look back at history will suggest why this is so.

Our first episode takes us back half a century and involves an icon of American industry, the Ford Motor Company. On September 2, 1957, amid pronouncements that "this product will raise the industry standard to a new level," Ford introduced a new automobile; its name was the Edsel. The car's unveiling culminated nearly 10 years of research and development costing roughly $1.5 billion in today's terms. The company's official goal for first-year sales of the Edsel was 200,000 vehicles. Little more than *half* this number were actually sold in the first *two* years of the model's existence. After several attempts to save the floundering wonder car (including a major reorganization of the Edsel division, and a complete redesign of the car) Edsel production was discontinued in November of 1959—just two years, two months, and 15 days after its much heralded introduction. The failure was so spectacular that the car became an object of derisive humor on a host of television shows, and one historian of the episode remarked that "compared with the Edsel, Custer's Last Stand was a victory." Overall, it appears that Ford lost more than $5 billion in today's terms—some 40 percent of the entire value of the company. The product that was supposed to restore it to industry leadership very nearly brought the company to its knees.

What went wrong? It certainly wasn't a lack of promotional efforts. By the time the Edsel was launched, Ford had recruited almost 1200 Edsel dealers to market and distribute the car. The advertising company handling the Edsel added 60 new employees to service the account and even opened a branch in Detroit, headquarters of Ford. The advertising campaign began in the fall of 1955, some two years before the Edsel hit the market. And the promotional effort was so intensive that shortly before the car's 1957 unveiling one Ford executive remarked, "When [consumers] find out it's got four wheels and one engine, just like the next car, they're liable to be disappointed."

And disappointed they were. Styling was one feature that Ford hoped would differentiate the Edsel from other cars, for it included a host of new features, including a vertically oriented grill with rounded corners. The problem, according to consumers, was that the car looked like "a Ford sucking a lemon." Perhaps the lemon analogy was appropriate, for within weeks of the Edsel's introduction, reports of manufacturing defects in the car became rampant—oil leaks, trunks that wouldn't open, inferior paint jobs, sagging springs, and incorrect rear axle ratios all became facts of life for Edsel buyers. The Edsel was different all right, and consumers quickly rejected it.

The Ford Motor Company is not the only corporate giant to have suffered at the hands of the consumers whom it supposedly controls. Consider the Coca-Cola Company, which on April 23, 1985, held a heavily publicized news conference to announce "the most significant soft drink marketing development in the company's history." Coca-Cola, the soft drink that had been the company's leading brand for nearly 100 years, was to be replaced with a formula (soon to be dubbed "New Coke") expected to be a more vigorous competitor for its chief rival, Pepsi. The announcement electrified millions across the country and became the lead story on the evening's national news broadcasts. According to *Time* magazine, 81 percent of the U.S. population knew of the change in formula within 48 hours, more people than were aware in July 1969 that Neil Armstrong had walked on the moon. By June, fully 96 percent of Americans knew of New Coke. Indeed, Coca-Cola executives estimated that the news stories generated by the decision to change the formula were worth the equivalent of $150 million in advertising expenditures. It is difficult to find another product in history that has been launched with anything like the attention received by New Coke. Success—and profits—it seemed, were assured.

There was just one problem: the company's customers didn't like the new formula. Within a month, the company was getting 5000 letters every week objecting to the change in formula, as well as that many complaining telephone calls *every day*. Perhaps more importantly, consumers backed up their complaints in the grocery stores and fast food restaurants, staying away from New Coke in droves. Company officials became increasingly concerned that their April decision had been a disastrous mistake, and on July 9 the board of directors decided to reverse that mistake.

Two days later, the original formula—newly dubbed "Coca-Cola Classic"—was back. By some estimates, the financial damage to the company was $1 billion in today's dollars.

It is tempting to think that mistakes such as those made by Ford and Coca-Cola are matters of history, unlikely to be repeated in the modern world of marketing focus groups and sophisticated computer-modeling of consumer behavior. The great Burger King french-fry fiasco suggests otherwise. Although Burger King has long led the nation in taste tests of hamburgers, its larger rival, McDonald's, has remained top dog in the french-fry department. This is a matter of some importance to all concerned, because with a profit margin as high as 80 cents on the dollar, fries are the most lucrative item on the fast food menu. Thus, after two years of intensive research and development, and armed with a $70 million marketing budget, Burger King launched a new line of french fries on January 2, 1998.

Burger King was determined to differentiate its product from McDonald's popular fry, hoping to do so with a special preparation that guaranteed extra crispiness. So exacting was the company that the specifications for preparing the new fries ran to 19 pages. And although the process was complicated, franchisees were excited. Said one, an owner of 41 Burger Kings, "This fry was supposed to be our salvation." For a while, it looked like it was. Intrigued by expensive Super Bowl advertising and a give-away of 15 million orders of fries on "Free Fryday," consumers swarmed into Burger Kings to try it out. By the middle of 1998, the company had sold 150 million more orders of fries than the same period the year before. But soon enough, consumers had enough: some said it was too salty, others too crispy. Some complained the fries clumped together, and others thought they were bitter. But whatever their words, their behavior said it all: they stayed away in droves, and by 1999 Burger King french-fry sales were down 14 percent. Soon thereafter, the company pulled the plug: the fry that was to be salvation is no more. And although the company is tight-lipped on how much the fry fiasco cost, the president of Burger King's National Franchise Association made it clear how the franchisees felt: "The g— d— fry was bad—horrendous." Consumers, it seems, agreed.

Of course, not all cases of product differentiation are like the disasters we have examined here. Indeed, if they were, no sensible business would seek to differentiate its goods from competitors'. The point instead is that product differentiation, for all of its oft-told stories of success, is far from being a road to riches. Like all economic endeavors, there are revenues, costs, and risks involved. There is no guarantee the profits will be positive, much less enough to warrant the risks. To hope to achieve even a competitive rate of return on differentiated products, companies must deliver to their customers a quality product at a reasonable price. This was a lesson that certainly made an impression on Donald Keogh, president of Coca-Cola in 1985. In announcing the return of the original formula to the shelves, Keogh apologized to consumers for the decision to launch New Coke. The episode, he said, had convinced him that "Our boss is the consumer." One guesses that Ford and Burger King would agree.

DISCUSSION QUESTIONS

1. If a firm can either devote resources to selling or improving an existing product, or to developing and differentiating a new product, what must be true about the profit rate on both activities in equilibrium?

2. Suppose that a large fraction of differentiated products fail. What will be true about the profit rate observed on differentiated products that happen to succeed? (Hint: Keep in mind your answer to Question 1.)

3. Suppose that product-differentiation activity is much riskier than most other business ventures. What would you expect the profit rate for product differentiation to be, compared to the average profit rate on other business activities?

Part Five

Political Economy

INTRODUCTION

The chief focus of economics has always been on explaining the behavior of the private sector. Yet dating back at least to the publication of Adam Smith's *Wealth of Nations* more than 200 years ago, economists have never missed an opportunity to apply their theories to additional realms of behavior. For the past 30 years or so, much of this effort has been devoted to developing theories that explain the actions of governments, as well as the consequences of those actions. This undertaking is often referred to as the study of political economy, for it often involves a mixture of politics and economics. As the selections in this section hint, economists do not yet have a unified theory of government. Nevertheless, they are making progress and are sometimes able to offer surprising insights.

It is fair (and no exaggeration) to say that farmers understand and have exploited the nuances of political economy as well as anyone in this nation, a point we elaborate upon in Chapter 20, "Raising Less Corn and More Hell." Beginning more than 70 years ago, American farmers convinced the federal government to guarantee that farmers receive prices for their crops well above the **equilibrium prices.** Not only that, these same farmers convinced the federal government that taxpayers and the consumers of food should bear the costs of making these high prices "stick." And pay we have: consumers face higher prices for many crops because of various **price support** or **target price** programs, and taxpayers face higher tax bills as well. At a minimum, over the next

10 years the average American household will pay almost $4400 in higher food prices and higher taxes, due to federal programs benefiting "farmers"—even though most all of this money will end up in the pockets of shareholders in giant agribusiness corporations, not in the pockets of small farmers. Moreover, as the experience of New Zealand reveals, government farm programs are *not* in fact necessary to protect the vitality or productivity of the farm sector. Some 20 years ago New Zealand brought a halt to all of its efforts to protect farmers from competition. The result has been innovation, cost-cutting, and aggressive international marketing by New Zealand farmers, who are now stronger and more productive than ever before.

One of the first things that economists had to learn about government decision making is that the costs of government policies are always higher than promised, and the benefits are always lower. This simple proposition forms the centerpiece of Chapter 21, "Killer Cars and the Rise of the SUV," which explores the implications of federal rules that specify the minimum fuel efficiency permitted for new cars sold in the United States. Sometimes the effects of the federal regulations are surprisingly pervasive—as when they induce one-third of American drivers to switch from cars to trucks in response to federal fuel economy rules. Sometimes the effects are at least moderately expensive—as when they induce companies to spend millions of dollars redesigning vehicles, not to make them more fuel-efficient but solely to satisfy the peculiar accounting conventions of the regulations. And, sadly, sometimes the effects of the regulations are tragic. Reliable estimates suggest that the federal fuel economy standards have forced automakers to downsize their cars to such an extent as to make them less crashworthy. It is estimated that 3000 Americans lose their lives in traffic accidents every year as a result of these particular regulations.

Crime rates that have gone up hand-in-hand with prison populations, coupled with criminals who seem impervious to law enforcement, have led many people to ask a simple if disturbing question: is there any effective way to fight crime? Although economic theory says the answer to this question is yes, the empirical estimates obtained by economists have said, well, "Maybe." Yet, as we see in Chapter 22, "Crime and Punishment," new evidence is shedding light on the answer to this question. Indeed, it is increasingly clear that the two central tools of traditional law enforcement—police to apprehend the criminals and prisons to punish them—may be every bit as effective as their proponents claim in discouraging criminal activity. Two lessons that emerge from this chapter are that politicians are likely to continue pouring more money into law enforcement, and those resources are going to have a growing impact in reducing crime in America.

For 30 years America struggled with the baby-boom generation as it graduated from bassinets to BMWs. For the next 30 years, we shall have to grapple with the problems that arise as the boomers progress from corporate boardrooms to nursing homes. As we see in Chapter 23, "The Graying of America," our nation is aging at the fastest rate in our history. It will not be long before all of America looks much like Florida, the retirement capital of the world, looks today. As America ages, two major problems in political economy are emerging. First, we must face the issue of paying the Social Security and Medicare bills of the rapidly growing elderly portion of the population. Second, as increasing numbers of people retire, there will be fewer workers capable of bearing the growing tax burden. America must learn new ways of utilizing the productive capabilities of the elderly and accept the fact that—as much as we may wish otherwise—sometimes the elderly may simply have to fend for themselves; otherwise, today's college students will soon find the financial burden beyond their capacity to bear.

20

Raising Less Corn and More Hell

When politician Mary Lease stumped the Kansas countryside in 1890, she urged the farmers to raise "less corn and more hell," and that is just what they have been doing ever since.

The two decades before World War I witnessed unparalleled agricultural prosperity in the United States. This "golden age of American farming" continued through the war, as food prices soared. The end of the war, combined with a sharp depression in 1920, brought the golden age to a painful halt. Even the long economic recovery from 1921 to 1929—the Roaring Twenties—did little to help American farmers. European countries were redirecting their resources into agricultural production, and new American **tariffs** on foreign goods severely disrupted international trade. Because food exports had been an important source of farmers' incomes, the decline in world trade reduced the demand for American agricultural products and cut deeply into food prices and farm income.

The sharply falling food prices of the 1920s led farmers to view their problem as one of relative overproduction. Numerous cooperative efforts were made, therefore, to *restrict* production, but virtually all of these efforts failed. Most crops were produced under highly competitive conditions, with large numbers of buyers and sellers dealing in products that were largely undifferentiated: One farmer's corn, for example, was the same as any other farmer's corn. Thus, producers were unable to enforce collective output restrictions and price hikes on a voluntary basis. But what farmers failed to do by voluntary means in the 1920s, they accomplished via government directives in the 1930s. An effective farm **price-support program** was instituted in 1933, marking the beginning of a policy of so-called farm subsidies in the United States that continues even today.

We can best understand the results of price supports and other government farm programs by first examining the market for agricultural commodities in the absence of government intervention. In that competitive market, a large number of farmers supply amounts of each commodity, such as corn. The sum of the quantities that individual farmers supply at various prices generates the **market supply schedule** of a commodity. Each farmer supplies only a small part of the market total. No one farmer, therefore, can influence the price of the product. If one farmer were to raise the price, anyone wishing to purchase corn could easily buy from someone else at the **market-clearing,** or **equilibrium, price.** And no farmers would sell below the market-clearing price. Thus, every unit of output sold by farmers goes for the same price. The price received for the last (or *marginal*) unit sold is exactly the same as that received for all the rest. The farmer will produce corn up to the point that, if one more unit were produced, its production cost would be greater than the price received. Notice that at higher prices, farmers can incur higher costs for additional units produced and still make a profit. Because all farmers face the same basic production decision, all farmers together will produce more at higher prices. Indeed, no farmer will stop producing until he or she stops making a profit on additional units. That is, each farmer will end up selling corn at the market-clearing price, which will equal his costs of production plus a normal profit.[1]

Now, how has the usual price-support program worked? The government has decided what constitutes a "fair price," often called the **target price.** The key to this vital determination is the ratio between the prices farmers historically paid for what they bought and the prices they received during "good" years, such as during agriculture's golden age. Except for the years of World War II, the "fair" price decreed by the government (called the **parity**

---

[1] For society as a whole, this is actually a cost of production, because it is required to keep the farmer growing corn instead of changing to an alternative occupation.

price) generally has been well above the market equilibrium price that would have prevailed in the absence of price supports. This has encouraged farmers to produce more, which ordinarily would simply push price right back down.

How has the government made the parity price "stick"? There have been two methods. For the first several decades of farm programs, it agreed to buy the crops, such as corn, at a price, called the **support price,** that was at or near the parity price. As a practical matter, these purchases have been disguised as "loans" from a government agency called the Commodity Credit Corporation (CCC), loans that never need be repaid. The government then either stored the crops it purchased, sold them on the world market (as opposed to the domestic market) at prices well below the U. S. support price, or simply gave them away to foreign nations under the Food for Peace program. In each instance, the result was substantial costs for taxpayers—and substantial gains for farmers. Under the support-price system, the American taxpayers routinely spent more than $10 billion e*ach year* for the benefit of corn farmers alone. Smaller but still quite substantial subsidies were garnered by the producers of wheat, peanuts, soybeans, sorghum, rice, and cotton, to name but a few.

In an effort to keep the size of the surpluses down, the government has often restricted the number of acres that farmers may cultivate. Under these various **acreage-restriction programs,** farmers wishing to participate in certain government subsidy programs were required to keep a certain amount of land out of production. About 80 million acres, an area the size of New Mexico, have at one time or another been covered by the agreements. Enticed by high support prices, farmers always have been ingenious in finding ways to evade acreage restrictions. For example, soybeans and sorghum are both excellent substitutes for corn as a source of livestock feed. So farmers agreed to cut their corn acreage, then planted soybeans or sorghum on the same land. This action aggravated the corn surplus and forced the government to extend acreage restrictions and price supports to soybeans and sorghum. Similarly, faced with limitations on the amount of land they could cultivate, farmers responded by cultivating the smaller remaining land far more intensively. They used more fertilizers and pesticides, introduced more sophisticated methods of planting and irrigation, and applied technological advances in farm machinery at every opportunity. As a result, agricultural output per man-hour is now *12 times* what it was 60 years ago.

There were a couple of problems with the support-price system. First, because it kept crop prices high, it kept consumers food bills high as well. People were spending an extra $5 to $10 billion on food each year. Another problem with the price-support system was the fact that the surplus crops piled up year after year in government warehouses. Storing the surpluses was not merely expensive, it also eventually became politically embarrassing. For example, at one point the federal government had enough wheat in its storage bins to make seven loaves of bread for every man, woman, and child in the *world*.

In the hopes of cutting costs and reducing its political liability, the federal government thus switched to a system in which it set a target price that was guaranteed to farmers, but let the price paid by consumers adjust to whatever lower level it took to get consumers to buy all of the crops. Then the government simply sent a check to farmers for the difference between the target price and the market price. This brought consumers' food bills down and eliminated government storage of surplus crops, but it also meant that the cost to taxpayers—up to $25 billion per year—was painfully clear in the huge checks being written to farmers.

The original price-support program hid its subsidies by making it appear as though the resulting crop surpluses were the result of American farmers simply being "too productive" for their own good. With the direct cash payments made under the target-price system, however, it became apparent that the government was taking money out of taxpayers' pockets with one hand and giving it to farmers with the other hand. Moreover, the target-price system, like our other agricultural programs, geared the size of the subsidies to the amount of output produced by the recipients. Thus, small farmers received trivial amounts, while giant farms— agribusinesses—collected giant subsidies. The owners of many huge cotton farms and rice farms, for example, received payments totaling more than $1 million apiece.

Faced with the prospect of a taxpayer revolt, Congress tried to fix things up with the Farm Security Act of 1985—and once again missed the mark. This legislation initially replaced cash payments to farmers with the payment-in-kind (PIK) program. Instead of writing checks to farmers, the PIK scheme authorized the U. S. Department of Agriculture to give farmers surplus commodities that were left over in storage from price supports. Farmers could use the commodities as livestock feed or simply sell them at the going market price. The PIK program got rid of leftover surpluses and encouraged exports initially, but only at great cost—roughly $30 billion a year. Moreover, the law locked many farmers into growing the same crop year after year, regardless of market conditions. If farmers didn't plant a specified percentage of their "crop base" each year, their subsidy payments were subsequently reduced. The result was huge crop costs for the government in the lucrative (for the farmers) corn and wheat programs.

The Farm Security Act of 1985 also tinkered with target prices for many crops—which brings us to oats instead of corn. The law created a 96-cents-a-bushel difference in subsidies for barley over oats. Not surprisingly, farmers in droves abandoned oats, just as consumer demand for oatmeal and other oat-based products was picking up. The farmers were happy growing barley, but cereal producers, in contrast, were, well, oatless. Indeed, when asked what he thought about the then current U.S. farm policy, the chief of procurement for General Mills remarked, "That's the silliest thing I've ever heard of." Can you blame him?

Throughout all of this, it is important to understand who actually benefits from federal farm programs. Although these programs traditionally have been promoted as a way to guarantee decent earnings for low-income farmers, most of the benefits have in fact gone to the owners of very large farms. Traditionally, the larger the farm, the bigger the benefit is from agricultural price supports. In addition, *all* of the benefits from price supports ultimately accrue to *landowners* on whose land price-supported crops can grow.

In the mid 1990s, the Republican-controlled Congress made what turned out to be a futile attempt to reduce agricultural subsidies. On April 5, 1996, *The New York Times* headline read "Clinton Signs Farm Bill Ending Subsidies," reflecting the fact that Congress had enacted and Clinton signed the seven-year Freedom to Farm act. The 1996 reforms were supposed to increase farmer flexibility and remove market distortions by moving away from price-support payments for wheat, corn, and cotton. In their place, farmers would instead receive "transition payments." The taxpayer was supposed to save billions of dollars.

Such was not to be. Beginning in 1998, Congress passed large farm "supplemental bills" each year, each costing billions of dollars per year—in money that goes directly from your paycheck to the bank accounts of the largest agribusiness corporations in America. Then, in 2002, Congress passed the most expensive farm bill in the history of the United States, with an advertised price tag of over $191 billion for a 10-year period. (The actual price tag likely will be even higher.) President Bush said, when he signed the bill, "This nation has got to eat." He further said, "Our farmers and ranchers are the most efficient producers in the world . . . we are really good at it." We are also really good at subsidizing farmers, and most of them are not very poor. Millionaires such as Ted Turner and David Rockefeller receive hundreds of thousands of dollars a year in taxpayer-financed agricultural subsidies. When you add to the $191 billion of direct subsidies the almost $300 billion of higher food prices that will be result over the 10 years of the program, you will see that the average American household will pay almost $4400 in higher food prices and higher taxes. As always, two-thirds of all farm subsidies will go to the highest 10 percent of farms, most which earn over $250,000 annually. In other words, large agribusinesses continue to be the chief beneficiaries of our generous agricultural policy.

In spite of all of this taxpayer money handed out to our farmers, American corn farmers still are not satisfied with their share of taxpayer subsidies. So they have lobbied for and obtained federal legislation that promotes and subsidizes ethanol, which is a corn-based fuel alcohol that can be added to regular gasoline. In fact, under the guise of "environmental protection," the U.S. Environmental Protection Agency mandates that either ethanol or MTBE (which is known to contaminate groundwater) be added to gasoline. Not only does the ethanol not result in cleaner air, it is also an uneconomic fuel. States that border on the two coasts, such as New York and California, have to ship it in from the farm belt. That transportation is not cheap. Producing ethanol also turns out to consume a lot of energy. Indeed, there is some evidence that ethanol production uses more in energy than the resulting ethanol produces when burned! But because corn farmers benefit from mandated ethanol usage, we'll end up using ethanol, even though it raises gas prices, fails to protect the environment, and wastes energy.

Perhaps we should not complain too much about farm programs in the United States, for at least we don't have *Japanese* farm programs. There a combination of subsidies for domestic farmers and tariffs on imported food have pushed farm incomes to a level roughly *double* the average income in the country as a whole. They also have driven up the price of an ordinary melon to $100 (yes, one hundred dollars).

Politicians from the farming states argue that we cannot abandon our farmers, because the United States would end up with too many bankrupt farms and not enough food. But there is evidence from at least one country that such a scenario is simply not correct. In 1984, New Zealand's Labor government ended all farm subsidies of every kind, going completely "cold turkey" without any sort of transition to the new era of free markets for food. Agricultural subsidies in New Zealand had accounted for more than 30 percent of the value of agricultural production, even higher than what has been observed in the United States. The elimination of subsidies in New Zealand occurred rapidly, and there were no extended phase-outs for any crops. Despite this, there was no outbreak of farm bankruptcies. Indeed, only 1 percent of farms have gone out of business in New Zealand since 1984. Instead, the farmers responded by improving their techniques, cutting costs, and aggressively marketing their products in export markets.

The results have been dramatic. The value of farm output in New Zealand has increased over 40 percent (in constant-dollar terms) since the subsidy phase-out. The share of New Zealand's total annual output attributed to farming has increased from 14 percent to 17 percent. Land productivity has increased on an annual basis of a little over 6 percent. Indeed, according to the Federated Farmers of New Zealand, their country's experience thoroughly debunked the myth that the farming sector cannot prosper without government subsidies.

Are any members of the U. S. Congress listening?

DISCUSSION QUESTIONS

1. American corn farmers receive at a minimum $10 billion in taxpayer subsidies per year. These subsidies allow them to sell their grain at prices below what it costs to produce them, particularly for export markets. How do corn subsidies hurt Mexican farmers?
2. If it is so obvious that farm subsidies hurt consumers, why do such subsidies continue to be voted in by Congress?
3. What groups would be the major beneficiaries of the elimination of farm subsidies in America?

21

Killer Cars and the Rise of the SUV

Things are not always what they seem.
—Phaedrus, circa A.D. 8

If there were a Murphy's Law of economic policy making, it would be this: *The costs are always higher than promised, and the benefits are always lower.* The federal law that regulates automobile fuel economy provides just one example of this fundamental principle and along the way demonstrates that what Phaedrus had to say two thousand years ago is true today.

Our story begins in the 1970s, when the United States was in the middle of a so-called energy crisis. The Organization of Petroleum Exporting Countries (OPEC), a cartel of major oil-producing countries, had succeeded in raising the prices of petroleum products (including gasoline) to record-high levels. Consumers reacted by conserving on their use of gasoline and other petroleum products, and Congress responded by enacting legislation mandating energy conservation as the law of the land. One of these laws, known as the corporate average fuel economy (CAFE) standard, requires that each auto manufacturer's passenger cars sold in this country meet a federally mandated fuel economy standard. The new car fleets for the year 2005, for example, had to average 27.5 miles per gallon (mpg) of gasoline. If an automaker sells a gas-guzzler that gets only 15 mpg, somewhere along the line it must also sell enough gas-sipping subcompacts so that the average fuel economy of the entire fleet of cars sold by the company works out to 27.5 mpg. If an automaker's average fuel economy is worse than 27.5 mpg, the corporation is fined $5 per car for each 0.1 mpg it falls short. For example, if General Motors were to fail to meet the CAFE standard by only one mpg, it could be subject to penalties of $200 million per year or more.

The CAFE standard was first introduced at a time when the price of gasoline, measured in terms of today's dollars, was about $3 per gallon. During the mid-1980s, price-cutting by members of the OPEC cartel, combined with a rise in oil production elsewhere, sent gasoline prices into free fall. With gasoline now about half as expensive (in inflation-adjusted dollars) as it was in the 1970s, the legally mandated CAFE standard of 27.5 mpg almost certainly results in cars that don't consume *enough* gasoline. This seems like a strange conclusion, so we want to be sure we understand why it is correct.

There is no doubt that conserving gasoline is a good thing, for gasoline is a scarce good. If we are able to accomplish the same objectives (such as making a trip to the grocery store) and use less gasoline in doing so, the money that would have been spent on the gas can now be spent on other goods. Yet conserving gasoline is itself a costly activity. In the extreme case, we could engage in 100 percent conservation of gasoline, but doing so would mean giving up automobiles altogether! Somewhat more realistically, reducing the amount of gasoline that cars burn requires that they be lighter, have smaller engines, and be smaller and sometimes less crash-resistant. To meet the CAFE standards, for example, automobile manufacturers had to switch to production techniques that are more costly, use materials (such as aluminum and high-tech plastics) that are more easily damaged in accidents and more costly to repair, and design engines that are less responsive and more difficult and costly to repair. Although these are all things that probably would make sense if the price of gas were $4 per gallon, many economists believe that with gas at $1.50 or even $2 per gallon the principal effect of the CAFE standard is to raise consumers' total transportation costs: The costs of conserving on gasoline exceed the savings from consuming less of it.

But the costs of the CAFE standard are measured not just in terms of the dollars and cents of reduced economic efficiency. They are also measured in terms of people whose lives are lost as the result of the law—thousands of lives every year.

The seemingly obvious way to respond to a law that requires enhanced fuel efficiency is to redesign engines so that they burn less fuel. Indeed, the automakers have done exactly this. But another highly effective means of reducing the fuel appetite of automobiles is to downsize them by making them smaller and lighter. A major study by Robert Crandall of The Brookings Institution and John Graham of Harvard found that the CAFE standard forced automakers to produce cars that are about 500 pounds lighter than they would have been without the law. A 500-pound weight reduction implies a 14 percent increase in the fatality risk for the occupants of a car involved in an accident. That translates into approximately 3000 additional deaths per year, plus another 15,000 or so serious nonfatal injuries each year.

Apparently, consumers have not been happy with the lighter and less powerful cars, nor with their higher attendant risk of death. Fortunately, consumers have found a way out. Light trucks, which include vans, pickups, and sport utility vehicles (SUVs) have been subject to a less demanding fuel economy standard. In contrast to the standard for cars, established in 1978 at 18.0 mpg, and now at 27.5 mpg, the CAFE standard for light trucks, initially set in 1980 at 17.5 mpg, is currently 20.6 mpg. Hence, the CAFE standards initially were less stringent for light trucks than for cars, and they have been raised less sharply (up 17 percent for light trucks, versus up 53 percent for cars).

Frustrated—and safety-conscious—consumers thus have been able to substitute light trucks for passenger cars and thereby escape some of the consequences that Congress otherwise would have inflicted on them. Indeed, according to research by economist Paul E. Godek, CAFE has induced millions of consumers to move away from small cars and into larger, higher-powered SUVs and other light trucks. Between 1975 and 1995, the light-truck share of passenger vehicles rose to 41.5 percent from 20.9 percent. Godek estimates that without CAFE the light-truck share would have been only 29.2 percent. Hence, about three-fifths of the rise in the light-truck market share has been induced by the CAFE standards. By the year 2005, the market share for SUVs and other light trucks reached fully 50 percent of the passenger vehicles sold each year, a remarkable transformation in the market in just 25 years.

The original goal of CAFE was (in part) to induce substitution from large cars to small ones. But the rise of the SUV has, to some extent, frustrated this intent. Two consequences have resulted. First, light trucks are less fuel-efficient than passenger cars, so fuel economy has risen less than if light-truck substitution had not been possible. A rough estimate is that overall fuel economy has been reduced by about 1.0 mpg.

More important are the consequences in the area of passenger vehicle safety. Despite their name, light trucks are heavier than cars. Because there are more light trucks on the road with CAFE-lightened cars, drivers of those cars are now at increased risk of death in crashes involving light trucks. This effect has made national headlines from time to time, as people have worried about the adverse effects for the occupants of small cars that tangle with large SUVs.

Beginning a few years ago, it also became apparent that, because of their high centers of gravity, SUVs and other light trucks are much more likely to roll over in accidents than are passenger vehicles. The results can be deadly, particularly for occupants who are not wearing their seat belts. Nevertheless, the higher mass of light trucks that protects their occupants from cars also protects them from heavy trucks, trees, wildlife, and so on. On balance, and particularly with recent improvements in the stability of SUVs, the substitution toward these vehicles may actually have reduced overall fatalities—meaning that CAFE is not killing quite as many extra people each year as it would without the rise of the SUV.

There remains one mystery in the CAFE story, which is why the law was originally enacted. If the real objective of CAFE was fuel economy (and thus, in part, environmental protection), this could have been accomplished much more cheaply with a direct tax on gasoline. According to Godek, the structure of the law suggests a different congressional motive. CAFE treats domestic and imported cars separately. Manufacturers must meet the standard for both fleets, so they can't simply import fuel-efficient cars to bring up the average mileage of their domestic cars. Instead, they must make more small cars here in America. Thus, CAFE has protected the jobs of domestic autoworkers—giving us one more example of a law supposedly enacted to achieve a high-minded goal that instead serves chiefly to insulate a U.S. industry from the rigors of competition.

So, the next time a minivan takes your parking place, or an oversized four-wheeler tailgates you, remember this: Their owners are just trying to prevent Congress from killing them to save jobs in Detroit.

DISCUSSION QUESTIONS

1. Why do you think Congress passed the CAFE standard?

2. Does your answer to Question 1 imply either (1) consumers do not know what is in their own best interest, or (2) firms will not voluntarily provide the goods (including fuel economy) consumers want to purchase?

3. Suppose Congress really knows what the best average fuel economy for automobiles is. How do you think "best" is (or should be) defined? Do the costs and benefits of achieving a particular level of fuel economy play a role in determining that definition?

4. If Congress wanted to increase the average fuel economy of cars, could it accomplish this by imposing a tax on gasoline? What are the advantages and disadvantages of using taxes rather than standards to achieve an improvement in fuel economy?

22

Crime and Punishment

The city of Detroit, Michigan, has twice as many police per capita as Omaha, Nebraska, but the violent crime rate in Detroit is four times as high as in Omaha. Does this mean police are the source of violent crime? If that sounds like an odd question, consider this: Since 1970 the number of Americans in prison has nearly quadrupled as a share of the population, even as the violent crime rate has doubled and the property crime rate has risen 30 percent. Does sending people to prison actually encourage them to commit crimes?

Few people would answer either of these questions with a yes, but there is still a widespread concern that crime pays and that there seems to be little that policymakers can do about it. In a nation in which more than 20 percent of all households can expect to be victimized by a serious crime in any given year, it is little wonder that people are asking some tough questions about law enforcement. Do harsher penalties really discourage people from committing crimes? Will longer prison sentences reduce the crime rate? Are more police the answer, or should we try something else? Given that crime costs its victims more than $200 billion every year in America, even as we are spending roughly $100 billion per year in public monies to prevent it, answers to questions such as these are clearly important.

There is one thing we can be sure of at the start: Uniformly heavy punishments for all crimes will lead to a larger number of *major* crimes. Let's look at the reasoning. All decisions are made at the margin. If theft and murder will be punished by the same fate, there is no marginal deterrence to murder. If a theft of $5 is met with a punishment of 10 years in jail and a theft of $50,000 incurs the same sentence, why not go all the way and steal $50,000? There is no marginal deterrence against committing the bigger theft.

To establish deterrents that are correct at the margin, we must observe empirically how criminals respond to changes in punishments. This leads us to the question of how people decide whether to commit a crime. A theory as to what determines the supply of criminal offenses needs to be established.

Adam Smith, the founder of modern economics, observed,

> The affluence of the rich excites the indignation of the poor, who are often both driven by want, and prompted by envy, to invade his possessions. It is only under the shelter of the civil magistrate that the owner of that valuable property, which is acquired by the labour of many years, or perhaps by many successive generations, can sleep a single night in security. He is at all times surrounded by unknown enemies, whom, though he never provokes, he can never appease, and from whose injustice he can be protected only by the powerful arm of the civil magistrate continually held up to chastise it. The acquisition of valuable and extensive property, therefore, necessarily requires the establishment of civil government. Where there is no property, or at least none that exceeds the value of two or three days' labour, civil government is not so necessary.[1]

Thus, Smith concluded, theft will be committed in any society in which one person has substantially more property than another. If Smith is correct, we can surmise that the individuals who engage in theft are seeking income. We can also suppose that, before acting, a criminal might be expected to look at the anticipated costs and returns of criminal activity. These could then be compared with the net returns from legitimate activities. In other words, those engaging in crimes may be thought of as doing so on the basis of a cost/benefit analysis in which the benefits to them outweigh their costs. The benefits of the crime of theft are clear: loot. The costs to the criminal would include, but not be limited to, apprehension by the police, conviction, and jail. The criminal's calculations are thus analogous to those made by an athlete when weighing the cost of

[1] Adam Smith, Book V, Chapter 1, *An Inquiry into the Nature and Causes of the Wealth of Nations,* 1776.

possible serious injury against the benefits to be gained from participating in a sport.

If we view the supply of offenses in this manner, we can devise ways in which society can lower the net expected benefit for committing any illegal activity. That is, we can figure out how to reduce crime most effectively. Indeed, economists have applied this sort of reasoning to study empirically the impact of punishment on criminal activity. The two areas on which they have focused are (1) the impact of increasing the probability that criminals will be detected and apprehended by, for example, putting more police on the street; and (2) the role of punishment by, for example, imprisonment.

Surprisingly, at least to an economist, the empirical answers to these questions came back rather mixed in early research studies. The estimated impact of imprisonment on crime rates appeared quite small, indeed often little different from zero. Moreover, a substantial majority of the early studies that attempted to estimate the impact of police on the crime rate found either no relationship or found that having more police on the force appeared to *increase* the crime rate!

The problem researchers have encountered in estimating the impact of police or prison terms on criminal activity is quite simple in principle but a difficult one to correct: Because people who live in areas with higher crime rates will want to take measures to protect themselves, they are likely to have larger police forces and to punish criminals more severely. Thus, even if more police and more severe penalties actually do reduce crime, this true effect may be masked or even seem to be reversed in the data, because high-crime areas will tend to have more police and higher prison populations.

Economic research has begun to unravel these influences, however, offering us the clearest picture yet of the likely effects of police and imprisonment on the crime rate. In a series of articles, Steven Levitt of the University of Chicago has looked for factors that strongly influence the number of police in a community or the size of a state's prison population but do not otherwise affect the crime rate. He has found such factors, and in so doing has revealed a much clearer picture of the true deterrence effect of law enforcement.

Levitt finds the strongest deterrent effect of police on violent crime such as murder, rape, and assault. In fact, he estimates the **elasticity** of violent crime with respect to police to be about –1.0. Accordingly, a 10 percent increase in a city's police force can be expected to produce about a 10 percent decrease in the violent crime rate in that city. With regard to property crimes, such as burglary, larceny, and auto theft, the impact of having more police is smaller but still significant. In this case, the estimated elasticity is about –0.3, meaning a 10 percent increase in the police force will yield about a 3 percent reduction in property crimes. The implications for a city like Detroit are quite striking. Increasing the police force by 10 percent would mean adding about 440 officers. Levitt's estimates imply that, as a result, the city could expect to suffer about 2100 fewer violent crimes each year and about 2700 fewer property crimes.

Levitt also has been able to isolate the role of imprisonment on deterring crime. He finds once again that the effects are strongest for violent crime. A 10 percent decrease in a state's prison population can be expected to increase the violent-crime rate in that state by about 4 percent. In the case of property crime, a 10 percent decrease in prison population will yield about a 3 percent rise in burglaries, larcenies, and auto thefts in the state. Perhaps not surprisingly, many states have been constructing new prisons.

In separate research, Levitt has found that juvenile criminals respond to incentives, just as their adult counterparts do. From the mid-1970s to the mid-1990s, juvenile crime soared relative to adult crime, which has led many commentators to worry about a generation of juveniles who are seemingly undaunted by the threat of imprisonment. In fact, it appears soaring juvenile crime was largely the result of changes in the incentives faced by juveniles: Over this same period of time, violent-crime imprisonment rates for juveniles fell 80 percent relative to those for adults. Hence, the chances of violent young criminals being jailed dropped to only about half that of violent adult criminals. Moreover, the change in penalties that occurs as youths become subject to adult laws (usually age 18) has a strong effect on their behavior. In states tough on youth but easy on adults, violent-crime rates rise 23 percent at age 18, but in states that are easy on juveniles and tough on adults, such crime drops 4 percent at age 18. Incentives, it seems, still matter.

Are the growing expenditures on crime prevention worth it? According to Levitt's results, the answer is yes. Adding another person to the prison population costs about $30,000 per year but can be expected to yield benefits (in terms of crime prevention) of more than $50,000 per year. Although adding an officer to the police force has an expected cost of about $80,000 per year, that officer can be expected to produce crime-prevention benefits of almost $200,000. If these numbers are anywhere close to being correct, we can expect further increases in spending on crime prevention in the years to come and perhaps even some noticeable reductions in the crime rate.

DISCUSSION QUESTIONS

1. The analysis just presented seems to make the assumption that criminals act rationally. Does the fact they do not necessarily do so negate the analysis?
2. In many cases, murder is committed among people who know each other. Does this mean that raising the penalty for murder will not affect the number of murders committed?
3. Consider the following prescription for punishments: "Eye for eye, tooth for tooth, hand for hand, foot for foot. . . ." Suppose our laws followed this rule, and further suppose we spent enough money on law enforcement to apprehend everyone who broke the law. What would the crime rate be? (*Hint:* If the penalty for stealing $10 was $10, and if you were certain you would be caught, would there be any expected gain from the theft? Would there be an expected gain from the theft if the penalty were only, say, $1, or if the chance of being caught were only 10 percent?)
4. In recent years, the penalty for selling illegal drugs has been increased sharply. How does that affect the incentive to sell drugs? For the people who decide to sell drugs anyway, what do the higher penalties for dealing do to their incentive to commit other crimes (such as murder) while they are engaged in selling drugs?

23

The Graying of America

America is aging. The 78 million baby boomers who pushed the Beatles and the Rolling Stones into stardom are well into middle age. Indeed, the future of America is now on display in Florida, where one person in five is over 65. In 25 years, almost 20 percent of all Americans will be 65 or older. Just as the post–World War II baby boom presented both obstacles and opportunities, so too does the graying of America. Let's see why.

Two principal forces are behind America's "senior boom." First, we're living longer. Average life expectancy in 1900 was 47. Today it is over 77 and is likely to reach 80 within the next decade. Second, the birthrate is near record low levels. Today's mothers are having far fewer children than their mothers had. In short, the old are living longer, and the ranks of the young are growing too slowly to offset that fact. Together, these forces are pushing up the proportion of the population over 65; indeed, the population of seniors is growing at twice the rate of the rest of the population. In 1970, the **median age** in the United States—the age that divides the older half of the population from the younger half—was 28; in 2005 the median age was 37 and rising. Compounding these factors, the average age at retirement has been declining as well, from 65 in 1963 to 62 currently. The result is more retirees relying on fewer workers to help ensure that their senior years are also golden years.

Why should a person who is, say, college age be concerned with the age of the rest of the population? Well, old people are expensive. In fact, people over 65 now consume over one-third of the federal government's budget. Social Security payments to retirees are the biggest item, now running over $500 billion a year. Medicare, which pays hospital and doctors' bills for the elderly, costs over $300 billion a year and is growing rapidly. Moreover, fully a third of the $250-billion-a-year budget for Medicaid, which helps pay medical bills for the poor of all ages, goes to those over the age of 65.

Under current law, the elderly will consume 40 percent of all federal spending within 15 years: Medicare's share of the gross domestic product (GDP) will double, as will the number of very old— those over 85 and most in need of care. Within 30 years, probably *one-half* of the federal budget will go to the old. In a nutshell, senior citizens are the beneficiaries of an expensive and rapidly growing share of all federal spending. What are they getting for our dollars?

To begin with, the elderly are already more prosperous than ever. Indeed, the annual discretionary income of those over 65 averages 30 percent higher than the average discretionary income of all age groups. Each year, inflation-adjusted Social Security benefits paid new retirees are higher than the first-year benefits paid people who retired the year before. In addition, for more than 30 years, cost-of-living adjustments have protected Social Security benefits from inflation. The impact of Social Security is evident even at the lower end of the income scale: The poverty rate for people over 65 is much lower than for the population as a whole. Retired people today collect Social Security benefits that are two to five times what they and their employers contributed in payroll taxes, plus interest earned.

Not surprisingly, medical expenses are a major concern for many elderly. Perhaps reflecting that concern, each person under the age of 65 in America currently pays an average of more than $1500 per year in federal taxes to subsidize medical care for the elderly. Indeed, no other country in the world goes to the lengths that America does to preserve life. Some 30 percent of Medicare's budget goes to patients in their last year of life. Coronary bypass operations—costing over $30,000 apiece—are routinely performed on Americans in their sixties and seventies. For those over 65, Medicare picks up the tab. Even heart transplants are now performed on people in their sixties and paid for by Medicare for those over 65. By contrast, the Japanese offer no organ transplants. Britain's National Health Service generally will not provide kidney dialysis for people over 55. Yet Medicare subsidizes dialysis for more than 100,000 people, half of them over 60. The cost: over $3 billion a year. Overall, the elderly receive Medicare benefits worth five to twenty times the payroll taxes (plus interest) they paid for this program.

The responsibility for the huge and growing bills for Social Security and Medicare falls squarely on current and future workers, because both programs are financed by taxes on payrolls. Thirty years ago, these programs were adequately financed with a payroll levy of less than 10 percent of the typical worker's earnings. Today, the tax rate exceeds 15 percent of median wages and is expected to grow rapidly.

By the year 2020, early baby boomers, born in the late 1940s and early 1950s, will have retired. Late baby boomers, born in the 1960s, will be nearing retirement. Both groups will leave today's college students, and their children, a staggering bill to pay. For Social Security and Medicare to stay as they are, the payroll tax rate may have to rise to 25 percent of wages over the next 20 years. And a payroll tax rate of 40 percent is not unlikely by the middle of the twenty-first century.

One way to think of the immense bill facing today's college students and their successors is to consider the number of retirees each worker must support. In 1946, the burden of one Social Security recipient was shared by 42 workers. By 1960, nine workers had to foot the bill for each retiree's Social Security benefits. Today, roughly three workers pick up the tab for each retiree's Social Security, plus his or her Medicare benefits. By 2030, only two workers will be available to pay the Social Security and Medicare benefits due each recipient. Thus a working couple will have to support not only themselves and their family, but also someone outside the family who is receiving Social Security and Medicare benefits.

Paying all the bills presented by the twenty-first century's senior citizens will be made more difficult by another fact: Older workers are leaving the workplace in record numbers. We noted earlier that the average retirement age is down to 62 and declining. Only 30 percent of the people age 55 and over hold jobs today, compared with 45 percent in 1930. Thus, even as the elderly are making increasing demands on the federal budget, fewer of them are staying around to help foot the bill.

Part of the exodus of the old from the workplace is due simply to their prosperity. Older people have higher disposable incomes than any other age group in the population and are using it to consume more leisure. Importantly, however, the changing work habits of older individuals have been prompted—perhaps inadvertently—by American businesses. Career advancement often slows after age 40—more than 60 percent of American corporations offer early retirement plans, whereas only about 5 percent offer inducements to delay retirement. Looking ahead to career dead-ends and hefty retirement checks, increasing numbers of older workers are opting for the golf course instead of the morning commute.

Recently, however, the private sector has begun to realize that the graying of America requires that we rethink the role of senior citizens in the workforce. Some firms are doing more than just thinking. For example, a major chain of home centers in California has begun vigorously recruiting senior citizens as salesclerks. The result has been a sharp increase in customer satisfaction: The older workers know the merchandise better and have more experience in dealing with people. Moreover, turnover and absenteeism have plummeted. People with gray hair, it seems, are immune to "surfer's throat," a malady that strikes younger Californians before sunny weekends.

Other firms have introduced retirement transition programs. Instead of early retirement at age 55 or 60, for example, older workers are encouraged to simply cut back on their workweek while staying on the job. Often, it is possible for workers to get the best of both worlds, collecting a retirement check even while working part-time at the same firm. Another strategy recognizes the importance of rewarding superior performance among older workers. At some firms, for example, senior technical managers are relieved of the drudgery of mundane management tasks and allowed to spend more time focusing on the technical side of their specialties. To sweeten the pot, a pay hike is often included in the package.

Congress and the president thus far seem unwilling to face the pitfalls and promises of an aging America. Although the age of retirement for Social Security purposes is legislatively mandated to rise to 67 from 65, the best that politicians in Washington, D.C., appear able to do is appoint commissions to "study" the problems we face. And the worst they can do? Well, we got a sample of it in 2003, with new legislation promising taxpayer-funded prescription drug benefits for senior citizens. Even those people in favor of the new program called it the largest expansion in **entitlement programs** in 40 years. Before passage of the law, the president claimed it was going to cost $35 billion a year, but within a couple of months, that estimate had been hiked to over $50 billion per year. In fact, the benefits of the program will be less than claimed, and the costs will be even higher, because more than three-quarters of senior citizens had privately funded prescription drug plans *before* the new law. You can be sure that these private plans are already disappearing, leaving seniors with fewer choices, and leaving you with a larger tax bill.

The sad fact is that there are currently programs out there that demonstrate how it is possible for government to responsibly address the crisis in funding programs for senior citizens. Chile, for example, faced a national pension system with even more severe problems than our Social Security system. Its response was to transform the system into one that is rapidly (and automatically, as time passes) converting itself into a completely private pension system. The result has been security for existing retirees, higher potential benefits for future retirees, and lower taxes for all workers. Americans could do exactly what the Chileans have done—if we chose to do so.

Many experts believe that significant changes in America's immigration laws could offer the best hope of dealing with the tax burdens and workforce shrinkage of the future. About a million immigrants come to America each year, the largest number in our nation's history. Yet more than 90 percent of new immigrants are admitted based on a selection system unchanged since 1952, under which the right of immigration is tied to family preference. As a result, most people are admitted to the United States because they happen to be the spouses, children, or siblings of earlier immigrants, rather than because they have skills or training highly valued in the American workplace. Both Canada and Australia have modified their immigration laws to expand opportunities for those immigrants who possess skills in short supply, with results that are generally regarded quite favorably in both nations. Unless Congress manages to overhaul America's immigration preference system, new immigrants are unlikely to relieve much of the pressure building due to our aging population.

In the meantime, if Social Security and Medicare are kept on their current paths, and older workers continue to be taxed out of the workforce, the future burden on those who are today's college students is likely to be unbearable. If we are to avoid the social tension and enormous costs of such an outcome, the willingness and ability of older individuals to retain more of their self-sufficiency must be recognized. To do otherwise is to invite a future in which the golden years are but memories of the past.

DISCUSSION QUESTIONS

1. How do the payroll taxes levied on the earnings of workers affect their decisions about how much leisure they consume?

2. When the government taxes younger people so as to pay benefits to older people, how does this affect the amount of assistance that younger people might voluntarily choose to offer older people?

3. When the government taxes younger people to pay benefits to older people, how does this affect the size of the bequests that older people are likely to leave to their children or grandchildren when they die?

4. In general, people who are more productive earn higher incomes and thus pay higher taxes. How would a change in the immigration laws that favored more highly educated and skilled individuals affect the future tax burden of today's American college students? Would the admission of better-educated immigrants tend to raise or lower the wages of American college graduates? On balance, would an overhaul of the immigration system benefit or harm today's college students?

Part Six

Property Rights and the Environment

INTRODUCTION

We saw in Part Four that monopoly produces outcomes that differ significantly from the competitive outcome and so yields gains from trade that fall short of the competitive ideal. In Part Six we see that when externalities are present—that is, when there are discrepancies between the private costs of action and the social costs of action— the competitive outcome differs from the competitive ideal. Typically, the problem in the case of externalities is said to be *market failure,* but the diagnosis might just as well be termed *government failure.* For markets to work efficiently, property rights to scarce goods must be clearly defined, cheaply enforceable, and fully trans- ferable, and it is generally the government that is believed to have a comparative advantage in ensuring that these conditions are satis- fied. If the government fails to define, enforce, or make transferable property rights, the market generally will fail to produce socially effi- cient outcomes, and it becomes a moot point as to who is at fault. The real point is this: What might be done to improve things?

Interestingly enough, as we see in Chapter 24 "Frankenfoods," an important source of improvement is likely to come from a most unlikely quarter. For at least 9000 years, humans have genetically en- gineered plants and animals to better suit our wishes. The result has been a level of wealth and health that otherwise would have been unattainable. In recent years, however, this genetic tinkering has in- volved **gene splicing,** in which the genetic material from one species is inserted into another species in the hopes of improving on Mother

Nature. Many people find this to be an ominous, even threatening environmental development, simply because the characteristics and behavior of such **transgenic species** seem so unpredictable. Many knowledgeable scientists believe that such species are actually more predictable than their relatively unsophisticated predecessors (derived from cross-breeding and grafting). Still, there is also good reason to proceed with some caution, simply because not all of the potential costs have been identified. At the same time, however, some major environmental benefits are already being derived from the new transgenic species. Bt cotton, for example, fights off insects on its own, necessitating less pesticide use and producing much higher crop yields. Roundup Ready soybeans permit the use of herbicides that are much less harmful to the environment, and even enable farmers to eliminate plowing, thereby reducing erosion and damage to streams and lakes. So, despite all the bad press that such **Frankenfoods** have received, if we proceed judiciously, the result may be a Green Revolution that both improves human welfare *and* the quality of the ecosystem that we and all other species depend upon.

As population and per capita income both rise, consumption rises faster than either, for it responds to the combined impetus of both. With consumption comes the residue of consumption, also known as plain old garbage. Many of us have heard of landfills being closed because of fears of groundwater contamination, or of homeless garbage scows wandering the high seas in search of a place to off-load; all of us have been bombarded with public service messages to recycle everything from aluminum cans to old newspapers. The United States, it seems, is becoming the garbage capital of the world. This is no doubt true, but it is also true that the United States is the professional football capital of the world—and yet pro football teams seem to have no problem finding cities across the country willing to welcome them with open arms. What is different about garbage? You probably are inclined to answer that football is enjoyable and garbage is not. True enough, but this is not why garbage sometimes piles up faster than anyone seems willing to dispose of it. Garbage becomes a problem only if it is not priced properly— that is, if the consumers and businesses that produce it are not charged enough for its removal, and the landfills where it is deposited are not paid enough for its disposal. The message of Chapter 25, "The Trashman Cometh," is that garbage really is not different from the things we consume in the course of producing it. As long as the trashman is paid, he will cometh, and as long as we have to pay for his services, his burden will be bearable. We will still have garbage, but we will not have a garbage problem.

We noted earlier that the property rights to a scarce good or resource must be clearly defined, fully enforced, and readily transferable if that resource is to be used efficiently—that is, in the manner that yields the greatest net benefits. This is true whether the resource in question is space in a landfill, water in a stream, or, as we see in Chapter 26, "Bye, Bye, Bison," members of an animal species. If these conditions are satisfied, the resource will be used in the manner that benefits both its owner and society the most. If these conditions are not satisfied—as they were not for American bison on the hoof or passenger pigeons on the wing—the resource generally will not be used in the most efficient manner. And in the case of animal species that are competing with human beings, this sometimes means extinction. What should be done when a species becomes endangered? If our desire is to produce the greatest net benefit to humanity, the answer in general is not to protect the species at *any* possible cost, for this would be equivalent to assigning an infinite value to the species. Instead, the proper course of action is to devise rules that induce people to act as though the members of the species were private property. If such rules can be developed, we shall not have to worry about spotted owls or African elephants becoming extinct any more than we currently worry about parakeets or cocker spaniels becoming extinct.

In Chapter 27, "Smog Merchants," property rights are again the focus of the discussion as we look at air pollution. We ordinarily think of the air around us as being something that we all own. The practical consequence of this is that we act as though the air is owned by none of us—for no one can exclude anyone else from using our air. As a result, we overuse the air in the sense that air pollution becomes a problem. This chapter shows that it is possible to define and enforce property rights to air, which the owners can then use as they see fit, which includes selling the rights to others. Once this is done, the users of clean air have the incentive to use it just as efficiently as they do all of the other resources (such as land, labor, and capital) utilized in the production process.

Air—or more generally, the atmosphere as a whole—reappears as the topic of Chapter 28, "Greenhouse Economics." There is a growing body of evidence that human action is responsible for rising concentrations of so-called greenhouse gases in the earth's atmosphere, and that left unchecked this growth may produce costly increases in the average temperature of our planet. Given the nature of the problem—a **negative externality**—private action taken on the individual level will not yield the optimal outcome for society. Thus the potential gains from government action, in the form of environmental regulations or taxation, are substantial. The key word here is potential, for government action, no matter how well-intentioned, does not automatically yield benefits that exceed the costs. As we seek solutions to the potential problems associated with greenhouse gases, we must be sure that the consequences of premature action are not worse than those of delaying action until the problem can be examined further. If we forget this message, greenhouse economics may turn into bad economics—and worse policy.

24

Frankenfoods

If you've ever eaten popcorn, you've eaten genetically modified food. Actually, almost all of the foods we eat, many of the clothes we wear, and even the pages on which these words are printed come from plant or animal species that have been genetically modified. Virtually all living things that form a pivotal role in our lives— including our household pets—have genetic structures today that have been shaped by conscious human decisions to make them that way.

Let's return to popcorn, because corn is probably the first living organism whose genetic structure was consciously modified by humans to suit their wishes. Beginning about 9000 years ago, the inhabitants of the Balsas River basin of southern Mexico began the process of transforming a plant called teosinte into corn (maize). Over the ensuing 3000 years they undertook breeding experiments that

- softened the hull of the kernel, so that it was more digestible;
- made the kernel stick more tightly to the cob, to reduce wastage; and
- transformed the architecture of the plant from many branches to one stalk, facilitating harvesting.

Eventually, the human experimentation even yielded a product that was more suitable for making tortillas. By 6000 years ago, teosinte had disappeared from fields, replaced with a crop very much identifiable as an ancestor of today's corn.

Although corn was first, human genetic experiments on cattle, rice, trees, horses, peas, wheat, cotton, pigs, and literally thousands of other plants and animals have formed the foundation for much of modern agriculture. The results of such genetic engineering, ranging from crossbreeding to plant grafting, now feed and clothe the world. In recent years, however, people around the globe have begun objecting to advances in the genetic modification of species. Genetically modified (GM) foods—often referred to as **Frankenfoods,** an allusion to Mary Shelley's fictional Frankenstein—are said to pose a threat to human health and the ecological system in which we live. Why, after 9000 years of success with genetic engineering, should people suddenly start to worry that it might yield catastrophic results? Just as importantly, what would be the likely results if we decided to bring genetic engineering to a halt, or even just slow its pace significantly?

The answer to the first question likely centers on the relatively new methods that are being to produce today's GM plants (and even animals). Instead of crossbreeding two existing plants, scientists are selecting individual genes, sometimes from species far removed, and inserting them into a plant of interest. The result is called a **transgenic species,** because its genes comes from two or more different species. For example, so-called "Bt cotton" is a form of cotton that has had inserted into it a toxin-producing gene from a soil bacterium known as *Bacillus thuringiensis*. The poison contained in the cotton is delivered only to bugs that eat cotton. The delivery of the toxin is so efficient that farmers who plant Bt cotton can use far less pesticides on their fields—pesticides that are toxic not merely to bugs, but also potentially life-threatening to many other species, including *Homo sapiens*.

The concern among people who object to the creation of such GM plants is that they are unlike anything seen before in the 9000 years of genetic engineering on record. There is simply no way to interbreed bacteria and plants. Unlike, say, peas, where crossbreeding of plants with red and white flowers reasonably can be expected to yield plants with pink flowers, when a gene from one species is inserted into another, radically different species, there is no possible way of predicting the result.

Therefore, say the opponents of modern genetic engineering, the results of today's GM experiments might yield transgenic crops that spread from fields into forest or other wildlands, becoming environmental nuisances along the way. Or they might cross-pollinate with neighboring wild plants, producing "superweeds" that could devastate huge swaths of previously productive agricultural lands. Indeed, say GM opponents, we might even end up with transgenic killers, species capable of threatening the continued existence of entire species, perhaps even human beings.

Are such outcomes possible? Yes, say scientists, something very unpleasant and very costly *might* result from modern gene-splicing techniques. But the likelihood is very small, probably even smaller than with traditional methods of genetic engineering, including those dating back 9000 years. The reason is that the current methods are highly targeted, involving the insertion of a single gene, with a known property, into a specific location in the genetic makeup of the recipient species. As a general rule, only *one* change in the recipient species is the result. This is in sharp contrast with older methods, in which a random "shotgun" approach is tried: interbreed two plants (or animals) and see what happens. Sometimes nothing (observable) happens, and sometimes many things change, but it is very difficult to predict just what will happen and whether or not it will be beneficial or harmful.

Given that we have been in the business of modern gene-splicing for about 8980 years less than we have been interbreeding by traditional means, it seems prudent to proceed with some caution, recognizing that there *may* be costs of the new methods that we have not thought of yet. At the same time, however, it is important to recognize that genetic engineering is absolutely central to the economic *and* environmental well-being of the world today, and that its beneficial future is likely to grow, if we let it.

Let's first consider the history of the so-called "Green Revolution," which started 40 years ago. In the mid-1960s scientists used genetic engineering to develop high-yielding varieties of rice and wheat that were subsequently released to farmers in Asia and Latin America. These crops spread rapidly in tropical and subtropical climates that had good irrigation systems or reliable rainfall, literally transforming the state of agriculture—and human nutrition—in dozens of developing nations.

On the nutritional side of the equation, crop yields soared, food prices fell, and both the caloric and nutritional intake of hundreds of millions of people improved sharply. Had there been no Green Revolution, food prices would have been roughly 50 percent higher, and caloric intake in the affected developing nations would have been nearly 15 percent lower. Significantly, both malnutrition and infant and child mortality rates would have been markedly higher.

On the environmental side of matters, the impact of the Green Revolution may have been even more profound. Because the GM rice, wheat, and other crops had much higher yields (in terms of bushels produced per acre), farmers were able to reduce the number of acres planted and still earn higher profits with the crops. Between about 1965 and 1990, for example, it is estimated that genetically engineered Green Revolution crops saved more than 100 million acres of wildlands in India. In recent years, the higher yields from GM crops have reduced forest-clearing in Honduras and the Philippines.

On a global scale, estimates have been made of the total impact of farming techniques and changes in yields since 1950. One expert, Dennis Avery of the Hudson Institute, says that absent these improvements, the world would have lost to agricultural cultivation an additional 20 million square *miles* of wildlife habitat, much of it forest. Given that there currently are 16 million square miles of forests in the world today, this implies that improvements in techniques and crop yields "have saved every square mile of forest on the planet," according to Avery.

Now, not all of this was due to GM crops, but a significant portion was, and the challenges we face in the future may be even greater. Many experts believe that most of the really big yield enhancements from traditional GM techniques have been exhausted. To be sure, improvements using crossbreeding are still being made, but no one believes they will be able to feed the additional 3 billion people who are likely to inhabit the earth by the year 2050. Modern gene-splicing techniques—and their resulting Frankenfoods—have that potential, however. Perhaps just as importantly, modern Frankenfood techniques promise to substantially *improve* the quality of the environment along the way.

Consider Bt cotton, which we mentioned earlier. In the United States, where farmers successfully have used pesticides to protect cotton, switching to Bt cotton has not significantly improved yields. What it has done, however, is permit farmers to drastically reduce their use of pesticides. This reduction in pesticides not only protects nontarget insects and other species in and around the cotton fields, it means there is much less pesticide runoff into streams and lakes. In India the benefits come in a different form. Cash-constrained farmers there use relatively little pesticides, so Bt cotton has enabled them to save only about $10 to $15 per acre on pesticide costs. But because of the low pesticide use, insect-caused crop losses in India historically have been huge. Thus the key impact of Bt cotton is on the yield side: Crop yields per acre in India are pushed up 60 percent when Bt cotton is planted. Higher yields not only raise the income of farmers and help push down prices for consumers, they also protect wildlands from further agricultural intrusion.

In a similar view, a variety of soybeans called Roundup Ready is transforming agricultural methods in the United States and elsewhere. These transgenic soybeans tolerate Roundup, an herbicide that kills many types of weeds and then quickly breaks down into environmentally harmless by-products. When farmers plant Roundup Ready soybeans, which now amount to one-third of the U.S. crop, they are able to switch from far more toxic chemical herbicides to Roundup. Moreover, they often no longer have to use plowing to aid them in controlling weeds. Less plowing means less soil erosion and less damaging runoff into adjacent bodies of water.

The promise of transgenic crops extends far beyond pesticides and plowing, however. For example, salt-resistant tomatoes and other crops have been developed that permit agriculture to take place on otherwise sterile lands, saving fertile savannahs and forests for wildlife. Similarly, crops are being developed that are able to tolerate aluminum, an element that is eminently useful in making airplanes but serves as a crop-killing contaminant in many soils around the world. There are even transgenic crops bred to thrive on the toxic wastes found in the worst industrial dump sites, crops capable of transforming such areas from wastelands to wildlife habitats.

Given the uncertainties and unknowns in any new field of scientific inquiry, it is certainly true that the potential costs of transgenic species—environmental as well as economic—should be carefully monitored and taken into account. Yet it is also important to remember the fate that likely would have befallen humankind had genetic manipulation been stopped in its tracks 9000 years ago. Instead of munching popcorn in front of wide-screen televisions, we might well be tilling teosinte in southern Mexico.

DISCUSSION QUESTIONS

1. How do the potential (environmental and economic) costs of transgenic crops differ from most of the traditional costs associated with agriculture, such as tractors and labor? (*Hint:* Who bears the costs: the farmer or others in society? Does this difference mean that we should think and act differently regarding these costs?)

2. How can the tools discussed in Chapters 1–3 help us understand some of policy issues involved with Frankenfoods?

3. Suppose one accurately took into account all of the costs and benefits of developing transgenic crops. Could you be sure that the economically efficient path to follow would be to permit the development of Frankenfoods?

4. Suppose that there are great economic benefits from transgenic crops, including improved nutrition, longer life spans, reduced infant mortality, and the like. But also assume that there are some modest potential environmental costs, for example, in the form of some species that are made extinct because they cannot compete with the new transgenic species. Should the existence of *any* environmental costs outweigh *all* possible economic benefits?

25

The Trashman Cometh

Is garbage really different? To answer this question, let us consider a simple hypothetical situation. Suppose a city agreed to provide its residents with all of the food they wished to consume, prepared in the manner they specified, and delivered to their homes for a flat, monthly fee that was independent of what or how much they ate. What are the likely consequences of this city food-delivery service? Most likely, people in the city would begin to eat more, because the size of their food bill would be independent of the amount they ate. They would also be more likely to consume lobster and filet mignon rather than fish sticks and hamburger because, once again, the cost to them would be independent of their menu selections. Soon the city's food budget would be astronomical, and either the monthly fee or taxes would have to be increased. People from other communities might even begin moving (or at least making extended visits) to the city, just to partake of this wonderful service. Within short order the city would face a food crisis as it sought to cope with providing a rapidly growing amount of food from a city budget that could no longer handle the financial burden.

If this story sounds silly to you, just change "food delivery" to "garbage pickup"; what we have just described is the way most cities in the country historically have operated their municipal garbage-collection services. The result during the late 1980s and early 1990s was the appearance of a garbage crisis—with overflowing landfills, homeless garbage scows, and drinking-water wells said to be polluted with the runoff from trash heaps. This seeming crisis—to the extent it existed—was fundamentally no different from the food crisis just described. The problem was not that (1) almost nobody wants garbage, nor that (2) garbage can have adverse environmental effects, nor even that (3) we had too much garbage. The problem lay in that (1) we often do not put prices on garbage in the way we put prices on the goods that generate the garbage, and (2) a strange assortment of bedfellows used a few smelly facts to make things seem worse than they were.

First things first. America produces plenty of garbage—about 230 million tons of household and commercial solid waste that either has to be burned, buried, or recycled. (That works out to over 1500 pounds per person.) About 36 percent of this is paper, whereas yard waste (such as grass trimmings) accounts for another 12 percent. Plastics amounts to about 20 percent of the volume of material that has to be disposed of, but because plastic is relatively light, it comprises only about 11 percent of the weight. More than 70 million tons of this trash is recycled.

Landfills are the final resting place for most of our garbage, although incineration is also widely used in some areas, particularly in the Northeast, where land values are high. Both methods began falling out of favor with people who lived near these facilities (or might eventually), as NIMBY (not-in-my-backyard) attitudes spread across the land. Federal, state, and local regulations also made it increasingly difficult to establish new waste disposal facilities, or even to keep old ones operating. The cost to open a modern 100-acre landfill rose to an estimated $70 million or more, and the permit process needed to open a new disposal facility soared to seven years in some states. Meanwhile, environmental concerns forced the closure of many landfills throughout the country and prevented others from ever beginning operations. By 1992, all but five states were exporting at least some of their garbage to other states. Today, most of the garbage from some densely populated states in the Northeast ends up in other people's backyards: New Jersey ships garbage to ten other states, while New York keeps landfill operators busy in thirteen different states. Across the country, some Americans have wondered where all of the garbage is going to go.

Although the failure of America's cities to price garbage appropriately led to an inefficient amount of the stuff, much of the appearance of a garbage crisis has been misleading. Rubbish first hit the headlines in 1987 when a garbage barge named *Mobro*, headed south with New York City trash, couldn't find a home for its load. As it turns out, the barge operator wanted to change his disposal contract after he sailed; when he tried to conduct negotiations over the radio while under way, operators of likely landfills (mistakenly) suspected he might be carrying toxic waste rather than routine trash. When adverse publicity forced the barge back to New York with its load, many people thought it was a lack of landfill space, rather than poor planning by the barge operator, that was the cause. This notion was reinforced by an odd combination of environmental groups, waste management firms, and the Environmental Protection Agency (EPA).

The Environmental Defense Fund wanted to start a major campaign to push recycling, and the *Mobro* gave things the necessary push. As one official for the organization noted, "An advertising firm couldn't have designed a better vehicle than a garbage barge." Meanwhile, a number of farsighted waste management companies had begun loading up on landfill space, taking advantage of new technologies that increased the efficient minimum size of a disposal facility. Looking to get firm contracts for filling this space, the trade group for the disposal industry started pushing the notion that America was running out of dump space. State and local officials who relied on the group's data quickly bought into the new landfills, paying premium prices to do so. The EPA, meanwhile, was studying the garbage problem but without accounting for the fact that its own regulations were causing the efficient scale of landfills to double and even quadruple in size. Thus the EPA merely counted landfills around the country and reported that they were shrinking in number. This was true enough, but what the EPA failed to report was that because landfills were getting bigger much faster than they were closing down, total disposal capacity was *growing* rapidly, not shrinking.

For a while, it seemed that recycling was going to take care of what appeared to be a growing trash problem. In 1987, for example, old newspapers were selling for as much as $100 per ton in today's prices, and many municipalities felt that the answer to their financial woes and garbage troubles was at hand. Yet as more communities began putting mandatory recycling laws into effect, the prices of recycled trash began to plummet. Over the next five years, 3500 communities in more than half the states had some form of mandatory curbside recycling; the resulting increase in the supply of used newsprint meant that communities soon were having to pay to have the stuff carted away. For glass and plastics, the story is so far much the same. The market value of the used materials is below the cost of collecting and sorting it. About a dozen states have acted to increase the demand for old newsprint by requiring locally published newspapers to utilize a minimum content of recycled newsprint. Even so, many experts believe that no more than 60 to 70 percent of all newsprint can be recycled, and we are already recycling 52 percent of it, up from 33 percent in 1988.

Just as significantly, recycling raises significant issues that were often ignored during the early rush to embrace the concept. For example, the production of a hundred tons of de-inked fiber from old newsprint produces about 40 tons of sludge that must be disposed of somehow. Although the total volume of material is reduced, the concentrated form of what is left can make it more costly to dispose of properly. Similarly, recycling paper is unlikely to save trees, for most virgin newsprint is made from trees planted expressly for that purpose and harvested as a crop: if recycling increases, many of these trees simply will not be planted. In a study done for Resources for the Future, A. Clark Wiseman concluded, "The likely effect of [newsprint recycling] appears to be smaller, rather than larger, forest inventory." Moreover, most virgin newsprint is made in Canada, using clean hydroelectric power. Makers of newsprint in the United States (the primary customers for the recycled stuff) often use higher-polluting energy such as coal. Thus one potential side effect of recycling is the switch from hydroelectric power to fossil fuels.

Some have argued that we should simply ban certain products. For example, Styrofoam cups have gotten a bad name because they take up more space in landfills than do paper hot-drink cups, and because Styrofoam remains in the landfill forever. Yet according to a widely cited study by Martin B. Hocking of the University of Victoria, the manufacture of a paper cup consumes 36 times as much electricity and generates 580 times as much wastewater as does the manufacture of a Styrofoam cup. Moreover, as paper degrades underground, it releases methane, a greenhouse gas that contributes to global climate change. In a similar vein, consider disposable diapers, which have been trashed by their opponents because a week's worth generates 22.2 pounds of post-use waste, whereas a week's worth of reusable diapers generates only 0.24

pound. Because disposable diapers already amount to 1 percent of the nation's solid waste, the edge clearly seems to go to reusable cloth diapers. Yet the use of reusable rather than disposable diapers consumes more than three times as many BTUs (British thermal units) of energy and generates ten times as much water pollution. It would seem that the trade-offs that are present when we talk about "goods" are just as prevalent when we discuss "bads" such as garbage.

It also appears that more government regulation of the garbage business is likely to make things worse rather than better, as may be illustrated by the tale of two states: New Jersey and Pennsylvania. A number of years ago, to stop what was described as price-gouging by organized crime, New Jersey decided to regulate waste hauling and disposal as a public utility. Once the politicians got involved in the trash business, however, politics very nearly destroyed the business of trash. According to Paul Kleindorfer of the University of Pennsylvania, political opposition to passing garbage-disposal costs along to consumers effectively ended investment in landfills. In 1972 there were 331 landfills operating in New Jersey; by 1988 the number had fallen to 13, because the state-regulated fees payable to landfill operators simply didn't cover the rising costs of operation. Half of New Jersey's municipal solid waste is now exported to neighboring Pennsylvania.

Pennsylvania's situation provides a sharp contrast. The state does not regulate the deals that communities make with landfill and incinerator operators; the market takes care of matters instead. For example, despite the state's hands-off policy, tipping fees (the charges for disposing of garbage in landfills) are below the national average in Pennsylvania, effectively limited by competition between disposal facilities. The market seems to be providing the right incentives; in one recent year, there were 31 pending applications to open landfills in Pennsylvania, but only 2 in New Jersey, despite the fact that New Jersey residents are paying the highest disposal rates in the country to ship garbage as far away as Michigan, Illinois, Missouri, and Alabama.

Ultimately, two issues must be solved when it comes to trash. First, what do we do with it once we have it? Second, how do we reduce the amount of it that we have? As hinted at by the Pennsylvania story and illustrated further by developments elsewhere in the country, the market mechanism can answer both questions.

The fact of the matter is that in many areas of the country, population densities are high and land is expensive. Hence a large amount of trash is produced, and it is expensive to dispose of locally. In contrast, there are some areas of the country where there are relatively few people around to produce garbage, where land for disposal facilities is cheap, and where wide-open spaces minimize the potential air pollution hazards associated with incinerators. The sensible thing to do, it would seem, is to have the states that produce most of the trash ship it to states where it can be most efficiently disposed of—for a price, of course. This is already being done to an extent, but residents of potential recipient states are (not surprisingly) concerned, lest they end up being the garbage capitals of the nation. Yet Wisconsin, which imports garbage from as far away as New Jersey, is demonstrating that it is possible to get rid of the trash without trashing the neighborhood. Landfill operators in Wisconsin are now required to send water-table monitoring reports to neighbors and to maintain the landfills for 40 years after closure. Operators also have guaranteed the value of neighboring homes to gain the permission of nearby residents and in some cases have purchased homes to quiet neighbors' objections. These features all add to the cost of operating landfills, but as long as prospective customers are willing to pay the price and neighboring residents are satisfied with their protections— and so far these conditions appear to be satisfied—then it would seem tough to argue with the outcome.

Some might still argue that it does not seem right for one community to be able to dump its trash elsewhere. Yet the flip side is this: Is it right to *prevent* communities from accepting the trash, if that is what they want? Consider Gilliam County, Oregon (pop. 1950), which wanted Seattle's garbage so badly it fought Oregon state legislators' attempts to tax out-of-state trash coming into Oregon. Seattle's decision to use the Gilliam County landfill generated $1 million per year for the little community—some 25 percent of its annual budget and enough to finance the operations of the county's largest school.

Faced with the prospect of paying to dispose of its garbage, Seattle quickly had to confront the problem of reducing the amount of trash its residents were generating. Its solution was to charge householders according to the amount they put out. Seattle thus began charging $16.10 per month for each can picked up weekly. Yard waste that has been separated for composting costs $4.25 per month, and paper, glass, and metal separated for recycling are hauled away at no charge. In the first year that per-can charges were imposed, the total tonnage that had to be buried fell by 22 percent. Voluntary recycling rose from 24 percent of waste to 36 percent—a rate almost triple the national average at the time. The "Seattle Stomp" (used to fit more trash into a can) became a regular source of exercise, and the city had trouble exporting enough garbage to fulfill its contract with Gilliam County.

The Seattle experience is paralleled by a similar program in Charlottesville, Virginia. A few years ago, this university town of 40,000 began charging 80 cents per 32-gallon bag or can of residential garbage collected at the curb. The results of the city's new policy suggest that people respond to garbage prices just as they do to all other prices: When an activity becomes more expensive, people engage in less of it. In fact, after controlling for other factors, the introduction of this unit-pricing plan induced people to reduce the volume of garbage presented for collection by 37 percent.

Where did all of the garbage go? Well, some of it didn't go anywhere, because many residents began practicing their own version of the Seattle Stomp, compacting garbage into fewer bags. Even so, the total weight of Charlottesville's residential garbage dropped by 14 percent in response to unit pricing. Not all of this represented a reduction in garbage production, because some residents resorted to "midnight dumping"—tossing their trash into commercial Dumpsters or their neighbors' cans during late-night forays. This sort of behavior is much like the rise in gasoline thefts that occurred in the 1970s when gas prices jumped to the equivalent of $3 to $4 per gallon. But just as locking gas caps ended most gas thefts, there may be a simple way to prevent most midnight dumping. Economists who have studied the Charlottesville program in detail suggest that property taxes or monthly fees could be used to cover the cost of one bag per household each week, with a price per bag applied only to additional bags. According to these estimates, a one-bag allowance would stop all midnight dumping by most one-person households and stop almost half the dumping by a hypothetical three-person household. Moreover, such a scheme would retain most of the environmental benefits of the garbage-pricing program.

The message slowly beginning to emerge across the country, then, is that garbage really is not different from the things we consume in the course of producing it. As long as the trashman is paid, he will cometh, and as long as we must pay for his services, his burden will be bearable.

DISCUSSION QUESTIONS

1. How do deposits on bottles and cans affect the incentives of individuals to recycle these products?

2. Why do many communities mandate recycling? Is it possible to induce people to recycle more without requiring that all residents recycle?

3. How do hefty per-can garbage pickup fees influence the decisions people make about what goods they will consume?

4. A community planning on charging a fee for trash pickup might structure the fee in any of several ways. It might, for example, charge (1) a fixed amount per can, (2) an amount per pound of garbage, or (3) a flat fee per month, without regard to amount of garbage. How would each of these affect the amount and type of garbage produced? Which system would lead to an increase in the use of trash compactors? Which would lead to the most garbage?

26

Bye, Bye, Bison

The destruction of animal species by humans is nothing new. For example, the arrival of human beings in North America about 12,000 years ago is tied to the extinction of most of the megafauna (very large animals) which then existed. The famous LaBrea Tar Pits of southern California yielded the remains of 24 mammals and 22 birds that no longer exist. Among these are the saber-toothed tiger, the giant llama, the 20-foot ground sloth, and a bison that stood seven feet at the hump and had six-foot-wide horns.

Although many experts believe that human hunting was directly responsible for the destruction of these species, and that a combination of hunting and habitat destruction by humans has led to the extinction of many other species, the link is not always as clear as it might seem at first glance. For example, it is estimated that only about 0.02 percent (1 in 5000) of all species that have ever existed are currently extant. Most of the others (including the dinosaurs) disappeared long before humans ever made an appearance. The simple fact is that all species compete for the limited resources available, and most species have been out-competed, with or without the help of *Homo sapiens*. Just as important is that basic economic principles can help explain why various species are more or less prone to meet their demise at the hands of humans, and what humans might do if they want to delay the extinction of any particular species.[1]

Let's begin with the passenger pigeon, which provides the most famous example of the role of human beings in the extinction of a

---

[1] We say "delay" rather than "prevent" extinction because there is no evidence to date that any species—*Homo sapiens* included—has any claim on immortality.

species. At one time these birds were the most numerous species of birds in North America and perhaps in the world. They nested and migrated together in huge flocks and probably numbered in the billions. When flocks passed overhead, the sky would be dark with pigeons for days at a time. The famous naturalist John James Audubon measured one roost at 40 miles long and 3 miles wide, with birds stacked from treetop down to nearly ground level. Although the Native Americans had long hunted these birds, the demise of the passenger pigeon is usually tied to the arrival of the white man, which increased the demand for pigeons as a source of food and sport. The birds were shot and netted in vast numbers; by the end of the nineteenth century, an animal species that had been looked on as almost indestructible because of its enormous numbers had almost completely disappeared. The last known passenger pigeon died in the Cincinnati Zoo in 1914.

The American bison only narrowly escaped the same fate. The vast herds that roamed the plains were an easy target for hunters; with the advent of the railroad and the need to feed railroad crews as the transcontinental railroads were built, hunters such as Buffalo Bill Cody killed bison by the thousands. As the demand for the fur of the bison increased, it became the target for more hunting. Like the passenger pigeon, the bison had appeared to be indestructible because of its huge numbers, but the species was soon on the way to becoming extinct. Despite the outcries of the Native Americans who found their major food source being decimated, it was not until late in the nineteenth century that any efforts were made to protect the bison.[2]

These two episodes, particularly that of the bison, are generally viewed as classic examples of humankind's inhumanity to our fellow species, as well as to our fellow humans, for many Native American tribes were ultimately devastated by the near demise of the bison. A closer look reveals more than simply wasteful slaughter; it discloses exactly why events progressed as they did and how we can learn from them to improve modern efforts to protect species threatened by human neighbors.

---

[2] For the bison's cousin, the eastern buffalo—which stood seven feet tall at the shoulder, was twelve feet long, and weighed more than a ton—the efforts came too late. The last known members of the species, a cow and her calf, were killed in 1825 in the Allegheny Mountains.

Native Americans had hunted the bison for many years before the arrival of white men and are generally portrayed as both carefully husbanding their prey and generously sharing the meat among tribal members. Yet the braves who rode their horses into the thundering herds marked their arrows so it was clear who had killed the bison. The marked arrows gave the shooter rights to the best parts of the animal. Tribal members who specialized in butchering the kill also received a share as payment for processing the meat. Indeed, the Native American hunting parties were organized remarkably like the parties of the white men who followed: *Once they were killed,* the ownership of the bison was clearly defined, fully enforced, and readily transferable. Moreover, the rewards were distributed in accord with the contribution that each had made to the overall success of the hunt.

Matters were different when it came to the ownership rights to living bison herds. Native Americans, like the whites who came later, had no economically practical way to fence in the herds. The bison could (and did) migrate freely from one tribe's territory into the territory of other tribes. If the members of one tribe economized on their kill, their conservation efforts would chiefly provide more meat for another tribe, who might well be their mortal enemies. This fact induced Native Americans to exploit the bison, so that the herds disappeared from some traditional territories on the Great Plains by 1840—before Buffalo Bill was even born.

Two factors made the efforts of the white man—the railroad hunters—more destructive, hastening the disappearance of the bison herds. First, the white population (and thus the demand for the meat and hides) was much larger than the Native American population. Second, white men used firearms on the bison—a technological revolution that increased the killing capacity of a given hunter by a factor of 20 or more, compared to the bow and arrow. Nevertheless, the fundamental problem was the same for the white man and Native American alike: The property rights to live bison could not be cheaply established and enforced. To own a bison one had to kill it, and so too many bison were killed.

The property rights to a scarce good or resource must be clearly defined, fully enforced, and readily transferable if that resource is to be used efficiently—that is, in the manner that yields the greatest net benefits. This is true whether the resource in question is the

American bison, the water in a stream, or a pepperoni pizza. If these conditions are satisfied, the resource will be used in the manner that best benefits both its owner and society.[3] If they are not satisfied— as they were not for bison on the hoof or passenger pigeons on the wing—the resource generally will not be used in the most efficient manner. In the case of animal species that are competing with human beings, this sometimes means extinction.

In modern times, the government has attempted to limit hunting and fishing seasons and the number of animals that may be taken, by imposing state and federal regulations. The results have been at least partially successful. It is likely, for example, that there are more deer in North America today than there were at the time of the colonists—a fact that is not entirely good news for people whose gardens are sometimes the target of hungry herds. In effect, a rationing system (other than prices) is being used in an attempt to induce hunters and fishermen to act as though the rights to migratory animals were clearly defined, fully enforced, and readily transferable. Yet the threatened extinction of many species of whales illustrates that the problem is far from resolved.

The pattern of harvesting whales has been the subject of international discussion ever since World War II, for migratory whales are like nineteenth-century bison: To own them, one must kill them. It was readily apparent to all concerned that without some form of restraint, many species of whales were in danger of extinction. The result was the founding of the International Whaling Commission (IWC) in 1948, which attempted to regulate international whaling. But the IWC was virtually doomed from the start, for its members had the right to veto any regulation they considered too restrictive, and the commission had no enforcement powers in the event a member nation chose to disregard the rules. Moreover, some whaling nations (such as Chile and Peru) refused to join the IWC, so commission quotas had little effect on them. Some IWC members have used nonmember flagships to circumvent agreed upon quotas,

[3] This does not mean that all species will be permanently protected from extinction, for reasons that are suggested in Chapter 3, "Flying the Friendly Skies?" It does mean that extinction will be permitted to occur only if the benefits of letting it occur exceed the costs.

while others have claimed that they were killing the whales solely for exempt "research" purposes.

The story of the decimation of a species is well told in the events surrounding blue whales, which are believed to migrate thousands of miles each year. This animal, which sometimes weighs almost 100 tons, is difficult to kill even with the most modern equipment; nevertheless, intensive hunting gradually reduced the stock from somewhere between 300,000 and 1 million to, at present, somewhere between 600 and 3000. In the 1930–1931 winter season, almost 30,000 blue whales were taken, a number far in excess of the species' ability to replenish through reproduction. Continued intense harvesting brought the catch down to fewer than 10,000 by 1945–1946, and in the late 1950s the yearly harvest was down to around 1500 per year. By 1964–1965, whalers managed to find and kill only 20 blue whales. Despite a 1965 ban by the IWC, the hunting of blues continued by nonmembers such as Brazil, Chile, and Peru.

Humpback whales have suffered a similar fate. From an original population estimated at 300,000, there remain fewer than 5000 today. Like the blues, humpbacks are now under a hunting ban, but the lack of monitoring and enforcement capacity on the part of the IWC makes it likely that some harvesting is still taking place. IWC conservation attempts designed to protect finbacks, minke whales, and sperm whales have also been circumvented, most notably by the Russians and Japanese, who simply announced their own unilateral quotas.

Whales are not the only seagoing creatures to suffer from an absence of clearly defined, cheaply enforceable, and transferable property rights. Codfish off the New England and eastern Canadian coasts were once so abundant, it was said, that a person could walk across the sea on their backs. The fish grew into six-foot-long, 200-pound giants, and generations of families from coastal communities knew they could count on the fish for a prosperous livelihood. The problem was that the fish had to be hauled from the sea before rights to it could be established. The result was overfishing, which led to declining yields and shrinking fish. Over the last 30 years alone, the catch has dropped more than 75 percent, and the typical fish caught these days weighs but 20 pounds. As a result, the Canadians have virtually closed down their cod fishery, and the American fleet is but a ghost of its former self.

The cod is not alone in its demise. In the northeastern Atlantic, haddock, mackerel, and herring are all in serious trouble. Along the West Coast of the United States, lingcod, rockfish, and bocaccio are in trouble as well. Worldwide, 30 percent of fish stocks, including orange roughy, shark, swordfish, and tuna, are declining due to overfishing, and another 40 percent or more of the commercial stocks are on the verge of trouble.

A number of nations have taken legislative action in the hope of stemming the decline. Beginning in 1996, for example, the U.S. National Maritime Fisheries Service was required to begin working with eight regional fishing councils around the country to come up with plans to stem the demise of traditional fish stocks. Yet not all the councils are actually following the plans they have laid out, so the overfishing continues. A more promising approach may be seen in Britain, where under the terms of European Union rules, the catch of all major fish stocks are limited by quotas, which specify the amount of fish that legally may be taken. The British innovation has been to make those quotas transferable—that is, the rights to catch specific numbers of fish can be purchased and sold just like any other good. The quotas assign rights to fish, and their transferability ensures that the lowest-cost, most sensible means of taking those fish will be used. With quotas set at levels consistent with the long-term survival of the fish, and the elimination of the pressure to "catch it or lose it," fish stocks in the affected areas have begun a turnaround.

The Canadian province of British Columbia has started a similar program covering its halibut fishery, with equally promising results. Since 1923 management of the Pacific halibut fishery has been regulated jointly by the United States and Canada. Yet despite stringent controls, which included limits on the number of vessels that could fish, and reductions in the length of the season, the halibut stock showed signs of collapse by the late 1980s.

Joint efforts by fishers and the Canadian Department of Fisheries and Oceans led to the creation of a system of individual vessel quotas (IVQs) in 1991. Existing license holders now own a percentage of the total allowable catch. In effect, each vessel owner has secure property rights to a specified poundage of fish each year, and the result has been to change their incentives and behavior drastically.

The allocation of individual vessel quotas eliminated the need for a short fishing season, originally created in a futile effort to halt overfishing. Prior to IVQs, the short season forced the fishers into the same prime areas at the same time, resulting in damaged and lost fishing gear and "ghost fishing," in which lost fishing gear continued to catch fish. From six days in 1990, the season has been lengthened to 245 days, with fishers allowed to choose when they will take the catch that belongs to them. Vessels no longer conflict with one another, preventing substantial losses of gear and fish each season. Moreover, before the individual quotas, vessels had extra crew on board to ensure the most rapid possible harvesting of fish. Under IVQs, the total number of crew members in the fleet quickly dropped by about 20 percent.

Before quotas, vessel owners felt compelled to fish regardless of weather conditions, because the loss of even a day of fishing could make the difference between profit and loss for the season. Now that pressure has been eliminated, greatly enhancing the safety of the fishers. The longer fishing season also has enabled fishers to sell higher quality and fresher fish. Prior to IVQs, only about half the catch could be sold as fresh fish, which are more valuable; now nearly all of it is sold fresh, yielding better product for consumers and higher profits for producers.

The IVQs are transferable (although with some restrictions) and the transferability has added to the benefits of the system. For example, the number of vessels has been reduced, because smaller, less efficient fishers have sold or leased their licenses to more efficient operators. This has decreased capital costs and helped reduce total crew in the fleet. Similarly, average vessel size has risen, increasing the safety of the crews. Transferability also gets the quotas into the hands of the "highliners," the skippers who are best at finding the fish and harvesting them in the lowest-cost manner. And, finally, the best news of all is reserved for the halibut themselves. Since the introduction of IVQs, fishers no longer need to harvest the halibut to establish rights to them, so they no longer have an incentive to overfish. As a result, halibut stocks in the Pacific fishery have begun to grow rapidly—one more illustration that the clear assignment of enforceable, transferable property rights remains the most effective way we know to protect other species from the depredations of *Homo sapiens*.

DISCUSSION QUESTIONS

1. Has there ever been a problem with the extinction of dogs, cats, or cattle? Why not?

2. Some argue that the only way to save rare species is to set up private game reserves to which wealthy hunters can travel. How could this help save endangered species?

3. Is government *ownership* of animals needed to protect species from extinction?

4. In the United States, most fishing streams are public property, with access available to all. In Britain, most fishing streams are privately owned, with access restricted to those who are willing to pay for the right to fish. Anglers agree that over the past 30 years, the quality of fishing in the United States has declined, while the quality of fishing in Britain has risen. Can you suggest why?

27

Smog Merchants

Pollution is undesirable, almost by definition. Most of us use the term so commonly it suggests we all know, without question, what it means. Yet there is an important sense in which "pollution is what pollution does." Consider, for example, ozone (O_3), an unstable collection of oxygen atoms. At upper levels of the atmosphere it is a naturally occurring substance that plays an essential role in protecting life from the harmful effects of ultraviolet radiation. Without the ozone layer, skin cancer would likely become a leading cause of death, and spending a day at the beach would be as healthy as snuggling up to an open barrel of radioactive waste. At lower levels of the atmosphere, however, ozone occurs as a by-product of a chemical reaction between unburned hydrocarbons (as from petroleum products), nitrogen oxides, and sunlight.[1] In this form it is a major component of smog, and breathing it can cause coughing, asthma attacks, chest pain, and possibly long-term lung-function impairment.

Consider also polychlorinated biphenyls (PCBs), molecules that exist only in human-made form. Because they are chemically quite stable, PCBs are useful in a variety of industrial applications, including insulation in large electrical transformers. Without PCBs, electricity generation would be more expensive, as would the thousands of other goods that depend on electricity for their production and distribution. Yet PCBs are also highly toxic; acute exposure (e.g., from ingestion) can result in rapid death. Chronic (long-term) exposure is suspected to cause some forms of cancer. Illegal dumping of PCBs into streams and lakes has caused massive fish kills

---

[1] Ozone is also produced as a by-product of lightning strikes and other electrical discharges. Wherever and however it occurs, it has a distinctive metallic taste.

and is generally regarded as a threat to drinking-water supplies. And because PCBs are chemically stable (i.e., they decompose very slowly), once they are released into the environment they remain a potential threat for generations to come.

As these examples suggest, the notion of pollution is highly sensitive to context. Even crude oil, so essential as a source of energy, can become pollution when it appears on the shores of Alaska's pristine shores. Despite this fact, we shall assume in what follows that (1) we all know what pollution is when we see, smell, taste, or even read about it, and (2) holding other things constant, less of it is preferred to more.

There are numerous ways to reduce or avoid pollution. Laws can be passed banning production processes that emit pollutants into the air and water or specifying minimum air- and water-quality levels or the maximum amount of pollution allowable. Firms would then be responsible for developing the technology and for paying the price to satisfy such standards. Or the law could specify the particular type of production technology to be used and the type of pollution-abatement equipment required in order to produce legally. Finally, subsidies could be paid to firms that reduce pollution emission, or taxes could be imposed on firms that engage in pollution emission.

No matter which methods are used to reduce pollution, costs will be incurred and problems will arise. For example, setting physical limits on the amount of pollution permitted discourages firms from developing the technology that will reduce pollution beyond those limits. The alternative of subsidizing firms that reduce pollution levels may seem a strange use of taxpayers' dollars. The latest solution to the air pollution problem—selling or trading the rights to pollute—may seem even stranger. Nevertheless, this approach is now being used around the nation, especially in Los Angeles, the smog capital of the country.

Under the plan that operates in the Los Angeles area, pollution allowances have been established for 390 of the area's largest polluters. Both nitrous oxide and sulphur dioxide, the two main ingredients of southern California's brown haze, are covered. Prior to the plan, which went into effect in 1994, the government told companies such as power plants and oil refineries what techniques they had to use to reduce pollutants. Under the new rules, companies are simply told how much they must reduce emissions each year, and they are then allowed to use whatever means they see fit to meet the standards. Over the initial 10 years of the plan, firms had their baseline emissions limits cut by 5 to 8 percent a year. By 2005, emissions of nitrous oxides from these sources were down by 75 percent and sulphur dioxide by 60 percent.

The key element in the program is that the companies are allowed to buy and sell pollution rights. A firm that is successful in reducing pollutants below the levels to which it is entitled receives emission reduction credits (ERCs) for doing so. The firm can sell those credits to other firms, enabling the latter to exceed their baseline emissions by the amount of credits they purchase.

Presumably, firms that can cut pollutants in the lowest cost manner will do so, selling some of their credits to firms that find it more costly to meet the standards. Because the total level of emissions is determined ahead of time by the area's Air Quality Management District, the trading scheme will meet the requisite air quality standards. Yet because most of the emissions reductions will be made by firms that are the most efficient at doing so, the standards will be met at the lowest cost to society.

A similar market-based plan covering sulphur dioxide has been adopted by the Environmental Protection Agency (EPA) on a nationwide level. This program was kicked off by an auction of 150,000 air pollution allowances granted by the EPA. Each allowance permits a power utility to emit one ton of sulphur dioxide (SO_2) into the air. Based on their past records, utilities have been given rights to emit sulphur dioxide into the air at a declining rate into the future. By the year 2000, for example, utility emissions of sulphur dioxide had to be cut in half. Companies can either use their allowances to comply with the clean air regulations, or they can beat the standards and sell their unused allowances to other utilities.

As it turns out, although the EPA auctions probably helped get the trading process started, the expansion in private trades has been so rapid and extensive that the auctions are now a minor part of the market. Perhaps more importantly, the private market in allowances seems to be quite efficient at doing what it was designed to do—move allowances to their highest-valued locations, permit equalization of control costs across sources, and generate a key source of information about the costs of reducing SO_2 emissions.

Research conducted by Paul Joskow, Richard Schmalensee, and Elizabeth Bailey has found that after an initial 12- to 18-month period in which there were few private trades and relatively high prices for the allowances—some $250 to $300 per ton—the market evolved rapidly. By mid-1994 prices had dropped below $150 per ton, and the volume of private trades exceeded the volume offered in the EPA auction. More recently prices have averaged $170 per ton, and private trading of allowances now greatly dwarfs the EPA auction.

This research also has uncovered two other quite important facts. First, the transaction costs of trading allowances are quite low—about 2 percent of the prevailing price. In addition, it appears that the prices at which trade takes place at any point in time are all quite close to one another. The spread between average bids and lowest winning bids at EPA auctions is only about 1 to 3 percent, and trading in the private market appears to be similarly concentrated around a single price at any point in time.

Because utilities can freely choose between either abating or emitting each ton of SO_2, they will pay for an allowance only what it will save them in abatement costs. Equivalently, a utility will pay no more for abatement than it would pay for an allowance to emit the SO_2. Thus, the existence of a common price for allowances assures us that the cost per ton of cutting emissions must be at that same level. That is, the costs of abating SO_2 emissions must be running about $170 per ton. According to the U.S. Council of Economic Advisers, the tradable permit plan for SO_2 has not only helped contribute to a 60 percent cut in SO_2 emissions from major sources, it has substantially reduced the costs of achieving this environmental improvement.

There are also EPA trading programs for the emissions produced by heavy-duty on-highway engines (such as found in large trucks) and for nitrogen oxide (NO_x) emissions from power plants. The general consensus seems to be that the heavy-duty engine program has significantly reduced the costs of complying with emissions standards. As yet, the nationwide NO_x program for power plants is still being implemented, so there is no data on its effectiveness, but a better established NO_x program covering the

Los Angeles area appears to be cutting the costs of achieving emissions reductions there.

Perhaps not surprisingly, the notion of selling the right to pollute has been controversial, particularly among environmental organizations. The activist group Greenpeace, for example, claims that selling pollution allowances "is like giving a pack of cigarettes to a person dying of lung cancer." Nonetheless, other environmental groups have chosen to buy some of the allowances and retire them unused. One such group was the Cleveland-based National Healthy Air License Exchange, whose president said, "It is our intent . . . to have a real effect on this market and on the quality of air."

Some observers have been disappointed that the government has taken so long to approve emissions-trading schemes. There appear to be two key reasons why progress has been so slow. First, many environmentalists are vigorously opposed to the very concept of tradable emissions, arguing that it amounts to putting a price on what traditionally has been considered a "priceless" resource—the environment. Because most of the cost savings that stem from tradable emissions rights accrue to the polluters and their customers, government agencies have proceeded carefully, to avoid charges that they are somehow selling out to polluters.

Ironically, the second reason for the delay in developing markets for tradable pollution rights has been the reluctance on the part of industry to push harder for them. Similar programs in the past involved emissions credits that could be saved up (banked) by a firm for later use or bartered on a limited basis among firms. Under these earlier programs, environmental regulators would periodically wipe out emissions credits that firms thought they owned, on the ground that doing so provided a convenient means of preventing future environmental damage.

Not surprisingly, some companies believe that any credits purchased under a tradable-rights plan might be subject to the same sort of confiscation. Under such circumstances, firms have been understandably reluctant to support a program that might not prove to be of real value.[2] Indeed, even under the tradable-emissions plan

---

[2] One can imagine the enthusiasm people would feel toward, say, the market for automobiles if the government announced that because cars were a source of pollution, the property rights to them might be revoked at any time, for any reason.

adopted for Los Angeles, the regulators have explicitly stated that the emissions credits are *not* property rights and that they can be revoked at any time. Sadly, unless obstacles such as these can be removed, achieving environmental improvement at the lowest **social cost** is likely to remain a goal rather than an accomplishment.

DISCUSSION QUESTIONS

1. Does marketing the right to pollute mean that we are allowing too much destruction of our environment?

2. Who implicitly has property rights to the air when the EPA auctions SO_2 permits? Does your answer depend on who gets the revenue raised by the auction?

3. Some environmental groups have opposed tradable pollution rights on the grounds that this puts a price on the environment, when in fact the environment is a priceless resource. Does this reasoning imply that we should be willing to give up *anything* (and therefore everything) to protect the environment? Does environmental quality have an infinite value? If not, how should we place a value on it?

4. Environmental regulations that prohibit emissions beyond some point implicitly allow firms and individuals to pollute up to that point at no charge. Don't such regulations amount to giving away environmental quality at no charge? Would it be better to charge a price via emissions taxes, for example, for the initial amount of pollutants? Would doing so reduce the amount of pollution?

28

Greenhouse Economics

The sky may not be falling, but it is getting warmer—maybe. The consequences will not be catastrophic, but they will be costly—maybe. We can reverse the process but should not spend very much to do so right now—maybe. Such is the state of the debate over the greenhouse effect—the apparent tendency of carbon dioxide (CO_2) and other gases to accumulate in the atmosphere, acting like a blanket that traps radiated heat, thereby increasing the earth's temperature. Before turning to the economics of the problem, let's take a brief look at the physical processes involved.

Certain gases in the atmosphere, chiefly water vapor and CO_2, trap heat radiating from the earth's surface. If they did not, the earth's average temperature would be roughly $0°$F instead of just over $59°$F, and everything would be frozen solid. Human activity helps create some so-called greenhouse gases, including CO_2 (mainly from combustion of fossil fuels), methane (from landfills and livestock), and chlorofluorocarbons (CFCs—from aerosol sprays, air conditioners, and refrigerators). We have the potential, unmatched in any other species, to profoundly alter our ecosystem.

There seems little doubt that humankind has been producing these gases at a record rate and that they are steadily accumulating in the atmosphere. Airborne concentrations of CO_2, for example, are increasing at the rate of about 0.5 percent per year; over the past 50 years, the amount of CO_2 in the atmosphere has risen a total of about 25 percent. Laboratory analysis of glacial ice dating back at least 160,000 years indicates that global temperatures and CO_2 levels in the atmosphere do, in fact, tend to move together, suggesting that the impact of today's rising CO_2 levels may be higher global temperatures in the future. Indeed, the National Academy of Sciences (NAS) has suggested that by the middle of the twenty-first century, greenhouse gases could be double the levels they were in 1860, and that global temperatures could rise by as much as $2°$ to $9°F$.[1] The possible consequences of such a temperature increase include the following: a rise in the average sea level, inundating coastal areas, including most of Florida; the spread of algal blooms capable of deoxygenating major bodies of water, such as the Chesapeake Bay; and the conversion of much of the midwestern wheat and corn belt into a hot, arid dust bowl.

When an individual drives a car, heats a house, or uses an aerosol hair spray, greenhouse gases are produced. In economic terms, this creates a classic **negative externality.** Most of the costs (in this case, those arising from global warming) are borne by individuals *other than* the one making the decision about how many miles to drive or how much hair spray to use. Because the driver (or sprayer) enjoys all the benefits of the activity but suffers only a part of the cost, that individual engages in more than the economically efficient amount of the activity. In this sense, the problem of greenhouse gases parallels the problem that occurs when someone smokes a cigarette in an enclosed space or litters the countryside with fast-food wrappers. If we are to get individuals to reduce production of greenhouse gases to the efficient rate, we must somehow induce them to act *as though* they bear all the costs of their actions. The two most widely accepted means of doing this are government regulation and taxation, both of which have been proposed to deal with greenhouse gases.

The 1988 Toronto Conference on the Changing Atmosphere, attended by representatives from 48 nations, favored the regulation route. The Conference recommended a mandatory cut in CO_2 emissions by 2005 to 80 percent of their 1988 level—a move that would have required a major reduction in worldwide economic output. The 1997 Kyoto conference on climate change, attended by representatives from 160 nations, made more specific but also more modest proposals. Overall, attendees agreed that by 2012, 38 developed

---

[1] This amount may not sound like much, but it does not take much to alter the world as we know it. The global average temperature at the height of the last ice age 18,000 years ago—when Canada and most of Europe were covered with ice—was $51°F$, just $8°$ or so cooler than today.

nations should cut greenhouse emissions by 5 percent relative to 1990 levels. Developing nations, including China and India (the two most populous nations in the world), would be exempt from emissions cuts. On the taxation front, one prominent U.S. politician has proposed a tax of $100 per ton on the carbon emitted by fuels. It is estimated that such a tax would raise the price of coal by $70 per ton (about 300 percent) and elevate the price of oil by $8 per barrel, or about 20 percent. These proposals, and others like them, clearly have the potential to reduce the buildup of greenhouse gases but only at substantial costs. It thus makes some sense to ask, what are we likely to get for our money?

Perhaps surprisingly, the answer to this question is not obvious. Consider, for example, the raw facts of the matter. On average over the past century, greenhouse gases have been rising and so has the average global temperature. Yet most of the temperature rise occurred before 1940, whereas most of the increase in greenhouse gases occurred after 1940. In fact, global average temperatures fell about 0.5° F between 1940 and 1970; this cooling actually led a number of prominent scientists during the 1970s to forecast a coming ice age!

Just as disconcerting is that the facts of global temperature change appear different depending on how and where temperature is measured. For example, if one looks only at ground-based measurements, the decade of the 1990s was clearly the warmest on record. Yet the upward trend in temperature that appears to hold true in these data is directly at odds with the results from other sources. Measurements taken using satellites and balloons, for example, suggest that there is *no* tendency for the average temperature of the atmosphere to rise. Why these discrepancies exist and what they mean for the future are issues still unresolved.

Nevertheless, let us suppose for the moment that, barring a significant reduction in greenhouse gas emissions, global warming is either under way or on the way. What can we expect? According to the most comprehensive study yet of this issue, a report by the prestigious National Academy of Sciences, the answer is a "good news, bad news" story.

The bad news is this: the likely rise in the sea level by one to three feet will inundate significant portions of our existing coastline; the expected decline in precipitation will necessitate more widespread use of irrigation; the higher average temperatures will compel more widespread use of air conditioning, along with the associated higher consumption of energy to power it; and the blazing heat in southern latitudes may make these areas too uncomfortable for all but the most heat-loving souls. The good news is that the technology for coping with changes such as these is well known and the costs of coping surprisingly small—on a scale measured in terms of hundreds of billions of dollars, of course. Moreover, many of the impacts that loom large at the individual level will represent much smaller costs at a societal level. For example, although higher average temperatures could prove disastrous for farmers in southern climes, the extra warmth could be an enormous windfall farther north, where year-round farming might become feasible. Similarly, the loss of shoreline due to rising sea levels would partly just be a migration of coastline inland—current beachfront property owners would suffer, but their inland neighbors would gain.[2]

None of these changes are free, of course, and there remain significant uncertainties about how global warming might affect species other than *Homo sapiens*. It is estimated, for example, that temperate forests can "migrate" only at a rate of about 100 kilometers per century, not fast enough to match the speed at which warming is expected to occur. Similarly, the anticipated rise in the sea level could wipe out between 30 and 70 percent of today's coastal wetlands. Whether new wetlands would develop along our new coastline and what might happen to species that occupy existing wetlands are issues that have not yet been resolved.

Yet the very uncertainties that surround the possible warming of the planet suggest that policy prescriptions of the sort that have been proposed—such as the cut in worldwide CO_2 emissions agreed to at Kyoto—may be too much, too soon. Indeed, the National Academy of Sciences recommended that we learn more before we leap too far. Caution seems particularly wise, because the exclusion of developing nations from any emissions cuts could result in huge costs for developed nations but little or no reduction in worldwide greenhouse gases. Some sense of the damage that can be wrought by ignoring such counsel and rushing into a politically popular response to a complex environmental issue is well illustrated by another atmospheric problem: smog.

---

[2] There would be a net loss of land area and thus a net economic loss. Nevertheless, the net loss of land would be chiefly in the form of less valuable inshore property.

Although gasoline is a major source of the hydrocarbons in urban air, its contribution to smog is plummeting because new cars are far cleaner than their predecessors. In the 1970s, cars spewed about 9 grams of hydrocarbons per mile; emissions controls brought this down to about 1.5 grams per mile by 1995. The cost of this reduction is estimated to be approximately $1000 for each ton of hydrocarbon emissions prevented—a number that many experts believe to be well below the benefits of the cleaner air that resulted. Despite the improvements in air quality, smog is still a significant problem in many major cities. Additional federal regulations aimed primarily at the nine smoggiest urban areas, including New York, Chicago, and Los Angeles, went into effect in 1995. Meeting these standards meant that gasoline had to be reformulated at a cost of about 6 cents per gallon. This brought the cost of removing each additional ton of hydrocarbons to about $10,000—some 10 times the per-ton cost of removing the first 95 percent from urban air.

Just as significantly, EPA rules require that gasoline have a minimum oxygen content to help it burn. But because gasoline does not naturally contain oxygen, these rules effectively require refiners to put additives in their gas. At this point, there are only two additives that meet the EPA requirements: ethanol (refined from corn), and methyl tertiary butyl ether (MTBE). Because adding ethanol would drive the cost of gas up sharply, refiners have felt compelled to add MTBE. Yet MTBE has contaminated water supplies, and concern over its possible carcinogenic properties had led officials in several states to ban its use.

The costs of the EPA oxygen standards for gasoline are estimated to add 21 cents per gallon to the price of gas. Moreover, the presence of multiple EPA standards across the country has left supplies of gasoline vulnerable to disruption, because fuel often cannot be transshipped from one area to another to meet temporary shortages. This fact has contributed substantially to large spikes in the price of gasoline in major Midwestern cities, such as Milwaukee and Chicago, every time there has been even a minor supply disruption.

Overall, the costs of EPA-mandated gasoline reformulation are huge, even though the EPA has never shown that the oxygen content requirement is necessary to meet its air quality standards. The potential benefits of reformulated gasoline appear to be trivial compared to the costs, yet we are stuck with this EPA mandate, because few politicians want to be accused of being in favor of smog.

There is no doubt that atmospheric concentrations of greenhouse gases are rising and that human actions are the cause. It is probable that, as a result, the global average temperature is, or soon will be, rising. If temperatures do rise significantly, the costs will be large, but the consequences are likely to be manageable. Given the nature of the problem, private action, taken on the individual level, will not yield the optimal outcome for society. Thus the potential gains from government action, in the form of environmental regulations or taxation, are substantial. But the key word here is *potential,* because government action, no matter how well intentioned, does not automatically yield benefits that exceed the costs. As we seek solutions to the potential problems associated with greenhouse gases, we must be sure that the consequences of action are not worse than those of first examining the problem further. If we forget this message, greenhouse economics may turn into bad economics—and worse policy.

DISCUSSION QUESTIONS

1. Why will voluntary actions, undertaken at the individual level, be unlikely to bring about significant reductions in greenhouse gases such as CO_2?

2. Does the fact that the CO_2 produced in one nation results in adverse effects on other nations have any bearing on the likelihood that CO_2 emissions will be reduced to the optimal level? Would the problem be easier to solve if all the costs and benefits were concentrated within a single country? Within a single elevator?

3. The policy approach to greenhouse gases will almost certainly involve limits on emissions, rather than taxes on emissions. Can you suggest why limits rather than taxes are likely to be used?

4. It costs about $80,000 per acre to create wetlands. How reasonable is this number as an estimate of what wetlands are worth?

Part Seven

International Trade and Economic Prosperity

INTRODUCTION

Many of the key public issues of our day transcend national borders or affect the entirety of our $12 trillion economy. The rapid developments in information processing, communications, and transportation over the past 25 years are gradually knitting the economies of the world closer together. Political developments, most notably the demise of the Iron Curtain and the dissolution of the Soviet Union, have contributed to this growing economic integration, as have reductions in long-standing barriers to international trade. Moreover, the last decade was a period of growing awareness that the economic vitality of individual markets was importantly determined by macroeconomic decisions made in Washington, D.C. The turn of the twenty-first century was also—briefly—the first time in three decades that the federal government managed to spend less than it collected in taxes, a development that surely warrants examination as a public issue.

The passage of the North American Free Trade Agreement (NAFTA) and the creation of the World Trade Organization (WTO) have substantially reduced the barriers to trade between the United States and most of the rest of the world. If we take advantage of these lower trade barriers, we have the opportunity to make ourselves far better off by specializing in those activities in which we have a **comparative advantage** and then trading the fruits of our efforts with other nations. Yet voluntary exchange also often redistributes wealth, in addition to creating it, so there will always be some individuals who oppose free trade. There are many smoke screens behind which the self-interested opposition to free trade is hidden, as we see in Chapter 29, "Free Trade, Less Trade, or No Trade?" Nevertheless, although **protectionism**—the creation of trade barriers such as tariffs and quotas—often sounds sensible, it is in fact a surefire way to reduce rather than enhance our wealth. If we ignore the value of free trade, we do so only at our peril.

To illustrate the tremendous damages that can be wrought when protectionism gains the upper hand, Chapter 30, "The $750,000 Steelworker," examines what happens when tariffs and quotas are imposed in an effort to "save" U.S. jobs from foreign competition. The sad facts are that (1) in the long run, it is almost impossible to effectively protect U.S. workers from foreign competition, and (2) efforts to do so not only reduce Americans' overall living standards, but they also end up costing the jobs of other Americans. The moral of our story is that competition is just as beneficial on the international scene as it is on the domestic front.

As its title makes clear, Chapter 31, "A Farewell to Jobs" also addresses the issue of jobs—in this case, the claim that American firms are exporting jobs. In recent years, a large number of American corporations have begun "outsourcing" service work (such as technical and customer support) to workers located in foreign lands, most notably India. Despite claims regarding the novelty—and supposed harm to the economy—of this activity, outsourcing is no different from any other form of international trade. When Americans purchase, say, an automobile made in Japan, that car is made by residents of Japan rather than by residents of the United States. Similarly, when Americans purchase technical support from a company in India, that service is provided by residents of India rather than by residents of the United States. Both are examples of international trade, and both, like all voluntary trade, create wealth for the trading partners. The residents of each land are making the most of their **comparative advantage** in producing different goods and services, and government restrictions on such activities will serve only to make us worse off.

Well before Americans worried about competition from cheap labor in India, they were worried about cheap labor in China. As we see in Chapter 32, "The Rise of the Dragon," China has been adopting capitalist institutions over the past 25 years. As it has done so, it has reaped the rewards of those institutions, most notably in the form of a rapidly rising standard of living for its people. But accompanying this has been the emergence of China as a major player in world markets. Indeed, China is now America's number two trading partner (after Canada) and may even have risen to number one by the time you read this. The growing volume of trade between the United States and China has created enormous wealth for people in both nations, albeit not without costly adjustments for some individuals. The crucial fact to keep in mind, however, is that international trade is fundamentally no different from interstate trade or interpersonal trade: as long as it is voluntary, the result is a higher standard of living for all participants.

29

Free Trade, Less Trade, or No Trade?

The last 15 years have been a time of great change on the international trade front. The North American Free Trade Agreement (NAFTA), for example, substantially reduced the barriers to trade among citizens of Canada, the United States, and Mexico. On a global scale, the Uruguay round of the General Agreement on Tariffs and Trade (GATT) was ratified by 117 nations including the United States. Under the terms of this agreement, GATT was replaced by the World Trade Organization (WTO), whose membership now numbers about 150, and **tariffs** were cut worldwide. Agricultural **subsidies** were reduced, patent protections extended, and the WTO is establishing a set of arbitration boards to settle international disputes over trade issues.

Many economists believe that both NAFTA and the agreements reached during the Uruguay round were victories not only for free trade, but also for the citizens of the participating nations. Nevertheless, many noneconomists, particularly politicians, opposed these agreements, so it is important we understand what is beneficial about NAFTA, the Uruguay round, and free trade in general.

Voluntary trade creates new wealth. In voluntary trade, both parties in an exchange gain. They give up something of lesser value in return for something of greater value. In this sense, exchanges are always unequal. But it is this unequal nature of exchange that is the source of the increased productivity and higher wealth that occurs whenever trade takes place. When we engage in exchange, what we give up is worth less than what we get—for if this were not true, we would not have traded. And what is true for us is also true for our trading partner, meaning that partner is better off, too.

Free trade encourages individuals to employ their talents and abilities in the most productive manner possible, and to exchange the fruits of their efforts. The **gains from trade** lie in one of the most fundamental ideas in economics: A nation gains from doing what it can do best *relative* to other nations, that is, by specializing in those endeavors in which it has a **comparative advantage.** Trade encourages individuals and nations to discover ways to specialize so that they can become more productive and enjoy higher incomes. Increased productivity and the subsequent increase in the rate of economic growth are exactly what the signatories of the Uruguay round and NAFTA sought—and are obtaining—by reducing trade barriers.

Despite these gains from exchange, free trade is routinely opposed by some (and sometimes many) people, particularly in the case of international trade. There are many excuses offered for this opposition, but they all basically come down to one issue. When our borders are open to trade with other nations, some individuals and businesses within our nation face more competition. As we saw in Chapter 18, most firms and workers hate competition, and who can blame them? After all, if a firm can keep the competition out, profits are sure to rise. And if workers can prevent competition from other sources, they can enjoy higher wages and greater selection among jobs. So the real source of most opposition to international trade is that the opponents to trade dislike the competition that comes with it. There is nothing immoral or unethical about this—but there is nothing altruistic or noble about this, either. It is self-interest, pure and simple.

Opposition to free trade is, of course, nothing new on the American landscape. One of the most famous examples of such opposition resulted in the Smoot-Hawley Tariff of 1930. This major federal government statute was a classic example of protectionism—an effort to protect a subset of American producers at the expense of consumers and other producers. It included tariff schedules for over 20,000 products, raising taxes on affected imports by an average of 52 percent.

The Smoot-Hawley Tariff encouraged beggar-thy-neighbor policies by the rest of the world. Such policies represent an attempt to improve (a portion of) one's domestic economy at the expense of foreign countries' economies. In this case, tariffs were imposed to discourage imports, in order that domestic import-competing industries would benefit. The beggar-thy-neighbor policy at the heart of the Smoot-Hawley Tariff Act of 1930 was soon adopted by the United Kingdom, France, the Netherlands, and Switzerland. The result was a massive reduction in international trade. According to many economists, this caused a worsening of the ongoing worldwide depression of the period.

Opponents of free trade sometimes claim that beggar-thy-neighbor policies benefit the United States by protecting import-competing industries. In general, this claim is not correct. It is true that some Americans benefit from such policies, but two large groups of Americans lose. First, there are the purchasers of imports and import-competing goods. They suffer from higher prices and reduced selection of goods and suppliers caused by tariffs and import **quotas.** Second, the decline in imports caused by protectionism also causes a decline in exports, thereby harming firms and employees in these industries. This follows directly from one of the most fundamental propositions in international trade: *in the long run, imports are paid for by exports.* This proposition simply states that when one country buys goods and services from the rest of the world (imports), the rest of the world eventually wants goods from that country (exports) in exchange. Given this fundamental proposition, a corollary becomes obvious: *any restriction on imports leads to a reduction in exports.* Thus any business for import-competing industries gained as a result of tariffs or quotas means at least as much business *lost* for exporting industries.

Opponents to free trade often raise a variety of objections in their efforts to restrict it. For example, it is sometimes claimed that foreign companies engage in dumping, that is, selling their goods in America below cost. The first question to ask when such charges are made is, below *whose* cost? Clearly, if the foreign firm is selling in America, it must be offering the good for sale at a price that is at or below the costs of American firms, or else it could not induce Americans to buy it. But the ability of individuals or firms to get goods at lower cost is one of the *benefits* of free trade, not one of its damaging features.

What about claims that import sales are taking place at prices below the foreign company's costs? This amounts to arguing that the owners of the foreign company are voluntarily giving some of their wealth to us, namely, the difference between their costs and the (lower) price they charge us. It is possible, though unlikely, they might wish to do this, as a way of getting us to try a product that we would not otherwise purchase. But if so, why would we want to refuse this gift? As a nation, we are richer if we accept it. Moreover, it is a gift that will be offered only in the short run: there is no point in selling at below cost unless one hopes to soon raise price profitably above cost!

Another argument sometimes raised against international trade is that the goods are produced abroad using unfair labor practices (such as the use of child labor) or using production processes that do not meet American environmental standards. It is surely the case that such charges are sometimes correctly levied. But we must remember two things here. First, although we may find the use of child labor (or perhaps 60-hour weeks with no overtime pay) objectionable, such practices were at one time commonplace in the United States. They used to be engaged in here for the same reason they are currently practiced abroad: the people involved were (or are) too poor to do otherwise. Some families in developing nations literally cannot survive unless all members of their family contribute. As unfortunate as this is, if we insist on imposing our tastes—shaped in part by our extraordinarily great wealth—on peoples whose wealth is far smaller than ours, we run the risk of making them worse off even as we think we are helping them.

Similar considerations apply to environmental standards.[1] It is well established that individuals' and nations' willingness to pay for environmental quality is very much shaped by their wealth: Environmental quality is a luxury good; that is, people who are rich (such as Americans) want to consume much more of it per capita than do people who are poor. Insisting that other nations meet environmental standards that we find acceptable is much like insisting that they wear the clothes we wear, use the modes of transportation we prefer, and consume the foods we like. The few people who manage to afford it will indeed be living in the style to which we are accustomed, but most people will not be able to afford much of anything.

Our point is not that foreign labor or environmental standards are, or should be, irrelevant to Americans. Our point instead is that

---

[1] There is one important exception to this argument. In the case of foreign air or water pollution generated near enough to our borders (for example with Mexico or Canada) to cause harm to Americans, good public policy presumably dictates that we seek to treat such pollution as though it were being generated inside our borders.

achieving high standards of either is costly, and trade restrictions are unlikely to be the most efficient or effective way to achieve them. Just as importantly, labor standards and environmental standards are all too often raised as smoke screens to hide the real motive: keeping the competition out.

If it is true that free trade is beneficial and that restrictions on trade generally are harmful, we must surely raise the question, how does legislation like the Smoot-Hawley Tariff (or any other trade restriction) ever get passed? As Mark Twain noted many years ago, the reason the free traders win the arguments and the protectionists win the votes is this: Foreign competition often clearly affects a narrow and specific import-competing industry such as textiles, shoes, or automobiles, and thus trade restrictions benefit a narrow, well-defined group of economic agents. For example, restrictions on imports of Japanese automobiles in the 1980s chiefly benefited the Big Three automakers in this country: General Motors, Ford, and Chrysler. Similarly, long-standing quotas on the imports of sugar benefit a handful of large American sugar producers. And when tariffs of up to 30 percent were slapped on many steel imports in 2002, an even smaller number of American steelmakers and their employees benefited. Because of the concentrated benefits that accrue when Congress votes in favor of trade restrictions, sufficient monies can be raised in those industries to convince members of Congress to impose those restrictions.

The eventual reduction in exports that must follow is normally spread in small doses throughout all export industries. Thus no specific group of workers, managers, or shareholders in export industries will feel that it should contribute money to convince Congress to reduce international trade restrictions. Additionally, although consumers of imports and import-competing goods lose due to trade restrictions, they too are typically a diffuse group of individuals, none of whom individually will be affected a great deal because of any single import restriction. It is the simultaneous existence of concentrated benefits and diffuse costs that led to Mark Twain's conclusion that the protectionists would often win the votes.

Of course, the protectionists don't win all the votes—after all, about one-seventh of the American economy is based on international trade. Despite the opposition to free trade that comes from many quarters, its benefits to the economy as a whole are so great it is unthinkable that we might do away with international trade altogether. Thus, when we think about developments such as the North American Free Trade Agreement (NAFTA) and the World Trade Organization (WTO), it is clear that both economic theory and empirical evidence indicate that, on balance, Americans will be better off after—and because of—the move to freer trade.

DISCUSSION QUESTIONS

1. During the late 1980s and early 1990s, American automobile manufacturers greatly increased the quality of the cars they produced, relative to the quality of the cars produced in other nations. What effect do you think this had on (1) American imports of Japanese cars, (2) Japanese imports of American cars, and (3) American exports of goods and services other than automobiles?

2. Over the last 20 years, some Japanese automakers have opened plants in the United States so that they could produce (and sell) "Japanese" cars in the United States. What effect do you think this had on (1) American imports of Japanese cars, (2) Japanese imports of American cars, and (3) American exports of goods and services other than automobiles?

3. For a number of years, Japanese carmakers voluntarily limited the number of cars they exported to the United States. What effect do you think this had on (1) Japanese imports of American cars and (2) American exports of goods and services other than automobiles?

4. Until recently, American cars exported to Japan had driver controls on the left side of the car (as in America) even though the Japanese drive on the left side of the road, and thus Japanese cars sold in Japan have driver controls on the right side. Suppose the Japanese tried to sell their cars in America with the driver controls on the right side. What impact would this likely have on their sales in this country? Do you think the unwillingness of American carmakers to put the driver controls on the correct side for exports to Japan had any effect on their sales of cars in that country?

30

The $750,000 Steelworker

In even-numbered years, particularly years evenly divisible by four, politicians of all persuasions are apt to give long-winded speeches about the need to protect U.S. jobs from the evils of foreign competition. To accomplish this goal, we are encouraged to buy American. If further encouragement is needed, we are told that if we do not voluntarily reduce the amount of imported goods we purchase, the government will impose (or make more onerous) either tariffs (taxes) on imported goods or quotas (quantity restrictions) that physically limit imports. The objective of this exercise is to save U.S. jobs.

Unlike black rhinos or blue whales, U.S. jobs are in no danger of becoming extinct. There are an infinite number of potential jobs in the American economy, and there always will be. Some of these jobs are not very pleasant, and many others do not pay very well, but there will always be employment of some sort as long as there is scarcity. Thus when a steelworker making $72,000 per year says that imports of foreign steel should be reduced to save his job, what he really means is this: He wants to be protected from competition so he can continue his present employment at the same or higher salary rather than move to a different employment that has less desirable working conditions or pays a lower salary. There is nothing wrong with the steelworker's goal (better working conditions and higher pay), but it has nothing to do with saving jobs. (Despite this, we may even use the term "saving jobs" in the discussion that follows, because it is such convenient shorthand.)

In any discussion of the consequences of restrictions on international trade, it is essential to remember two facts. First, *we pay*

208

for imports with exports. It is true that in the short run we can sell off assets or borrow from abroad if we happen to import more goods and services than we export. But we have only a finite amount of assets to sell, and foreigners do not want to wait forever before we pay our bills. Ultimately, our accounts can be settled only if we provide (export) goods and services to the trading partners from whom we purchase (import) goods and services. Trade, after all, involves *quid pro quo* (literally, something for something). The second point to remember is that *voluntary trade is mutually beneficial to the trading partners.* If we restrict international trade, we reduce those benefits, both for our trading partners and for ourselves. One way these reduced benefits are manifested is in the form of curtailed employment opportunities for workers. In a nutshell, even though tariffs and quotas enhance job opportunities in import-competing industries, they also cost us jobs in export industries; the net effect seems to be *reduced* employment overall.

What is true for the United States is true for other countries as well: They will buy our goods only if they can market theirs, because they too have to export goods to pay for their imports. Thus any U.S. restrictions on imports to this country—via tariffs, quotas, or other means—ultimately cause a reduction in our exports, because other countries will be unable to pay for our goods. This implies that import restrictions inevitably must decrease the size of our export sector. So imposing trade restrictions to save jobs in import-competing industries has the effect of costing jobs in export industries.

Just as important, import restrictions impose costs on U.S. consumers as a whole. By reducing competition from abroad, quotas, tariffs, and other trade restraints push up the prices of foreign goods and enable U.S. producers to hike their own prices. Perhaps the best documented example of this is found in the automobile industry, where voluntary restrictions on Japanese imports were put in place.

Due in part to the enhanced quality of imported cars, sales of domestically produced automobiles fell from 9 million units in 1978 to an average of 6 million units per year between 1980 and 1982. Profits of U.S. automobile manufacturers plummeted as well, turning into substantial losses for some of them. U. S. automobile manufacturers and autoworkers' unions demanded protection from import competition. They were joined in their cries by politicians from automobile-producing states. The result was a voluntary agreement entered into by Japanese car companies (the most important competitors of U.S. firms) that restricted U.S. sales of Japanese cars to 1.68 million units per year. This agreement—which amounted to a quota even though it never officially bore that name—began in April 1981 and continued into the 1990s in various forms.

Robert W. Crandall, an economist with the Brookings Institute, has estimated how much this voluntary trade restriction has cost U.S. consumers in terms of higher car prices. According to his estimates, the reduced supply of Japanese cars pushed their prices up by $1600 apiece, measured in 2005 dollars. The higher price of Japanese imports in turn enabled domestic producers to hike their prices an average of $640 per car. The total tab in the first full year of the program was about $7 billion. Crandall also estimated the number of jobs in automobile-related industries that were saved by the voluntary import restrictions; the total was about 26,000. Dividing $7 billion by 26,000 jobs yields a cost to consumers of about $275,000 *per year* for every job saved in the automobile industry. U.S. consumers could have saved over $2 billion on their car purchases each year if, instead of implicitly agreeing to import restrictions, they had simply given $75,000 to every autoworker whose job was preserved by the voluntary import restraints.

The same types of calculations have been made for other industries. Tariffs in the apparel industry were increased between 1977 and 1981, saving the jobs of about 116,000 U.S. apparel workers at a cost of $45,000 per job each year. At about the same time, the producers of citizens band (CB) radios also managed to get tariffs raised. Approximately 600 workers in the industry kept their jobs as a result but at an annual cost to consumers of over $85,000 per job.

The cost of protectionism has been even higher in other industries. Jobs preserved in the glassware industry due to trade restrictions cost $200,000 apiece each year. In the maritime industry, the yearly cost of trade protection is $270,000 per job. In the steel industry, the cost of preserving a job has been estimated at an astounding $750,000 per year. If free trade were permitted, each worker losing a job could be given a cash payment of half that amount each year, and the consumer would still save a lot of money.

THE $750,000 STEELWORKER   211

Even so, this is not the full story. None of these studies estimating the cost to consumers of saving jobs in import-competing industries have attempted to estimate the ultimate impact of import restrictions on the flow of exports, the number of jobs lost in the export sector, and thus the total number of jobs gained or lost.

When imports to the United States are restricted, our trading partners can afford to buy less of what we produce. The resulting decline in export sales means fewer jobs in exporting industries. And the total reduction in trade leads to fewer jobs for workers such as stevedores (who unload ships) and truck drivers (who carry goods to and from ports). On both counts—the overall cut in trade and the accompanying decline in exports—protectionism leads to job losses that might not be obvious immediately.

Several years ago, Congress tried to pass a domestic content bill for automobiles. In effect, the legislation would have required that cars sold in the United States have a minimum percentage of their components manufactured and assembled in this country. Proponents of the legislation argued that it would have protected 300,000 jobs in the U.S. automobile manufacturing and auto parts supply industries. Yet the legislation's supporters failed to recognize the negative impact of the bill on trade in general and its ultimate impact on U.S. export industries. A U.S. Department of Labor study did recognize these impacts, estimating that the domestic content legislation would actually cost more jobs in trade-related and export industries than it protected in import-competing businesses. Congress ultimately decided not to impose a domestic content requirement for cars sold in the United States.

More recently, when President Bush decided in 2002 to impose tariffs of up to 30 percent on steel imports, the adverse effects on the economy were substantial and soon apparent. To take but one example, prior to the tariffs, the Port of New Orleans relied on steel imports for more than 40 percent of its revenues, in part because once steel coming into the port is offloaded, the ships are cleaned and refilled with U.S. grain for export. By reducing imports, the tariffs slashed economic activity at the port and cut U.S. grain exports. Businesses and farms all up and down the Mississippi River were adversely affected. More broadly, the higher costs of imported steel produced a decline in employment in U.S. industries that use steel as an input. Indeed, one study estimated that, due to the tariffs, some 200,000 people lost their jobs in 2002 in these industries alone—a number that exceeded the total number of people actually employed by the steel manufacturing firms protected by the tariff.

In principle, trade restrictions are imposed to provide economic help to specific industries and to increase employment in those industries. Ironically, the long-term effects may be just the opposite. Researchers at the World Trade Organization (WTO) examined employment in three industries that have been heavily protected throughout the world: textiles, clothing, and iron and steel. Despite stringent trade protection for these industries, employment actually declined during the period of protection, in some cases dramatically. In textiles, employment fell 22 percent in the United States and 46 percent in the European Union. The clothing industry had employment losses, ranging from 18 percent in the United States to 56 percent in Sweden. Declines in employment in the iron and steel industry ranged anywhere from 10 percent in Canada to 54 percent in the United States. In short, WTO researchers found that restrictions on free trade were no guarantee against job losses—even in the industries supposedly being protected.

The evidence seems clear: The cost of protecting jobs in the short run is enormous. And in the long run, it appears that jobs cannot be protected, especially if one considers all aspects of protectionism. Free trade is a tough platform on which to run for office. But it looks as if it is the one that will yield the most general benefits if implemented. Of course, this does not mean that politicians will embrace it, and so we end up "saving" jobs at a cost of $750,000 each.

DISCUSSION QUESTIONS

1. Who gains and who loses from import restrictions?

2. What motivates politicians to impose tariffs, quotas, and other trade restrictions?

3. If it would be cheaper to give each steelworker $375,000 per year in cash than impose restrictions on imports of steel, why do we have the import restrictions rather than the cash payments?

4. Most U.S. imports and exports travel through our seaports at some point. How do you predict that members of Congress from coastal states would vote on proposals to restrict international trade? What other information would you want to know in making such a prediction?

31

A Farewell to Jobs

Let's take a trip back at the late 1980s. The foremost problem on some economists' minds is the merciless competition that American firms face from Asian manufacturers. "Japan, Inc." and its neighbors, for example, have started turning out computer memory chips at ever lower prices. The result is sharply declining profits for U.S. chipmakers, and—according to chipmakers and their political supporters—a dire threat to U.S. jobs. The issue of looming job losses in this and other industries dominates the political scene. Chip-industry leaders try to persuade members of Congress that the United States will lose its technological edge—unless, of course, the federal government will step in to protect U.S. chipmakers. Experts are even prophesying that without government protection and help, U.S. microelectronics will be "reduced to permanent, decisive inferiority within 10 years."

Now, flash forward to the mid-2000s, when the most frequently recurring issue in domestic-policy debates has been much the same. To be sure, the details—which country is "stealing" jobs from which industry—have changed, but not by much. Indeed, by the early stages of the presidential election of 2004, so-called foreign **outsourcing** of **white-collar jobs** had become as un-American as desecrating our flag. A well-known TV business analyst on CNN, Lou Dobbs, even began a listing of all of the "unpatriotic" American-based companies that were "sending this country's jobs overseas." The House of Representatives tried to pass measures to prevent any type of outsourcing for the Department of State as well as for the Department of Defense. Representative Don Manzullo (R.-Ill.) said, "You just can't continue to outsource overseas time after time after time, dilute the strategic military base, and then expect this Congress to sit back and see the jobs lost and do nothing." (This was from a member of the same House of Representatives that, 20 years before, tried to outlaw competition from foreign automakers because the U.S. auto industry supposedly faced "imminent collapse.")

According to Craig Barrett, CEO of Intel (the world's largest chipmaker), American workers today face the prospect of "300 million well-educated people in India, China, and Russia who can do effectively any job that can be done in the United States." In a similar vein, Forrester Research has predicted that 3.3 million service jobs will "move offshore" by 2015. Five hundred thousand of those jobs supposedly will be in computer software and services. Democratic presidential nominee John Kerry had a name for the leaders of companies that "export" such jobs: "Benedict Arnold CEOs." And when the chair of the Council of Economic Advisors publicly stated that foreign outsourcing of services jobs wasn't such a bad idea, Kerry, as well as numerous other politicians, lambasted the Bush administration, arguing that foreign outsourcing of U.S. service jobs was the biggest plague ever to hit the U. S. economy.

To understand this hot-button issue of outsourcing service employment to workers located abroad, you have to go back to our chapter-opening scenario. What actually happened after the "Asian invasion" of computer chips and other high-tech items in the late 1980s? The result was not the demise of Silicon Valley. Rather, American high-tech companies responded to the challenge by finding those things at which they were best and leaving the rest to their foreign competitors. They became innovative. They led the way in personal computing and the development of the Internet. They became the engine of job creation throughout the 1990s. Indeed, we can look back through American business history and find numerous other periods in which foreign competition has threatened a particular sector of the economy. In spite of that competition—and regardless of the outcome for the sector involved—the American economy has always continued to prosper.

What we have witnessed is a continual testing of a concept that is central to all of economics: **comparative advantage.** The nineteenth-century economist David Ricardo got it right 200 years ago, and no one has disproved him since—although U. S. corporate executives facing stiff foreign competition try to all the time. In a nutshell, the principle of comparative advantage says that if an individual, firm, or nation is singularly well-suited at doing one thing (i.e., has low costs of doing it), then that entity must, *by definition,* be poorly suited at doing other things (i.e., face high costs of doing them.) Comparative advantage implies that there is a niche for everyone, and that those niches can best be filled (and our wealth increased the most) if we permit unfettered freedom of trade, both domestically and internationally.

To better understand comparative advantage, consider the current situation: Just as is the case for their counterparts in the United States, engineers and technicians in India have the capacity to provide both computer programming and to create innovative new technologies. Indian programmers and high-tech engineers earn one-fifth of what their counterparts earn in the United States. Consequently, India is able to do both jobs at a lower dollar cost than in the United States: India has an **absolute advantage** in both. In other words, it can produce a unit of programming for fewer dollars than in the United States, and it can also produce a unit of technology innovation for fewer dollars. Does that mean that the United States will lose not only programming jobs but technology-innovation jobs, too? Does that mean that our standard of living will fall if the United States and India engage in international trade?

Economist David Ricardo would have answered no to both questions—as do your authors today. While India may have an absolute advantage in both activities, that fact is *irrelevant* in determining what India or the United States will produce. India has a comparative advantage in doing programming in part because such activity requires little **capital.** The flip side is that the United States has a comparative advantage in technology innovation partly because it is relatively easy to obtain capital in this country to undertake such long-run projects. The result is that Indian programmers will do more and more of what U.S. programmers have been doing in the past. In contrast, American firms will shift to more and more innovation. The United States will specialize in technology innovation; India will specialize in programming. The business people in each country will specialize in those activities in which they have a comparative advantage. As in the past, the U.S. economy will continue to concentrate on what are called the "most best" activities.

The principle here is no different from what we regularly observe in world-class athletes. Typically, they have the physical and mental skills that would enable them to beat virtually anyone else in any of several sporting activities. They have an absolute advantage in athletics. Yet they invariably end up specializing in *one* sport, the one in which they have a comparative advantage. They do this because they are so good in that sport *relative* to other sports that their earnings would be lower if they "wasted" their time in those other sports. Exactly the same thing is happening with the Indian engineers and technicians, just as it happens in all other endeavors.

Let's return to the general issue of outsourcing services to foreign workers. Computer programming is just one area in which such outsourcing is occurring. This outsourcing also extends, somewhat amazingly, to U.S. income tax return preparation. The fact is that accounting firms small and large use workers in India to prepare returns for U.S. clients. By now at least a quarter of a million returns each year are being prepared by Indians in Bangalore and Bombay. Moreover, U.S. hospitals are sending (via the Internet, of course) computer-image X-rays to India for physicians and medical technicians there to prepare before the images are resent to the United States for a final diagnosis.

Sending overseas white-collar jobs that are labor-intensive— answering simple complaints, taking orders over the phone, explaining basic computer setup, and reading simple medical-test results—is no different from what we did when we bought lower-priced computer chips from Japan and other Asian countries in the 1980s. Nor is it fundamentally any different than what we did when we started importing more labor-intensive textiles in the 1980s and 1990s. Because of foreign competition, specific industries throughout time have been forced to be more innovative and cost-conscious, but overall the number of jobs in the United States has consistently grown, decade after decade. Indeed, at least for the high-tech industrial sector, what happened after the "Asian invasion" of the 1980s was a **productivity** boom.

Let's go back to the arguments for and against foreign outsourcing of services. Even those who agree that international trade and globalization have raised living standards, not only in the United States but elsewhere, seem troubled by the current phenomenon of outsourcing services. According to *Business Week* editor Kathleen Madigan, "This is no longer about a few low-wage or manufacturing jobs. Now, one out of three jobs is at risk. These jobs could be shipped overseas in the name of cost cutting." She argues further that proponents of unfettered international trade "underestimate the risk of being overtaken as skill and education levels rise elsewhere." Her policy suggestion is to focus on maintaining a better-educated workforce.

The fact is that there is little evidence that, overall, well-paying jobs are being "sent overseas." The average unemployment rate for college-educated workers in the post-recession year 2003 was only 3 percent. The average for 1992, the last post-recession year, was higher—3.2 percent. During 2003–2004, employment growth among college-educated workers was six times greater than for less-educated workers.

Certainly jobs disappear in this economy and everywhere else—normally because of technological change. (Actually, jobs "disappear" in the U.S. economy at a rate of 1 million per *week* as workers quit or are fired; but in a typical year, slightly *more* than a million jobs per week are "created" as workers accept new employment.) It is also true that manufacturing employment has not recovered since the last recession at the beginning of the 2000s. But the decline in manufacturing jobs is not unique to the United States. Indeed, despite talk of "losing" manufacturing jobs to China and elsewhere, the number of manufacturing jobs in foreign countries such as China is shrinking *faster* than it is in the United States!

Wealth-enhancing **technological change** is relieving human beings of the necessity of performing mind-numbing, repetitive, dangerous factory jobs. It is making us more productive, and we are collectively better off as a result, even though some individuals may be worse off. But the only way to protect *everyone* from the effects of technological change is to prevent all technological change. Not only would this impoverish us if we tried it, we would fail in our attempts, because other nations around the world would gleefully step into the technology-leading shoes we had vacated.

Indeed, the reason that U.S. companies can outsource service jobs to India, China, and elsewhere is *because* of technological change—dramatic improvements in telecommunications and computing. One thing you can be absolutely certain of is this: The political brouhaha over "exporting" jobs will die out and may even be dead by the time you read this, but technological change will never stop. We don't know what the next great innovation cycle will be, nor which sectors will be affected. When they are affected, though, some politicians will jump on the bandwagon and declare that a new threat to the American economy has emerged. You'll then hear much pontification about how foreigners are destroying the U. S. economy. But remember this: for the last 250 years it has been technological change that has enabled us to get richer; indeed, in the United States every generation over this span has been roughly 50 percent richer than the one that preceded it. It is true that, along the way, some people in the whale blubber-rendering industry and the buggy-whip industry have had to move on to other employments. But as long as humans can think, technology will change. Our only option is to decide whether we want to get rich by embracing these changes or get poor by rejecting them.

DISCUSSION QUESTIONS

1. What is the difference between buying automobiles, clothes, and DVD players from abroad and buying low-cost labor services, such as call-center services, from abroad?

2. Given the possibility of continued outsourcing of programming services abroad, what do you think will happen to the demand for degrees in computer sciences in the United States over time?

3. In what way can immigration be thought of as "insourcing" jobs, that is, bringing the people into America to do the jobs here? Suppose we had decided a century ago (as many politicians advocated at the time) to stop this "insourcing" threat to Americans by eliminating all immigration into America. Would our nation be better or worse off? Would you be an American?

32

The Rise of the Dragon

Back in the 1980s, a select group of economies in Asia came to be known as the "Asian tigers" because of their aggressive approach to economic growth. Included among the tigers were Singapore, Malaysia, Thailand, and Indonesia. All took the view that a combination of low wages and high export sales represented the fast track to economic growth and prosperity. Now these tigers are being overtaken by the "dragon" of Asia—China—which is following the same path, with perhaps even more success.

For decades after the Communists' rise to power in 1949, China was best known for poverty and repression, and its aggression came mostly on the military front. But in recent years *economic* aggression has become the byword. Although both poverty and repression are still the norm, both are changing for the better. China, it seems, is trying to learn from capitalism, even if not converting to it.

China's economic offensive began roughly 25 years ago in its southeastern province of Guangdong. The Chinese leadership decided to use this province as a test case, to see if capitalist **direct foreign investment** could stimulate **economic growth** in a way that could be politically controlled. The experience was deemed a success—economic growth soared amid political stability. What the government learned from the experience helped it smooth the 1999 transition of Hong Kong from British to Chinese control. Most important in terms of China's long-term economic aspirations, many foreign investors came to view the Guangdong experiment as solid evidence that they could invest in China without fear that the Communist government would confiscate their capital. Beginning about 1992, foreign investment began to soar in China.

The annual rate of such investment is nearly 10 times greater than it was at the beginning of the 1990s.

There are two powerful forces that are attracting economic investment to China: **demand** and **supply.** On the demand side, 1.3 billion people live there, some 20 percent of the world's population. Although **per capita income** is still low by world standards, it has been growing at better than 6 percent per year, after adjusting for inflation. At that rate, the standard of living for the Chinese people—and thus their **purchasing power** in world markets—is doubling every decade or so. China is already the world's largest cell phone market, with 200 million customers. Within a few years, it is estimated, China will account for 20 percent of the world's purchases of personal computers. Indeed, China now spends about $40 billion per year on information technology and services, and this amount is growing at a rate of nearly 30 percent per year. Sometime in the next 20 to 30 years, the Chinese economy will almost surely supplant the economy of the United States as the world's largest.

With its population of 1.3 billion individuals, China also offers attractions on the supply side. Although American and European firms with operations in China choose to pay their workers considerably more than state-owned enterprises pay, labor is still relatively inexpensive. Manufacturing and production workers employed by U.S. or European firms, for example, earn under $4 per hour, only about one-fourth what the foreign firms would have to pay in their home markets. And when it comes to highly skilled workers, the Chinese labor market is even more attractive. China's universities produce more than 450,000 engineering graduates each year, including 50,000 in computer science. (By comparison, there are about 30,000 new computer science graduates each year in the United States.) Most importantly, firms can hire those engineers for salaries that are only 10 to 20 percent of the cost of hiring engineers in America or Europe.

The fact that, in many cities, the Chinese workforce is generally well-educated and often English-speaking has helped make China even more attractive to foreign employers. Collaborative scientific ventures between Chinese researchers and U.S. firms are becoming increasingly common. A research team at Beijing University played a role in deciphering the genetic makeup of rice, for example. American computer hardware and software firms Intel, IBM, Oracle, and Microsoft have shifted some key components of their research to China in recent years. American firms are even setting up customer service-call centers there. Microsoft customers from the United States who call in for help may well find themselves talking with one of that company's 400 engineers who are located in Shanghai.

A single episode in China's recent history offers a fascinating look at the forces at work in that country. Not long ago computer-makers began offering what has become one of the hot-selling items of recent years, the tablet PC, equipped with software that reads handwriting. The development of the software used by the tablet PC illustrates the key elements of China's recent growth.

The Chinese language has thousands of individual characters and no alphabet. As a result, it cannot be easily accommodated on computer keyboards. This fact significantly slowed the sales of computer hardware and software in China during the 1980s and 1990s. In the hopes of tapping the huge Chinese market, Microsoft established a major research lab in Beijing, China's capital, in-structing its engineers to devise a means of making computers eas-ier for the Chinese to use. For more than a year, researchers fed a computer a steady stream of handwritten documents, including notes, diagrams, and even shopping lists. Gradually, with the aid of many hours of human programming and learning-by-doing on the part of the computer, the Chinese researchers developed a pro-gram that could distinguish words from everything else, and then turn the words into typed text. And what worked for handwriting in China would work for handwriting anywhere. Equipped with this software, a viable tablet PC was born.

Both elements of China's growth—demand and supply—were clearly at work in this process. Without the huge potential market in China, this project wouldn't have been given the priority it was, and might not have been undertaken at all. Moreover, without well-trained, English-speaking Chinese computer scientists at the heart of the project, it is unlikely that Microsoft could have been successful. And the upshot of the project is that a product whose primary impetus came from China is yielding benefits around the world—and making the computer market in China even more al-luring to U.S. firms.

China's rapid economic expansion has caused a huge increase in its demand for raw materials and other inputs, many of which are being supplied by Malaysia, Thailand, and Singapore. Although these Asian tigers are grateful for the boom in exports, they are also concerned by the growing competition they face from their neighbor to the north. Chinese medium- and high-tech industries are starting to cut into the market share of the very sectors that have helped fuel the growth of the Asian tigers over the past 20 years. The situation is even more critical in Japan, where wages are much higher than in China, but whose technological lead over China is gradually eroding. "Are we to become a vassal of the Chinese dynasty again?" asked one Japanese official, clearly concerned that his nation's manufacturing firms were having trouble competing with Chinese firms.

Although lower wages among the tigers are keeping them competitive for now, they are concerned about the future, because competition for foreign investment is particularly intense. China's 2001 entry into the **World Trade Organization (WTO)** prompted a surge in foreign investment there, even as China's rivals in the region saw their foreign investment shrink. Without fresh outside capital, the economies of Malaysia, Singapore, and Thailand may all start looking like Japan's, where growth has been essentially zero since the mid-1990s, and where high unemployment is a chronic problem. Eventually, Japan as well as China's other neighbors will adjust to the growing economic presence of China, but the transition may be unpleasant.

Most Americans, however, are more concerned about the likely impact on the U.S. economy of China's capitalist ambitions. Will the dragon consume American firms and jobs as it grows? The short answer is "No." The long answer is that China, like all nations, must in the long run import goods equal in value to those it exports (unless China intends to *give* its exports away, which so far no one is claiming). This means that just as China is becoming a potent supplier of many goods and services, so too it is becoming a potent demander of still other goods and services.

Thus far, the Chinese demand for goods has not been as visible in American markets, because American firms tend to produce goods and services designed for higher income consumers, and China as yet has relatively few of those. In the meantime, the demand-side influence of the Chinese economy is already showing up, albeit in odd places. To take one example, right now China's most important import from the United States is trash. Ranging from used newspapers to scrap steel, Chinese companies buy billions of dollars of the stuff every year to use as raw materials in the goods they produce. In addition to yielding profits (and employment) in these U.S. export industries, this exportation of U.S. trash reduces the burden on U.S. landfills and, by pushing up the prices of recyclable scrap, encourages more recycling in the United States.

Eventually, of course, we'd like to be sending China more than our rubbish, but that time is coming. As China's economy grows, so too will the number of affluent Chinese, and with 1.3 billion or so potential candidates, that ultimately means *plenty* of consumers for America's high-end goods. Thus, the long-run effects of China's growth will mean a different American economy—we'll be producing and consuming different mixes of goods and services—but America will also be a richer nation. Voluntary exchange, after all, creates wealth, and the Chinese dragon is big enough to create a lot of wealth.

As we saw in Chapter 4, political and legal **institutions** are crucial foundations for sustained economic growth. Despite the advances China has made over the last 25 years, its wealth-creating future may be clouded unless it can successfully deal with two crucial institutional issues. First, there is the matter of resolving the tension inherent when a Communist dictatorship tries to use capitalism as the engine of economic growth. Capitalism thrives best in an environment of freedom, and itself creates an awareness of and appreciation for the benefits of that freedom. Yet freedom is antithetical to the ideological and political tenets of the Communist government of China. Will the government be tempted to confiscate the fruits of capitalist success to support itself? Or will growing pressure for more political freedom force the government to repress the capitalist system to protect itself? Either route would likely bring economic growth in China to a swift halt.

The second potential long-run problem faced by China lies in that nation's cultural attitude toward intellectual property. In a land in which imitation is viewed as the sincerest form of flattery, it is routine to utilize the ideas of others in one's own pursuits. As a result, patent and copyright laws in China are far weaker than in western nations. Moreover, actions elsewhere considered to be commercial theft (such as software piracy) are largely tolerated in China. If foreign firms find they cannot protect their economic assets in the Chinese market, foreign investment will suffer accordingly, and so too will the growing dragon that depends so heavily upon it.

DISCUSSION QUESTIONS

1. Currently AIDS is spreading rapidly in China, importantly as a result of contaminated blood supplies. If the government fails to stop the spread of AIDS, what are the likely consequences for future economic growth in China?

2. In 1989 a massive protest against political repression in China was halted by the government's massacre of more than 150 individuals at Tiananmen Square in Beijing. What impact do you think that episode had on foreign investment and growth in China during the years immediately after the episode?

3. Most of the advances in institutions in China have come in the cities rather than the countryside. Indeed, local officials in farming villages actively redistribute wealth among villagers to keep the distribution of income among local farmers roughly equal. Thus, a given farmer's success or failure with his crops has little impact on his family's standard of living. Given these facts, where do you think the economic growth in China has occurred over the last 25 years, in the cities or on the farms? Explain.

Glossary

Absolute advantage: Ability to produce more of a good, without regard for the costs of forgone output of other goods.

Acreage-restriction program: Federal government limit on the number of acres that a farmer can plant with a particular crop.

Capital: Nonhuman productive resources.

Capital stock: Collection of productive assets that can be combined with other inputs, such as labor, to produce goods and services.

Cartel: Group of independent businesses, often on an international scale, that agree to restrict trade, to their mutual benefit.

Civil law system: Legal system in which statutes passed by legislatures and executive decrees, rather than judicial decisions based on precedent, form the basis for most legal rules.

Common law system: Legal system in which judicial decisions based on precedent, rather than executive decrees or statutes passed by legislatures, form the basis for most legal rules.

Comparative advantage: Ability to produce a good at a lower opportunity cost than others; the principle of comparative advantage implies that individuals, firms, and nations will specialize in producing those goods for which they have the lowest opportunity cost compared to other entities.

Competition: Rivalry among buyers or sellers of outputs, or among buyers or sellers of inputs.

Congestion costs: Costs (such as excess travel time) caused by too many users attempting to simultaneously access a facility such as a highway or a computer network.

Constant-dollar price: Price corrected for changes in the purchasing power of the dollar; one that takes account of inflation and deflation.

Copyright infringement: Action that deprives the owner of a copyright of his or her rightful payment for use of the intellectual property protected by the copyright.

Cost: Highest-valued (best) forgone alternative; the most valuable option that is sacrificed when a choice is made.

Demand: The willingness and ability to purchase goods.

Demand curve: Graphic representation of the demand schedule; a negatively sloped line showing the inverse relationship between the price and the quantity demanded.

Demand schedule: Set of number pairs showing various possible prices and the quantities demanded at each price. This schedule shows the rate of planned purchases per time period at different prices of the good.

Direct foreign investment: Resources provided to individuals and firms in a nation by individuals or firms located in other countries, often taking the form of foreign subsidiary or branch operations of a parent company.

Economic good: Any good or service that is scarce.

Economic growth: Sustained increases over time in real per capita income.

Economies of scale: Cost structure for the firm that has the characteristic that the average costs of production decline as the level of output increases. *See also* Increasing returns.

Elastic demand: Characteristic of a demand curve in which a given percentage change in price will result in a larger inverse percentage change in quantity demanded. Total revenues and price are inversely related in the elastic portion of the demand curve.

Elasticity: Measure of the responsiveness of one variable to changes in the value of another variable; it equals percentage change in the dependent variable, divided by the percentage change in the independent variable.

Elasticity of demand: Responsiveness of the quantity of a commodity demanded to a change in its price per unit. *See also* Price elasticity of demand.

Elasticity of supply: Responsiveness of the quantity of a commodity supplied to a change in its price per unit. *See also* Price elasticity of supply.

Equilibrium price: Price that clears the market when there is no excess quantity demanded or supplied; the price at which the demand curve intersects the supply curve. Also called *Market-clearing price.*

Externalities: Benefits or costs of an economic activity that spill over to a third party. Pollution is a negative spillover or externality.

File sharing: The activity of downloading files, making files available for other users to download, over the Internet or other networks.

Fixed exchange rates: System of legally fixed prices (rates) at which two or more national currencies trade (exchange) for one another.

Frankenfoods: Slang term for genetically modified organisms, generally reserved for those created using modern gene-splicing techniques.

Free good: Any good or service available in larger quantities than desired at a zero price.

Full cost: Combined measure of all of the things that must be given up to undertake an activity; includes both the money price (i.e., other goods that must be sacrificed) and the value of the time that must be sacrificed.

Gains from trade: Extent to which individuals, firms, or nations benefit by engaging in exchange.

Gene splicing: Combining genetic code from two different organisms, often organisms form different species.

Human capital: Accumulated training, education, and knowledge of workers.

Incentives: Perceived consequences of actions or decisions; they may be positive or negative and monetary or non-monetary.

Increasing returns: Cost structure for the firm that has the characteristic that the average costs of production decline as the level of output increases. *See also* Economies of scale.

Inelastic demand: Characteristic of a demand curve in which a given change in price will result in a less than proportionate inverse change in the quantity demanded. Total revenue and price are directly related in the inelastic region of the demand curve.

Institutions: Basic rules, customs, and practices of society.

Intellectual property: Creative ideas and expressions of the human mind that possess commercial value and receive the legal protection of a property right, such as through the issuance of a patent, copyright, or trademark.

Labor force participation rate: Sum of all people who are working or are available for and looking for work, divided by the population; both numerator and denominator are generally restricted to persons age 16 and above.

Law of demand: Law stating that quantity demanded and price are inversely related—more is bought at a lower price, less at a higher price (other things being equal).

Law of supply: Law stating that a direct relationship exists between price and quantity supplied (other things being equal).

Marginal analysis: Analysis of what happens when small changes take place relative to the status quo.

Marginal benefits: Additional (marginal) benefits associated with one more unit of a good or action; the change in total benefits due to the addition of one more unit of production.

Marginal costs: Change in total costs due to a change in one unit of production.

Market-clearing price: *See* Equilibrium price.

Market share: Proportion of total sales in an industry accounted for by the sales of a specific firm or group of firms in that industry.

Market supply: Total quantities of a good offered for sale by suppliers at various prices.

Median age: Age that exactly separates the younger half of the population from the older half.

Merger: The joining together into common ownership of two or more formerly independent companies.

Minimum wage: Lowest hourly wage firms may legally pay their workers.

Models, or theories: Simplified representations of the real world used to make predictions or to better understand the real world.

Monopolist or **Monopoly:** Literally, a single supplier. More generally, it is a firm that faces a downward-sloping demand curve for its output and therefore can choose the price at which it will sell the good; an example of a *price searcher.*

Monopsonist or **Monopsony:** Literally, a single buyer. More generally, it is a firm that faces an upward-sloping supply curve for its input and therefore can choose the price at which it will buy the good; an example of a *price searcher.*

Natural monopoly: Monopoly that arises when there are large *economies of scale* relative to the industry's demand.

Natural-resource endowments: Collection of naturally occurring minerals (such as oil and iron ore) and living things (such as forests and fish stocks) that can be used to produce goods and services.

Negative externality: Cost associated with an economic activity that is paid by third parties. Pollution is a negative externality because, for example, someone other than the driver of an automobile bears part of the cost of the car's exhaust emissions.

Network effect: Change in the benefit that an agent derives from a good when the number of other agents consuming (or using) the same kind of good changes.

Oligopoly: Firm that is one of very few sellers (or buyers) in a market; in such a case, each firm reacts to changes in the prices and quantities of its rivals.

Opportunity cost: Highest valued alternative that must be sacrificed to attain something or to satisfy a want.

Outsourcing: Practice of having workers located in foreign lands perform tasks (typically services) that traditionally have been performed by domestic workers.

Parity price: Hypothetical price (relative to input costs) that, if received by farmers, will keep them on a par or parity with farmers early in the twentieth century.

Peer-to-peer (P2P) networking: Technology that allows Internet users to access files on other users' computers.

Perfectly elastic: An infinite value for the ratio of the percentage change in quantity over the percentage change in price, measured along a demand or supply curve; visually, a perfectly elastic curve appears horizontal.

Positive-sum game: Process or setting in which more than one participant gains. Voluntary exchange is said to be a positive-sum game because both parties are simultaneously made better off.

Preliminary injunction: Order by a court to stop a particular activity.

Price discrimination: Selling at prices that do not reflect differences in marginal costs; different prices with the same marginal costs, for example, or the same prices with different marginal costs.

Price elasticity of demand: Percentage change in quantity demanded divided by the percentage change in price. *See also* Elasticity of demand.

Price elasticity of supply: Percentage change in quantity supplied divided by the percentage change in price. *See also* Elasticity of supply.

Price searcher: Literally, a firm that must search for the profit-maximizing price, because it faces a downward-sloping demand curve (if it is a seller) or an upward-sloping supply curve (if it is a buyer); often used as a synonym for *monopoly* or *monopsony*.

Price-support program: Government agricultural program that mandates minimum prices for crops.

Price taker: Any economic agent that takes the market price as given; often used as a synonym for a firm operating in a market characterized by *pure competition*.

Private costs: Costs incurred by the relevant decision maker.

Product differentiation: The distinguishing of products by brand name, color, and other minor attributes.

Productivity: Amount of output produced per unit of input.

Profit: Income generated by selling something for a higher price than was paid for it. In production, the income generated is the difference between total revenues received from consumers who purchase the goods and the total cost of producing those goods.

Property and contract rights: Legal rules governing the use and exchange of property, and the enforceable agreements between people or businesses.

Property rights: Set of rules specifying how a good may be used and exchanged.

Protectionism: Set of rules designed to protect certain individuals or firms from competition, usually competition from imported goods.

Pure competition: Market structure in which participants individually have no influence over market prices; all act as *price takers*.

Quota: Limit on the amount of a good or activity; often used in international trade to limit the amount of some foreign good that legally may be imported into a country.

Rate of return: Net benefit, in percentage terms, of engaging in an activity. For example, if the investment of $1.00 yields a gross return of $1.20, the net benefit is $0.20 and the rate of return is equal to ($0.20/$1.00) = 20 percent.

Real per capita income: Gross domestic product (GDP) corrected for inflation and divided by population.

Regulated monopoly: A *price searcher* whose key business decisions, such as the price at which it sells its output, are regulated by a government agency.

Rent control: System in which the government tells building owners how much they can charge for rent.

Resource: Input used in the production of desired goods and services.

Rule of law: Principle that relations between individuals, businesses, and the government are governed by clearly enumerated rules that apply to everyone in society.

Scarce good: Any good that commands a positive price.

Scarcity: State of nature in which resources are limited even though wants are unlimited. Scarcity means that nature does not freely provide as much of everything as people want.

Shortage: Situation in which an excess quantity is demanded or an insufficient quantity is supplied; the difference between the quantity demanded and the quantity supplied at a specific price below the market clearing price.

Social cost: The full cost that society bears when a resource-using action occurs. For example, the social cost of driving a car is equal to all private costs plus any additional cost that other members of society bear (e.g., air pollution and traffic congestion).

Stock: Quantity of something at a point in time. An inventory of goods is a stock. A bank account at a point in time is a stock. Stocks are defined independent of time, although they are assessed at a point in time.

Subsidies: Government payments for the production of specific goods, generally designed to raise the profits of the firms receiving the subsidies and often intended to increase the output of the subsidized goods.

Supply: The willingness and ability to sell goods.

Supply curve: Graphic representation of the supply schedule, which slopes upward (has a positive slope).

Supply schedule: Set of prices and the quantity supplied at each price; a schedule showing the rate of planned production at each relative price for a specified time period.

Support price: Set by the federal government, the minimum price that farmers are guaranteed to receive for their crop; if the market price falls below the support price, the government purchases enough of the crop to bring the market price up to the support price.

Surplus: Excess quantity supplied or an insufficient quantity demanded; the difference between the quantity supplied and the quantity demanded at a price above the market clearing price. As applied to the government budget, an excess of tax receipts over expenditures.

Tangible assets: Assets that have a physical presence, such as cars, buildings, and jets, as contrasted with intangible assets such as copyrights, patents, bonds, and stocks.

Target price: Set by the federal government, the minimum price that farmers are guaranteed to receive for their crop; if the market price falls below the target price, farmers receive a payment equal to the difference between the two (multiplied by their production of the crop).

Tariff: Tax levied on imports.

Technological change: A change in the set of feasible production possibilities, typically the result of the productive implementation of new knowledge.

Trade barriers: Any rules having the effect of reducing the amount of international exchange. *Tariffs* and *quotas* are trade barriers.

Trade-off: Term relating to opportunity cost. In order to get a desired economic good, it is necessary to trade off (give up) some other desired economic good in a situation of scarcity. A trade-off involves making a sacrifice in order to obtain something.

Transgenic species: Species containing genes from two or more different species, generally because humans have spliced one or more genes from one species into another.

Type I error: Error of commission, such as might arise when an unsafe drug is errantly permitted to be sold.

Type II error: Error of omission, such as might arise if a beneficial drug is errantly prevented from reaching the market.

White-collar jobs: Employment in which workers rely chiefly on their intellect and knowledge rather than their physical skills.

World Trade Organization (WTO): Association of more than 145 nations around the world that helps reduce trade barriers among its members and handles international trade disputes among them.

Selected References

Chapter 1—Killer Airbags

Cumulative Regulatory Effects on the Cost of Automobile Transportation (RECAT): Final Report of the Ad Hoc Committee. Office of Science and Technology, Washington, DC: Government Printing Office, 1972.

Peterson, Steven, George Hoffer, and Edward Millner. "Are Drivers of Air-Bag-Equipped Cars More Aggressive? A Test of the Offsetting Behavior Hypothesis." *Journal of Law & Economics* 38, no. 2 (1995): 251–264.

http://nhtsa.gov/. Official Web site of the National Highway Traffic Safety Administration.

Chapter 2—Terrible Trade-off

Peltzman, Sam. "The Effects of Automobile Safety Regulation." *Journal of Political Economy* 83, no. 4 (1975): 677–725.

Kazman, Sam. "Deadly Overcaution: FDA's Drug Approval Process." *Journal of Regulation and Social Cost* 1, no. 1 (1990): 35–54.

Walker, Steven. "S.O.S. to the FDA." *The Wall Street Journal Online,* August 26, 2003.

Chapter 3—Flying the Friendly Skies?

Mitchell, Mark L., and Michael T. Maloney. "Crisis in the Cockpit? The Role of Market Forces in Promoting Air Travel Safety." *Journal of Law & Economics* 32, no. 2 (1989): 139–184.

http://www.airsafe.com. More statistics on airline safety than you ever wanted to know.

http://www1.faa.gov/. Official Web site of the Federal Aviation Administration.

Chapter 4—The Mystery of Wealth

Easterly, William, and Ross Levine. "Tropics, Germs, and Crops: How Endowments Influence Economic Development." *NBER Working Paper* no. 9106. Boston: National Bureau of Economic Research, Inc., 2002.

Mahoney, Paul G. "The Common Law and Economic Growth: Hayek Might Be Right." *Journal of Legal Studies* 30, no. 3 (2001): 503–525.

Chapter 5—Sex, Booze, and Drugs

Benjamin, Daniel K., and Roger LeRoy Miller. *Undoing Drugs: Beyond Legalization.* New York: Basic Books, 1993.

Hardy, Quentin. "Inside Dope." *Forbes,* November 10, 2003, pp. 146–154.

Miron, Jeffrey A., and Jeffrey Zwiebel. "Alcohol Consumption During Prohibition." *American Economic Review* 81, no. 2 (1991): 242–247.

Chapter 6—Expanding Waistlines

Chou, Shin-Y., Michael Grossman, and Henry Saffer. "An Economic Analysis of Adult Obesity: Results from the Behavioral Risk Factor Surveillance System." *NBER Working Paper Series* 9247. Boston: National Bureau of Economic Research, 2002.

Cutler, D. M., E. L. Glaeser, and J. M. Shapiro. "Why Have Americans Become More Obese?" Harvard Department of Economics, Working Paper, 2003.

Lakdawalla, D., and T. Philipson. "The Growth of Obesity and Technological Change: A Theoretical and Empirical Analysis." *NBER Working Paper* no. 8946. Boston: National Bureau of Economic Research, 2002.

Chapter 7—Is Water Different?

Anderson, Terry, and Pamela S. Snyder. *Water Markets: Priming the Invisible Pump.* Washington, DC: Cato Institute, 1997.

Hanke, Steve. "Demand for Water Under Dynamic Conditions." *Water Resources Research* 6, no. 5 (1970): 1253–1261.

Chapter 8—Slave Redemption in Sudan

Miniter, Richard. 1999. "The False Promise of Slave Redemption." *Atlantic Monthly* 284, no. 1 (1999): 63–70.

Vick, Karl. "Ripping Off Slave 'Redeemers.'" *Washington Post,* February 26, 2002, p. A01.

Walsh, Declan. "Fake Slaves Con Aid Agency in Sudanese Liberation Scam." *The Scotsman,* February 24, 2002. (http://scotlandonsunday. scotsman.com/index.cfm?id=212232002)

Chapter 9—Choice and Life

Blank, Rebecca, Christine George, and Rebecca London. "State Abortion Rates: The Impact of Policies, Providers, Politics, Demographics, and Economic Environment." *Journal of Health Economics* 15, no. 5 (1996): 513–553.

Sklar, June, and Beth Berkov. "Abortion, Illegitimacy, and the American Birth Rate." *Science* 185 (September 1974): 909–915.

Chapter 10—Smoking and Smuggling

Bartlett, Bruce. "Cigarette Smuggling." *Brief Analysis No. 423* National Center for Policy Analysis, October 30, 2002. (http://www.ncpa.org/ pub/ba/ba423)

Benjamin, Daniel K., and William R. Dougan. "Efficient Excise Taxation: The Evidence from Cigarettes." *Journal of Law & Economics* 40, no. 1 (1997): 113–136.

Yurekli, Ayda A. & Ping Zhang. "The Impact of Clean Indoor-Air Laws and Cigarette Smuggling on Demand for Cigarettes: An Empirical Model," *Health Economics* 9, no. 1 (2000): 159–170.

Chapter 11—Bankrupt Landlords, from Sea to Shining Sea

Downs, Anthony. *Residential Rent Controls: An Evaluation.* Washington, DC: Urban Land Institute, 1988.

Glaeser, Edward L., and Erzo F. P. Luttmer. "The Misallocation of Housing Under Rent Control." *American Economic Review* 93, no. 4 (2003): 1027–1046.

Chapter 12—Rationing Health Care

Esmail, Nadeem, and Michael Walker. *Waiting Your Turn: Hospital Waiting Lists in Canada,* 13th ed. Vancouver: Fraser Institute, 2003.

General Accounting Office. *Veterans Health Care: VA Needs Better Data on Extent and Causes of Waiting Times.* Washington, DC: General Accounting Office, 2000.

Pollard, Stephen. "The Genie of Choice: Has It Been Let Loose in Britain?" *National Review,* June 30, 2003.

Chapter 13—The Effects of the Minimum Wage

Baker, Michael, Dwayne Benjamin, and Shuchita Stanger. "The Highs and Lows of the Minimum Wage Effects: A Time-Series Cross-Section Study of the Canadian Law." *Journal of Labor Economics* 17, no. 2 (1999): 318–350.

Card, David, and Alan Krueger. "Minimum Wages and Employment: A Case Study of the Fast-Food Industry in New Jersey and Pennsylvania." *American Economic Review* 84, no. 3 (1994): 772–793.

Neumark, David, and William Wascher. "Minimum Wages and Employment: A Case Study of the Fast-Food Industry in New Jersey and Pennsylvania." *American Economic Review* 90, no. 5 (2000): 1362–1396.

Rottenberg, Simon (ed.). *The Economics of Legal Minimum Wages.* Washington, DC: American Enterprise Institute, 1981.

Chapter 14—Heavenly Highway

Singer, Jason. "Lonesome Highways: Japan's Hefty Tolls Drive Cars Away." *The Wall Street Journal,* September 15, 2003, p. A1.

Wheatley, Malcolm. "How IT Fixed London's Traffic Woes." *CIO Magazine,* July 15, 2003. (http://www.cio.com/archive/071503/london.html)

Chapter 15—Give Me MP3 or Give Me Death

Forbes, Steve. "The Freeloaders." *Forbes,* November 24, 2003, p. 31.

Miller, Roger LeRoy, et al. *Essentials of the Legal Environment.* Cincinnati: South-Western Publishing, 2005, chapter 13.

Smith, Ethan. "Copyright Law Faces Uncertain Future," *The Wall Street Journal,* October 21, 2003, p. A6.

Chapter 16—Contracts, Combinations, and Conspiracies

Zimbalist, Andrew. *Unpaid Professionals: Commercialism and Conflict in Big-Time College Sports.* Princeton, NJ: Princeton University Press, 2001.

Kanfer, Steven. *The Last Empire: DeBeers, Diamonds, and the World.* New York: Farrar Straus Giroux, 1993.

www.eia.doe.gov. Official Web site of the Energy Information Administration.

Chapter 17—Coffee, Tea, or Tuition-Free?

Chevalier, Judith, and Austan Goolsbee. "Measuring Prices and Price Competition Online: Amazon.com Versus BarnesandNoble.com." *Quantitative Marketing and Economics* 1, no. 2 (2003): 203–222.

Odlyzko, Andrew. "Privacy, Economics, and Price Discrimination on the Internet." St. Paul: Digital Technology Center, University of Minnesota, 2003.

"They're Watching You." *The Economist,* October 18, 2003, p. 77.

Chapter 18—Keeping the Competition Out

Lipton, Eric. "Finding the Intersection of Supply and Demand." *New York Times,* November 23, 2003, Late Edition Final, section 1, p. 31, col. 2.

http://www.schallerconsult.com/taxi/topics.htm. Loaded with facts on the New York City taxicab and taxi medallion markets.

Chapter 19—The Perils of Product Differentiation

Brooks, John. 1963. *The Fate of the Edsel & Other Business Adventures.* New York: Harper & Row, 1963.

Oliver, Thomas. *The Real Coke, The Real Story.* New York: Penguin, 1987.

Chapter 20—Raising More Hell and Less Corn

Becker, Elizabeth. "U.S. Corn Subsidies Said to Damage Mexico: Study Finds Farmers Lose Livelihoods." *New York Times,* August 27, 2003, p. C4.

Edwards, Chris, and Dan DeHaven. "Save the Farms—End the Subsidies." *CATO Working Paper,* March 6, 2002.

Fackler, Martin. "Japanese Farmers Losing Clout." *The Wall Street Journal,* February 20, 2004, p. A10.

Chapter 21—Killer Cars and the Rise of the SUV

Crandall, Robert W., and John D. Graham. "The Effect of Fuel Economy Standards on Automobile Safety." *Journal of Law and Economics* 32, no. 1 (1989): 97–120.

Godek, Paul. "The Regulation of Fuel Economy and the Demand for 'Light Trucks.'" *Journal of Law and Economics* 40, no. 2 (1997): 495–517.

Chapter 22—Crime and Punishment

Levitt, Stephen. "The Effect of Prison Population Size on Crime Rates: Evidence from Prison Overcrowding Litigation." *Quarterly Journal of Economics* 111, no. 2 (1996): 319–351.

Levitt, Stephen. "Using Electoral Cycles in Police Hiring to Estimate the Effect of Police on Crime." *American Economic Review* 87, no. 3 (1997): 270–290.

Levitt, Stephen. "Juvenile Crime and Punishment." *Journal of Political Economy* 106, no. 6 (1998): 1156–1185.

Chapter 23—The Graying of America

Miron, Jeffrey A., and David N. Weil. "The Genesis and Evolution of Social Security." In Michael D. Bordo, Claudia Goldin, and Eugene N. White (eds.), *The Defining Moment: The Great Depression and the American Economy in the Twentieth Century.* Chicago: University of Chicago Press, 1998, pp. 297–322.

Council of Economic Advisors. "Restoring Solvency to Social Security," *Economic Report of the President.* Washington, DC: Government Printing Office, 2004, chapter 6.

Chapter 24—Frankenfoods

Evenson, R. E., and D. Gollin. "Assessing the Impact of the Green Revolution, 1960 to 2000." *Science* 300 (May 2003): 758–762.

Federoff, Nina. "Prehistoric GM Corn." *Science* 302 (November 2003): 1158–1159.

Qain, Matin, and David Zilberman. "Yield Effects of Genetically Modified Crops in Developing Countries." *Science* 299 (February 2003): 900–902.

Rauch, Jonathan. "Will Frankenfood Save the Planet?" *Atlantic Monthly,* October 2003.

Chapter 25—The Trashman Cometh

Benjamin, Daniel K. *Eight Great Myths of Recycling.* Policy Series PS-28. Bozeman, MT: Property and Environment Research Center, 2003.

Fullerton, Don, and Thomas C. Kinnaman. "Household Responses to Pricing Garbage by the Bag." *American Economic Review* 88, no. 2 (1996): 971–984.

Hocking, Martin B. "Paper versus Polystyrene: A Complex Choice." *Science* 251(Feb. 1991): 504–505.

———. Disposable Cups Have Eco-merit. *Nature* 369(May 1994): 107.

Rathje, William, and Cullen Murphy. *Rubbish: The Archeology of Garbage.* New York: HarperCollins, 1992.

Chapter 26—Bye, Bye Bison

Adler, Jonathan. "Bad for Your Land, Bad for the Critters." *The Wall Street Journal,* December 31, 2003, p. A8.

Anderson, Terry L., and Peter J. Hill. *The Not So Wild, Wild West: Property Rights on the Frontier.* Stanford: Stanford University Press, 2004.

Coase, Ronald. "The Problem of Social Cost." *Journal of Law and Economics* 3, no. 2 (1960): 1–40.

Grafton, R. Quentin, Dale Squires, and Kevin J. Fox. "Private Property and Economic Efficiency: A Study of A Common-Pool Resource." *Journal of Law & Economics* 43, no. 2 (2000): 679–713.

Lueck, Dean, and Jeffrey A. Michael. "Preemptive Habitat Destruction under the Endangered Species Act." *Journal of Law & Economics* 46, no. 1 (2003): 27–60.

Chapter 27—Smog Merchants

Foster, Vivien, and Robert W. Hahn. "Designing More Efficient Markets: Lessons from Los Angeles Smog Control." *Journal of Law and Economics* 38, no. 1 (1995): 19–48.

Joskow, Paul L., Richard Schmalensee, and Elizabeth M. Bailey. "The Market for Sulfur Dioxide Emissions." *American Economic Review* 88, no. 5 (1998): 669–685.

http://www.epa.gov/airmarkets/trading. EPA Web site for tradeable emissions.

Chapter 28—Greenhouse Economics

Bradsher, Keith. "China's Boom Adds to Global Warming Problem." *New York Times,* October 22, 2003, p. A1.

Castles, Ian, and David Henderson. "The IPCC Emission Scenarios: An Economic-Statistical Critique." *Energy and Environment* 14, nos. 2, 3 (2003).

Lomborg, Bjorn. *The Skeptical Environmentalist.* New York: Cambridge University Press, 2001.

Sohngen, Brent, and Robert Mendelsohn. "Valuing the Impact of Large-Scale Ecological Change in a Market: The Effect of Climate Change on U.S. Timber." *American Economic Review* 89, no. 4 (1999): 686–710.

Chapter 29—Free Trade, Less Trade, or No Trade?

Eichengreen, Barry. "The Political Economy of the Smoot-Hawley Tariff." *Research in Economic History* 12, no. 1 (1989): 1–43.

Federal Reserve Bank of Dallas. *The Fruits of Free Trade.* Annual Report. Dallas, TX: 2002.

Irwin, Douglas A. "From Smoot-Hawley to Reciprocal Trade Agreements: Changing the Course of U.S. Trade Policy in the 1930s." In Michael D. Bordo, Claudia Goldin, and Eugene N. White, (eds.), *The Defining Moment: The Great Depression and the American Economy in the Twentieth Century.* Chicago: University of Chicago Press, 1998, pp. 325–352.

Chapter 30—The $750,000 Steelworker

Crandall, Robert W. "The Effects of U.S. Trade Protection for Autos and Steel." *Brookings Papers on Economic Activity,* 1987, pp. 271–288.

Berry, Steven, James Levinsohn, and Ariel Pakes. "Voluntary Export Restraints on Automobiles: Evaluating a Trade Policy." *American Economic Review* 89, no. 3 (1999): 400–430.

Chapter 31—A Farewell to Jobs

Federal Reserve Bank of Dallas. *The Fruits of Free Trade.* Annual Report. Dallas, TX: 2002.

Browning, Lynnley. "Outsourcing Abroad Applies to Tax Returns, Too." *New York Times,* February 15, 2004, p. 12.

Madigan, Kathleen. "Outsourcing Jobs: Is It Bad?" *Business Week,* August 25, 2003, pp. 36–38.

Chapter 32—The Rise of the Dragon

Eckholm, Erik, and Joseph Kahn. "China's Power Worries Neighbors." *New York Times,* December 1, 2002, p. 7.

Goodman, Peter S. "China Takes Pivotal Role in High-Tech Production." *International Herald Tribune,* December 5, 2002, p. 2.

Restall, Hugo. "New Property Rights for Chinese Farmers?" *The Wall Street Journal Europe,* October 3–5, 2003, p. A7.

Index

iPod, 108
Iran
    OPEC and, 111
    war with Iraq and, 112
Iraq
    OPEC and, 111
    war with Iran and, 112
iRiver, 108
Italy, cigarette smuggling in, 68
iTunes, 105, 108
IVQs (individual vessel quotas), 184–185
IWC (International Whaling Commission),
    182–183

J
Japan
    abortions legal in, 61
    automobiles imported from, restrictions
        on, 206, 209–210
    competition with China and, 223
    computer chips bought from, 214, 217
    dealing with traffic congestion in, 95–96
    economic growth and, 223
    farm programs in, 142
    Kyoto, conference on climate change in
        (1997), 194–195, 196
    organ transplants and, 155
    price control laws on drugs in, 107
    whaling and, 183
Jitneys, government regulation and, 126
Jobs
    manufacturing, lost in U.S., 218
    scarcity and, 208
    service, outsourcing of, 200, 214–219,
        221–222
    white-collar, outsourcing of, 200,
        214–219, 221–222
Jobs, Steve, 108
Joskow, Paul, 190
Jukebox, 105

K
KaZaA, 106
Kazakhstan, caviar cartel and, 113
Kefauver, Estes, 11
Keogh, Donald, 132
Kerry, John, 215
Klein, Daniel, 126

Kleindorfer, Paul, 175
Krueger, Alan, 89
Kuwait, OPEC and, 111
Kyoto, conference on climate change in
    (1997), 194–195, 196

L
Labor force participation rate of women,
    42–43
LaBrea Tar Pits, 179
Landfill(s)
    closing of, 162, 172, 175
    fees paid to, 175, 176
    government regulations and, 172, 173,
        175
    neighboring homes purchased by
        operators of, 176
    New Jersey's experience with, 175
    operation of, costs of, 175, 176
    Pennsylvania's experience with, 175
    Styrofoam in, 174
    trash exported to China from, 224
    waste management companies acquire
        land for, 173
    Wisconsin's experience with, 176
Law(s)
    of demand. *See* Law of demand
    immigration, 158–159
    rule of, 3, 23
    of supply. *See* Law of supply
Law of demand
    cigarettes and, 67
    college financial aid and, 119
    defined, 29
    price of food and, 41
    prostitution, alcohol, illegal drugs and,
        33
    rental housing and, 71
    water and, 31, 46–52, 48, 49
Law of supply
    defined, 29
    rental housing and, 71
Lawyers, protected by government regula-
    tion, 124
Lease, Mary, 136
Levine, Ross, 25
Levi's, 128
Levitt, Steven, 151–152, 153